European Immigrants and American Society

A Collection of Studies and Dissertations

•

Edited by
Timothy Walch and
Edward R. Kantowicz

•

A Garland Series

Irish and German Families and the Economic Development of Midwestern Cities, 1860–1895

•

James K. Benson

Garland Publishing, Inc. • New York & London • 1990

Library of Congress Cataloging-in-Publication Data

Benson, James K. (James Kasper)
Irish and German families and the economic development of Midwestern cities, 1860–1895/ James K. Benson.
p. cm.—(European immigrants and American society)
Thesis (Ph. D.)—University of Minnesota, 1980.
Includes bibliographical references.
ISBN 0-8240-7422-X (alk. paper)
1. Irish Americans—Minnesota—Saint Paul—Families.
2. Irish Americans—Minnesota—Saint Paul—Economic conditions. 3. German Americans—Minnesota—Saint Paul—Families. 4. German Americans—Minnesota—Saint Paul—Economic conditions. 5. Ethnicity—Minnesota—Saint Paul.
6. Saint Paul (Minn.)—Economic conditions.
I. Title. II. Series.
F614.S4B46 1990
305.83'10776581'09034—dc20 90-41582

Printed on acid-free, 250-year-life paper.
Manufactured in the United States of America

Design by
Julie Threlkeld

TABLE OF CONTENTS

LIST OF TABLES

Table		Page

Table		Page

Table Page

Table	Page

Table		Page

Table		Page

Table		Page

Table		Page

Title	Page

Table | Page

Table | Page

Acknowledgments

I am grateful to Rudolph J. Vecoli and John Modell, who provided guidance, criticism and encouragement at all stages of this project. Also, I am obligated to Robert E. Kennedy, Jr., George Green, Clyde Griffen and Jeylan T. Mortimer for helpful suggestions on specific issues.

For many courtesies extended during my research, I wish to thank the staffs of the Minnesota Historical Society, the library of the University of Minnesota, and the Immigration History Research Center of the University of Minnesota.

The Bush Foundation and the University of Minnesota provided financial support.

My family helped in more ways than I can acknowledge here. This work would not have been completed except for the constant help and encouragement of Ann, my wife. My mother, Mabel Benson, generously provided her time and skill in typing the final draft. And my perception of the ethnic dimension of family life draws upon the experience of both my parents and grandparents.

Introduction

Our historical knowledge of the process of urban growth in America has broadened and deepened rapidly over the past decade of research and writing on the topic. Drawing upon insights from several disciplines, the general shape of a broad historical explanation of the process of urbanization has begun to emerge. Urbanization in the nineteenth and twentieth centuries is coming to be viewed as a vast interaction of economic forces and demographic transition on a global scale. Within this emerging framework, the international migrations from Europe to America in the last half of the nineteenth century are viewed as an important contributing factor to the pace of urban growth in America. Immigration to American cities was a secondary response within this framework to the underlying process of economic transformation, which contributed to economic dislocations at the European points of origin and provided the stimuli of attractive employment opportunities.

The size of the immigration from Europe to America, the timing of the great waves during peak years of economic growth, and the concentration of immigrants in the age range in which new households typically are formed, all have been identified as important factors in the pace of development of American cities. Contributing both to labor supply and to the household demand for goods and services, immigration pushed urban economic growth to higher levels than internal migration alone would have made possible, and speeded the rapid urbanization of American society after the middle of the nineteenth century. The young adult age of most of the immigrants (a characteristic which they shared with internal migrants) also ensured a lingering influence on consumption demand for consumer goods after the peaks of the great waves of immigration had passed.

The purpose of the present study is to raise and examine the possibility that Irish and German immigrants affected this general pattern of American urban growth in distinctive ways stemming from culturally distinctive patterns of behavior among either or both of these groups. For the most part, the specific ethnic origins of immigrants has been neglected in the broad study of urbanization as an economic-demographic phenomenon because of the usual "economic man" assumption that ethnic differences in the behavior of immigrants in the marketplace were marginal at most and of little importance to a study of urban growth. Another reason for neglecting ethnic origins may be the assumption that matters of ethnic preference or taste are difficult to isolate independently of the mesh of economic constraints which influenced everyday decisions in the past. This study is an attempt to test both of these assumptions.

Irish and German immigrants constituted the bulk of European immigration to American cities between 1850 and 1900 and represented more than half of the foreign-born population of the country as late as 1900. In the following chapters we will evaluate a variety of historical records to determine, first, whether actual differences in group economic and demographic behavior existed among the Irish, Germans and persons of "native" parentage. As far as available sources will allow we will attempt to sort out differences in group behavior which may have been caused by ethnic values as contrasted with responses only to economic constraints. Finally, and most importantly, we will analyze the significance of ethnic differences for altering the pattern of urban development in the late nineteenth century. The major focus will be the process of economic interaction between specific immigrant populations and the American cities in which they resided.

Obviously, a subject of this size required drastic delimitation and it is nearly as important to clarify what this study is not as to state its main purpose. The Irish and German immigrants are studied here as populations with common ethnic origins for whom a central tendency of behavior is to be isolated. The religious and other subgroup characteristics which divided especially the Germans are recognized in subsequent chapters and, in the case of such factors as age and occupational composition are directly analyzed as demographic data permit, but the main concern is the central pattern. Irish and German immigrant populations also are treated as components of the city populations of which they were a part, and their relative contributions to the average characteristics of city populations are measured. For the most part this is an effort to isolate and evaluate a few group characteristics using the quantitative tools of demographic analysis. The study leaves to others the important work of writing a social history of the urban Germans and Irish, though the findings will contribute to that task.

For the sake of comparability across several sets of data, four basic indicators of urban development were chosen for study:

- the rate of household formation;
- the proportion of population residing in single family dwellings;
- the proportion of household heads who owned their own homes;
- The amount of above- average concentration in "typical" occupational sectors for ethnic workers.

Identifying German and Irish differences in these measures allows one to evaluate the relative contribution of each of the immigrant subpopulations both to housing demand and to labor supply in certain employment sectors. Changes over time in these rates for cities as a whole also help trace stages of urban development. Rising rates of household formation, homeownership, or single family home residence would signal an expansion phase, while declining rates would typify a period of slowed development. Depending upon the particular mix of employment sectors in a city and its relative rate of development, the above-average concentration of Irish or German workers in a particular employment sector could either add or detract from further growth.

The subject was limited further by my choice of St. Paul, Minnesota for intensive local study during the period 1860 to 1895, and by my use of census data for all American cities of 100,000 or more population in 1890 to test the importance of ethnic differences at the national level. The choice of St. Paul also led to a particular emphasis upon young, newly-developing Midwestern cities. An unexpected cyclic pattern of development was discovered in St. Paul from 1860 to 1895, and this pattern is generalized using census date for the set of 26 large cities in 1890. Though in many respects the following chapters present a local case study as an exemplar of longer trends, a local history of St. Paul or of its ethnic population is not the main purpose here. The St. Paul setting was analyzed only to help explain general patterns of development.

Finally, the study of those ethnic values which influenced the economic and demographic behavior of Irish and German immigrants has been narrowed to a search for statements reflecting attitudes toward marriage, homeownership and occupation in the "verbal" documents of the two groups in a few Midwestern cities. The methodological problems of inferring values from such a collection of statements are difficult to overcome but an attempt was made to suggest the contours of a more systematic study. Again, no attempt is made to describe German or Irish ethnic cultures as a whole, though the findings presented should contribute to that effort. The main purpose of including data on cultural values is to provide a partial explanation of the causes of ethnic differences after demographic and economic constraints on behavior have been taken into account. If real ethnic differences existed in the rate of formation of households, in the level of homeownership and in above-average concentration in certain occupations, the ultimate cause, it is argued, lay beyond the immediate context of economic action and at least partly within the realm of ethnic cultural values as learned from childhood in the family. Previous studies of the ethnic group behavior during this period have often speculated about the possible link between ethnic values and action. An attempt is made here to study the matter directly.

The reasons for delimiting the subject in these ways are partly personal, partly practical, and partly methodological. I have a personal interest in the study of European immigrants because of my awareness of my own family's origins. The selection of St. Paul and the Midwest for particular emphasis came naturally from my roots in this area. I also have a keen interest in the emerging framework of historical explanation for urban growth however, and this study's main purpose is to contribute to that framework. Every effort was made to place the behavior of St. Paul's Irish and German populations in the broader context of American urban development, out of a conviction that local histories have significance primarily as cases of larger patterns of societal development.

I also was concerned that the study employ a broad range of historical documents as a means of checking the validity of the conclusions drawn. If important ethnic differences emerged in a demographic analysis of immigrants within one city, it seemed important to ask whether immigrants discussed the meaning of their behavior in their remaining "verbal" records, and whether the differences had some effect on the larger society. Conclusions based on converging evidence from several kinds of sources and more than one "level of analysis" (e.g. individuals, ethnic groups, cities, national system of cities) should be more convincing than those based more narrowly on one kind of documentation, and if there is a disjunction, such a paradoxical finding would be no less of methodological or of substantive interest.

The practical difficulties of focusing several kinds of data on a single subject also shaped the design of this study. The manuscript census records for St. Paul did not provide information on homeownership, hence the addition of the "residence in single family dwellings" as a related indicator. The paucity of direct statements about marriage age, homeownership or occupational preference in the available verbal documents in St. Paul led to a search of ethnic newspapers and letters in other Midwestern cities. Ready access to a wide variety of local economic records helped to convince me that the selection of St. Paul for intensive study made sense for practical reasons.

Though a variety of methods are used to analyze demographic, economic and "verbal" sources, the general emphasis is to apply "controls" for such associated factors as age, income and household relationship when measuring ethnic differences in behavior. Using two and three-way cross tabulation techniques and multiple regression and factor analysis where appropriate, the goal was to isolate the ethnic-origin explanation from related influences on behavior and to assess the "independent" influence of ethnic origin. Such an approach permits an analysis of the context of economic constraint which modified the efforts of the Irish and Germans to apply ethnic values to economic decisions in the American city. The most extensive attempt to assess the interplay of cultural values and economic constraint is provided in Chapter Four where the occupational distributions of Irish and German workers in St. Paul are considered. The context of external constraint on the application of ethnic values is emphasized throughout the study and analyzed directly as far as the data allowed.

The study begins in Chapters One and Two with a measurement of ethnic differences as to household formation, household composition, and residence in single family dwellings in the City of St. Paul between 1860 and 1895. Chapter Three evaluates statements about marriage, family and property holding in the "verbal" records of Irish and German immigrants in St. Paul, Minneapolis, Milwaukee and Chicago during the period, searching for evidence of distinctive ethnic values. The interplay of economic conditions and ethnic values and resources is evaluated in Chapter Four to explain ethnic occupational patterns. In Chapter Five, the group tendencies identified in St. Paul are evaluated with census data for the 26 cities of 100,000 population or more in 1890, looking for the effect, if any, of these differences on the development patterns of large cities.

Did the specific ethnic origins of Irish and German immigrants modify the development pattern of American cities beyond what one could expect from the sheer numbers of these immigrants? The main significance of this study lies in the answers provided to this question. Along the way to this goal, the study also will provide a demographically-based evaluation of the adjustment of certain ethnic values and behavior of Irish and German immigrants in the American milleau. A cyclic pattern of development for frontier cities of the Midwest will be elaborated. Hopefully, our understanding both of urban processes and of the role of immigrants in American history will be enlarged by the effort.

Chapter 1

Ethnicity and Households in St. Paul: An Explanation of Irish and German Household Formation Patterns, 1860-1895

Until quite recently immigration studies in the United States have dealt only in a peripheral way with the family life of immigrant groups. Perhaps in part because much of the documentary evidence deals extensively with issues of intergroup conflict and with reportage of the affairs of ethnic organizations, historians of immigrant groups have usually emphasized those aspects of group life in their writings.[1] Both documentary evidence, and for twentieth century immigrants oral evidence, about immigrant family life has been recognized and sometimes used to briefly characterize the family life of groups.[2] Discussions of childhood and family relationships have been woven into biographies of individuals based on family papers, diaries and reminiscences.[3] Inter-generational conflict between immigrants and their children has been reviewed in a general way.[4] The implications for family life of the American schooling of immigrant children has received some attention.[5] On the whole, though, very few studies have tried to analyze systematically the cluster of behavior, structures, and norms which characterized the families of specific immigrant groups.[6]

A study of family life will illuminate many of the prevailing issues in immigrant and ethnic historiography. Though the clubs, associations and religious bodies of immigrant communities helped to socialize the second generation in ethnic ways, the family surely played a central role in this process. The entire issue of intergenerational relationships, of passage from immigrant group to ethnic community, involves the family in an intimate way. And group relationships with other ethnic groups and the broader structures of society intersected the family and household at many points. The choice of residence and workplace, of political affiliation, of schooling for children, of styles of consumption generally -- all of these important interactions with the economy and institutions of society included family and household decision-making processes where cultural norms were applied and relations with other groups considered.[7]

Because family life develops in stages (matrimony, child-bearing, child "launching", for example) and because migration typically occurred immediately before or after young adults left their parents to form their own families, a careful demographic study of the timing of these stages during early adulthood is especially important as a starting point for the analysis of immigrant family differences. If cultural norms usually cannot be derived directly from demographic measurements of the average family and household behavior of groups, it is nevertheless true that, when cultural norms affected such measurable events as endogomous mate selection, delayed marriage, and child-spacing, demography can identify accurately the <u>range</u> of group difference in behavior which needs to be explained. The use of statistical correlation methods to test the strength of association between family behavior and such socioeconomic factors as occupation can also help to identify probable causes, though any <u>explanation</u> which includes cultural norms must rely on inferences from both quantitative and "verbal" information.[8]

To a limited extent a comparative demographic analysis of the family and household behavior of American immigrant groups already has begun on the local level, usually relying on the state and federal census manuscripts for the period 1850 to 1880, supplemented by local marriage and death records. Since the censuses used the "household" or co-resident group sharing the same quarters (including lodgers, servants and secondary families unrelated to the head) as the basic reporting unit, some studies of social and geographic mobility in effect have compared the <u>household</u> behavior of immigrant groups by using heads of household as the unit of analysis.[9] Other studies have compared endogamy rates, proportions single, sex ratios, fertility and mortality rates, female employment rates, the frequency of female-headed families, and the distribution of household and family types generally.[10] Studies by Sennett, Glasco, Walkowitz, Laslett, Modell and Hareven have begun to illuminate difference in the timing of family and household formation stages among immigrant groups and to identify related socioeconomic factors.[11] Meanwhile, another set of demographic studies of the European countries of origin has been published, identifying family formation patterns which might be expected in the United States among immigrants if Old World tendencies persisted.[12]

From these studies it is now possible to predict the direction, if not the precise level, of group differences in important aspects of family and household formation among the largest immigrant groups in the nineteenth century America, the Irish and Germans, and the native-born.[13] Though any summary of the family and household formation patterns of Table 1 must be tentative since social class, age-sex structure and other relevant controls were not always applied and the sample of local areas was slim, it seems useful to suggest first approximations. On the whole, German and Irish immigrants were somewhat more likely to form new households earlier than did the native-born, and Germans had the greater tendency of the three. The higher

Table 1

Approximate Group Differences in Demographic Aspects of Family and Household Formation, Germans, Irish and U. S. -born, Late Nineteenth Century Urban Areas, Eastern United States

	Irish	Germans	U. S.-born
a. Fertility[a]	High	High	Low
b. Mortality, age-specific	High	Middle	Low
c. Males per 100 females, ages 20-29	Low	High	Middle
d. Endogamy	High	High	----
e. Proportion single, males age 20-29	High	Low	High
f. Proportion single, females, age 20-29	High	Middle	Low
g. Household Headship Rate,[b] males, 20-29	Middle	High	Low
h. Household Headship Rate,[b] females, age 20-29	Low	High	Low
i. Proportion of households, one-parent head	High	Low	High
j. Proportion of households extended[a,c]	High	Low	High

a. Controls for occupational level.
b. "Household headship rate" is the proportion of all adults who were heads of household; wives with co-resident husbands also considered heads for calculating this rate.
c. "Extended households" means households with one or more extended families (i.e. families with non-conjugal kin).

Source: See footnote number 13.

tendency to form households among the Irish and Germans compared to the native-born in some cases might be simply the result of differences in age-sex structure; since a large proportion of immigrants were concentrated in the young adult age group, comparisons with the native-born should be made with internal migrants only. Irish-German comparisons avoid this difficulty since both were immigrants and here group differences seem to be explained by the longer postponement of marriage among the Irish. On the average, Germans married and formed new households earlier and fewer of their households contained non-conjugal kin as compared to the Irish.

This assessment of American urban trends among the Irish and Germans is consistent with trends in Ireland and Germany in the nineteenth century. Beginning in the mid-nineteenth century, and accelerating rapidly after 1890, proportions of Irish men and women who postponed marriage or remained permanently single became the highest in Europe by the 1930's.[14] The situation in Germany is more difficult to interpret because of substantial regional differences, but one study of the Ruhr region, where much of the mid-nineteenth century German emigration to America began, indicated that marital fertility rates declined only very slightly from 1851 to 1901 except in the great cities.

Women in Protestant areas of the Ruhr region tended to marry at a younger age than women in Catholic areas. On the whole, a somewhat lower proportion of German women married between ages 15 to 29, but a higher proportion were married by ages 25 to 29 as compared to women in an adjacent region of France.[15]

Irish and German marriage patterns have persisted from first to second generations in the United States in the twentieth century. A study of data from the 1950 Census found that a "moderate positive correlation" existed between the proportions single among American ethnic groups (first and second generation) and their corresponding countries of origin, and that there was "probably at least a moderate tendency for marriage norms brought to this country by immigrants to persist among their American offspring".[16] The Irish in America, like their counterparts in Ireland ranked highest in their propensity to marry late or never to marry in 1950.[17] Though twentieth century patterns cannot simply be superimposed on the nineteenth century setting, there seems to be no obvious reason why persistence between generations should not have occurred also in the earlier, less industrialized society.

So far, efforts to interpret the social and psychological meaning of differences in the timing of family stages and the structure of family and household in the nineteenth century have been quite limited. Though his emphasis on the significance of the extended family is questionable, Richard Sennett's study of "Union Park" in Chicago creatively attempted to suggest the personal meanings of postponed marriage and other family life cycle phenomena.[18] Daniel J. Walkowitz's study of the mostly Irish women mill workers in Cohoes, New York attempted to connect Irish family values to the labor force participation and postponed marriage rates of women workers.[19] A cluster of studies mostly of black families has tried to assess the meaning of single parent households.[20] Another study of boarding and lodging finds that lodgers served as surrogate family members at specific family life cycle stages, and that a distinct tendency existed for householders to take in lodgers of the same ethnicity.[21] Much more could be made of the psychological meaning and social implications of family patterns, however, if verbal sources were used more extensively. Michael Anderson's important study of family structure in Preston, England in the nineteenth century, for example, used effectively a wide variety of verbal reports on family life from newspapers, local and parliamentary poor relief agencies, personal papers, and contemporary novels to illuminate the "phenomenal" aspects of family trends.[22]

Another reason for studying the families and households of immigrant groups is to increase our knowledge of the process of urban growth and development in the nineteenth century. A recent study by Richard Easterlin indicates that both the total population and the labor force of urban areas in the United States grew in a "long swing" pattern which "arose very largely from corresponding movements in immigration" before 1920.[23] The effect of immigration upon urban growth patterns was greater than the total number of immigrants would suggest, Easterlin argues, because like migrants generally the foreign immigrants were concentrated in the young adult age group, at or near the early family life cycle stages when new households were formed and the consumption of such durables as furniture and single family houses was high.[24] If important ethnic differences existed in the timing and levels of migration and family and household formation--and recent studies suggest that this was probably so, all else being equal -- then the study of ethnic differences in household formation should contribute to our understanding of the "long swing" of urban growth. We will then be able to clarify the role of the ethnic composition of urban populations in local variations of the cyclic trend.

In addition to overall cyclic trends of urban growth, a study of the interactions of immigrant families and households with the economy of the nineteenth century city can help to clarify other broad economic and social changes. During the early stages of industrialization in cotton milling areas of England in the same period, for example, Anderson found that while only about a third of parents with teenage children were able to offer children employment in a family enterprise, most parents had a major role in the recruitment of their children for jobs outside the household, either directly as when employers allowed them to subcontract their children's services as assistants or indirectly when employers gave hiring preference to their workers' children.[25] Virginia Y. McLaughlin's study of Italians and other immigrant groups in Buffalo in the early twentieth century found similar patterns of a familial role in job recruitment there.[26] Still another economic role of the family and household was the taking in of lodgers and boarders to supplement household income, a practice which was much more widespread in the early stages of urbanization and industrialization as compared to today. Thus, in both the production of income and the consumption of goods and services, families and households in the nineteenth century had more economic functions than their counterparts today, and the study of the timing and size of these changes becomes an important way of understanding the development process. If immigrant groups adapted the economic functions of their households differently to the changing nature of the marketplace, once again it becomes important to include the ethnic factor in the study of the internal processes of urban development.

Both the cultural and the economic implications of differences in family and household formation patterns among nineteenth century immigrants remain largely unexplored territory. To what degree did ethnic differences reflect the demographic and cultural character of the sending country? What kinds of adjustments were made in family and household formation patterns in the American setting because of such factors as imbalanced sex ratios and economic opportunities and how were these adjustments perceived by each immigrant group? How much did ethnic differences in household formation affect the demand for rental and sales housing in urban areas over the "long swing"? These questions can be addressed at the local level in the nineteenth century with three major kinds of data: federal and state census manuscripts, housing permits, and the verbal records of ethnic groups. To understand the social and economic meaning of the family patterns of immigrant groups it is appropriate to move beyond the present stage of descriptive research toward an explanation of the size and trend of ethnic differences and toward an assessment of their economic effects especially on the cities to which so many immigrants were drawn.

Problems of Method

Most economic analyses of consumption use the household rather than the family as the unit of analysis.[27]

One obvious reason for this, of course, is that some households do not contain families (such as apartments shared by unrelated adults) and an inclusive study of consumption would include both the private households of single adults and public "households" such as hotels, jails and hospitals. Both the family and the household (in its broadest economic sense) must be considered separately to fully understand the process of household formation among young adult immigrants and to judge the probable effect of household formation patterns upon consumption levels. Marriage, for example, may have had the effect of increasing the number of households by one (if neither spouse previously headed a household), not changing the number of households (if one of the pair previously headed a household), or even of decreasing the number of households (if both previously headed separate households).

Tamara Hareven has recently argued that historians of the family who rely on cross-sectional analysis of the household or its co-resident family groups as found in manuscript census schedules have failed to catch important ethnic differences in the timing of family life cycle stages, and she suggested that longitudinal tracing of families be substituted for cross-sectional analysis.[28] A study of the timing of family life cycle stages with cross-sectional data is in fact possible in two ways:

a) by comparisons of the family patterns of persons born in specific years (i.e. "cohorts") from one census year to the next, and b) by comparisons of the distribution of family patterns of age groups at each census year. This dual comparison of age-graded differences in ethnic family patterns from one census year to the next (using such rates as "proportions single") will identify differences in the average transition point from one family and household stage to the next for ethnic groups across the time period enclosed by the census years, and will compare the distribution of family behaviors at both ends of the period.[29]

At the same time the household behavior of immigrant groups can be compared in the same way (using such rates as "household headship") so that the probable economic impact of family patterns can be assessed. A thorough analysis of the effect of family patterns upon the demand for housing, for example, requires a detailed study of the various components of households including those without families.[30] Households may contain "primary families" and "secondary families" (the latter unrelated to the household head). They may be headed by "primary individuals" or by "primary family heads" and contain "secondary individuals" (such as lodgers and servants). The "primary family" or family of the household head may contain "sub-families" such as a co-resident son and his wife. All of these components tend to be concentrated within specific stages of the household life cycle (as distinct from the family life cycle) and the housing needs of the household tend to differ within each stage. Rented housing in multi-unit structures, for example, is more readily accepted by the households of single young adults and retired people than by middle-aged parents with several children.[31]

While it is true that comparisons of cohorts across time and comparisons of age groups at single points in time do not in fact follow individuals across a time period (except for those individuals in a cohort who remain in a locality from one census year to the next and happen to be selected in both samples) such comparisons nevertheless represent average age group tendencies and permit the historian to evaluate the importance of immigrant group differences within specific age groups. Another time dimension available to the historian of immigrant groups is the generational factor. The overwhelming personal importance of the act of migrating from one culture and society to another and the similarity of the psychological and social adjustment process for the first and second generations of each immigrant group makes this temporal sequence of central importance in immigration studies. In sum, three kinds of comparisons across time are useful with cross-sectional data: a) distributional comparisons of family and household patterns in each census year, b) comparison of cohort(or birth-group) trends from one census to the next, and c) comparison of ethnic generations both within and across ethnic groups in each census year.

Design of the Study

To examine closely the extent to which ethnic differences in the timing of family and household formation were affected by, and in turn helped to shape, the society and economy of receiving areas, a local study of household formation patterns and housing starts in St. Paul, Minnesota was undertaken for the period 1860 to 1895. Three major issues were looked into: a) how much did Irish and German immigrants differ from each other and from native-born migrants in the timing of new household formation, and how far can these differences be explained by cultural, demographic, and economic factors? b) how far did ethnic differences in the timing of new household formation affect the total number of housing starts during the period? c) how were adjustments of ethnic marriage and family norms to meet demographic and economic conditions perceived and justified by the Irish and German immigrants themselves?

In this chapter we will take up the first major question, attempting to outline demographic factors affecting ethnic differences in household headship. We will also examine the economic effects of differences in household income and wealth upon ethnic headship rates. After explaining these demographic and economic effects we will assess the probable range of cultural preference in household formation patterns. Then in later chapters we will address the other two major questions of the study: the effects of ethnic differences in headship rates on housing costs in St. Paul, and the differences in patterns of ethnic cultural adaptation in household formation patterns.

The principal types of historical evidence used in this study included: random samples of about 500 households each taken from the census manuscript schedules for St. Paul in 1860 and 1895;[32] published data on housing permits and the "tenure composition" (i.e. the ratio of sales to rental housing) of the housing stock in St. Paul, 1885-1900; and verbal evidence from Irish and German manuscript and newspaper sources in St. Paul. The years 1860 and 1895, from which the census samples were drawn, are analytically important for two reasons: a) they were both very close to "trough" years economically, both of short term business cycles and of the long swing of urban housing construction nationally,[33] and it is reasonable to expect that household incomes locally were low and thus economic stress on family and household formation patterns was high; and, b) in St. Paul, the years enclose a period of both rapid growth and of substantial economic diversification, allowing the impact of local urban development on household behavior to be compared directly.

Because the mushrooming collection of local urban studies produced recently has been criticized for choosing "arbitrarily defined" locales of study[34] it is important to consider the representativeness of a case study of Irish and Germans in St. Paul in the late nineteenth century. The choice of an urban rather than a rural area makes sense because Easterlin's study at the national level found that the impact of immigrant households on economic growth was greatest in urban areas.[35] Selecting a city with substantial proportions of Irish and German (as in St. Paul) is useful because Irish and Germans composed more than half of the total immigrant population of the United States as late as 1890.[36] And the selection of a newly-founded frontier city in the Midwest is helpful because the economic effects of immigration there would not be confounded by the previously established structures and populations of older cities. The mid-century wave of Irish and German immigration was reflected in St. Paul's population from the earliest years of settlement, and the German and Irish immigrants and their offspring represented a substantial proportion of the city's population late into the century. (see Table 2)[37]

It is probable also that the rapid pace of population growth in St. Paul helped to highlight the effect of immigration on housing construction. St. Paul's population grew from 10,400 in 1860 to 140,000 by 1895, increasing especially rapidly in the 1880's during a national "wave" of immigration.[38] Hence, much of the new construction of residential housing documented by St. Paul's housing permit data must have been immediately occupied by immigrants in the 1880's, unlike an established city such as Boston where immigrants for the most part occupied older structures left vacant by the native-born.[39] Growing from 41,400 in 1880 to 111,400 in 1885,[40] St. Paul did not have a sufficient stock of older housing to accomodate the dramatic inflow of population during the boom years. Rather than simply decreasing the vacancy rate for older residential units, then, immigration to St. Paul affected housing construction by directly creating additional demand for new housing.[41]

Within its regional setting, St. Paul's economic

Table 2

Irish and German Adult Populations
As Proportions of Total Adult Populations,
St. Paul, 1860 - 1895

	Percent German		Percent Irish	
	German-born	Second gener.[a]	Irish-born	Second gener.[a]
1860	23.5	---	26.0	---
1880	16.4	11.9	10.8	8.7
1890[b]	(12.2)	(12.5)	(4.5)	(7.6)
1895	13.4	---	6.3	---

a. U. S.-born persons having either father or mother or both parents born in each foreign state.

b. Ethnic populations of all ages as proportion of total population of all ages. Second generation definition in 1890 excludes persons of mixed foreign parentage.

Sources: Sample data for 1860, 1880 and 1895; U. S. Census Bureau, Eleventh Census, 1890, Vol. 1, Population, 203,671,704-729.

development was quite representative of other medium-sized frontier urban centers in the nineteenth century, though its proximity to Minneapolis created a division of economic functions in the Twin Cities, especially before 1880. St. Paul emerged quickly as a commercial center with a large wholesale and commission trade extending over a rapidly spreading area of the Northwest as the Northern Pacific Railroad and other roads pushed into frontier regions in the 1870's. Minneapolis, in part because of the proximity of a large commercial center, early concentrated its economy on milling flour and lumber, and exporting grain. After 1880, St. Paul's small manufacturing sector grew in relative size as clothing, boots and shoes, printing and publishing, and meat-packing industries expanded. At the same time Minneapolis' commercial sector grew in proportion to its manufacturing sector. By 1900 the Twin Cities had achieved near economic integration as a metropolitan area.[42]

The construction sector, of course, was also relatively large in the Twin Cities throughout the period, reflecting dramatic population increases. During the 35 year period from 1860 to 1895, the combined populations of the two cities grew from about 13,000 to 333,000, doubling in size more than four times, though most of the growth occurred in the 1880's.[43] Table 3

Table 3

Industrial Distribution of Gainfully Occupied Men and Women Aged 15 Years and Older, St. Paul, 1860 and 1895

	Percent of total gainfully occupied adults in each year	
	1860	1895
Agriculture	2.6	0.5
Extractive	1.4	0.6
Textiles, Leather	0.4	0.2
Apparel	5.4	4.3
Wood Products	3.6	1.6
Metal Products	2.1	3.8
Food Products	3.0	1.5
Other Manufactures	3.0	5.8
Construction	13.2	8.9
Unskilled Labor	16.7	12.5
Commerce	19.3	25.1
Transport	8.4	13.0
Public Service	2.2	5.8
Domestic Service	13.2	8.9
Professional	3.3	1.3
Education-Government Service	2.2	6.0
Total Percent	100.0	100.0
N	661	1062

Source: Sample data, census manuscript schedules.

provides detailed information on the industrial distribution of the gainfully occupied workforce in St. Paul in both years.

For comparative purposes, Table 4 shows proportions of the gainfully occupied workforce in each economic sector for St. Paul and five cities in the more urbanized East -- Buffalo, Kingston and Poughkeepsie, New York, and Hamilton, Ontario and Philadelphia, Pennsylvania in 1860.[44] St. Paul's manufacturing sector is clearly smallest in relative size and the difference would probably be even more marked if a proper share of unskilled laborers were assigned to the "Construction" sector in St. Paul. On the whole, though, there is a striking similarity of workforce structure among the six cities despite the frontier setting of St. Paul, a fact which seems to increase the generality of St. Paul as a case of nineteenth century urban growth, at least at the beginning of our period.

Still another issue in the question of St. Paul's representativeness within its region is that of regional migration flows of both internal migrants and foreign immigrants. Scattered evidence suggests that Chicago and to some extent St. Louis were major entry points into the region during the 1860's but that after about 1870

Table 4

Industrial Distributions of the Workforce,[a]
St. Paul and Five Eastern Cities, 1860

	St. Paul (Minn.)	Buffalo (N.Y.)	Hamilton (Ont.)	Kingston (N.Y.)	Pough-keepsie	Phia-delphia
Agriculture and Extract.	4	6	2	15	6	5
Manufacturing and Labor	34	46	48	41	49	48
Construction	13	22	19	11	12	11
Transport	8	5	2	18	8	8
Commerce and Professions	23	18	23	13	19	20
Other	8	3	6	2	6	8
Total Percent	100	100	100	100	100	100

a. Except for the St. Paul sample of total workforce, the samples represent only workers reporting occupations which appeared in the samples with sufficient frequency to be included in a list of major occupations only. The list of occupations was selected by ranking occupations in order of frequency reported and including only those which accounted for 75% of the sample of workmen.

Source: St. Paul percentages from Table 3; others from Theodore Hershberg, *et al.*, "Occupation and Ethnicity in Five Nineteenth-Century Cities: A Collaborative Inquiry," *Historical Methods Newsletter*, 7 (June, 1974), 193.

most German and Irish immigrants entered the Upper Midwest via railroad from Chicago, Milwaukee and to a much lesser degree by water from St. Louis.[45] Given these probable paths of migration, one would expect that relatively smaller proportions of Irish and German immigrants would settle in inland cities like St. Paul, Minneapolis, and Kansas City, Missouri because of the greater "intervening opportunities" for employment in Chicago, Milwaukee and St. Louis.[46] Table 5 seems to bear out this idea. The "inland" cities including St. Paul, had relatively smaller proportions of Irish and German immigrants in their workforces as compared to the larger cities on the margin of the region, though St. Paul's proportions occupied approximately a mid-point between the two geographical types.

A related issue is the problem of the internal migration of second-generation Irish and Germans from other areas of the region or from elsewhere in the United States. Because of the well-known phenomena of "chain migration," or the gradual accumulation of family members in an area attracted by family ties, one would expect that centers of German and Irish concentration would help to attract such second-generation Irish and German "internal migrants" more strongly than areas with lesser concentrations. Table 6 seems to support this idea.

Table 5

Proportions of Gainfully Occupied Workforce Who Were Born in Germany and Ireland, St. Paul and Five Other Midwestern Cities, 1880 and 1890

	Percentage German		Percentage Irish		Combined Percentage	
	1880	1890	1880	1890	1880	1890
Chicago	21	19	13	9	34	28
Milwaukee	39	37	4	2	43	39
St. Louis	21	20	11	7	32	27
Kansas City	5	6	9	5	14	11
Minneapolis	7	6	5	3	12	9
St. Paul	16	15	10	6	26	21

Table 6

Proportions of Gainfully Occupied Workforce Who Were Second Generation Germans and Irish, St. Paul and Five Other Midwestern Cities, 1900[a]

	Percentage Second Gener. German	Percentage Second Gener. Irish	Combined Percent
Chicago	25	14	39
Milwaukee	48	5	53
St. Louis	37	13	50
Kansas City	9	8	17
Minneapolis	11	8	19
St. Paul	23	13	46

a. U. S.-born persons having both parents born in each foreign country or one parent U. S.-born and one parent born in the foreign country is the definition of "second generation."

Source: U. S. Census Bureau, Twelfth Census, 1900, Special Report on Occupations, 516-715.

Though of course natural increase within each city accounted for some of the population of second-generation Germans and Irish, the table supports the proposition that second-generation ethnic migrants reinforced the migration paths of the first-generation. In the second-generation as well, St. Paul's ethnic composition occupied a midway position between inland and entrepot cities in the region.

In sum, one would expect that St. Paul's status as a medium-sized, rapidly-growing frontier city with moderately high proportions of first and second generation Irish and German immigrants in some ways would highlight the economic impact of ethnic household formation patterns and in other ways would be broadly representative of that impact. The "frontierness" of St. Paul would accentuate the effects of immigration upon the creation of housing demand because of rapid growth rates and a lack of an established housing stock. On the other hand, St. Paul's population and economic structure were sufficiently similar both to other cities in the Midwest and even to rapidly-growing, commercially-oriented cities in the East that it can be taken as a representative case of larger urban trends as well.

Trends in Irish and German Household Formation Patterns

How much did Irish and German immigrants differ from one another and from U.S. -born migrants in the timing of new household formation in St. Paul in the late nineteenth century? If substantial differences in household headship rates existed among these groups, how far can they be explained by cultural, demographic and economic factors unique to each group? To answer these questions we turn first to census data to examine trends in household size and in the ratio of households to total adult population in St. Paul from 1860 to 1900. As Table 7 indicates, after the initial period of settlement when mean size was small, household size in St. Paul increased rapidly and then began the steady downward trend typical of households in the United States from 1790 to the present.[47] During the same period the ratio of households to adults changed in a mildly-cyclical fashion, declining to a low in the mid-1880's (probably because of a housing shortage during that decade of immense population growth) then increasing to 1895. Comparing the years 1860 and 1895, the tendency for adults to reside in separate households dropped by about 20% while average household size increased by about 10%.

Our sample data for the years 1860 and 1895 allow us

Table 7

Average Household Size and
Number of Households per 100 Adults, St. Paul,
1860 to 1900

	Average Household Size[a]	Number of Households per 100 Adults[b]
1860	4.8	41
1865	5.5	--
1870	--	--
1875	5.9	34
1880	5.7	32
1885	5.6	28
1890	5.2	32
1895	5.2	33
1900	5.3	31

a. The census publications used the word "family" to denote households; see definition of the word "family" in: U. S. Census, Eleventh Census, 1890, Vol. 1, <u>Population</u>, Part 1, clxxxviii. The Census of 1900 for the first time also reported the number of "private families," in Vol. 2, Part 2, clxii.

b. The number of adults for 1860 and 1880 are all men and women age 21 years and over. The number of adults for 1875 and 1885 were estimated from the number of males age 21 years and over, using the proportion of females to males in the total population to estimate female population age 21 and over. Adults for 1890, 1895, and 1900 are all men and women age 20 and over, including those with "age unknown."

Sources: Sample data for 1860, 1880 and 1895; *Minnesota Executive Documents*: (1865), 435; (1875), Vol. 1, 83,98; (1886), Vol. 1, 373,477. Data for 1890 and 1900 from: U. S. Census Bureau, Eleventh Census, 1890, Vol. 1, *Population*, Part 1, cxci, and Part 2, 129; and Twelfth Census, 1900, Vol. 2, *Population*, Part 2, clxii, 343.

to measure the decline in the propensity of adults to reside in separate households more precisely and to partition the decline by age, sex, and ethnic group, to find which of these sub-groups contributed most to the trend. The measure of this tendency used here is "household headship rate" which is the proportion of men or women in a specified age or other category who are either heads of household or the spouse of a head of household. A related measure is "secondary family headship rate" which is the proportion of men or women in a specified age or other category who are family heads (or spouses) of <u>secondary</u> families in a household (i.e. families in a household whose members are unrelated to the head of household). The "secondary family headship rate" is useful as a measure of the degree to which families "doubled up" in households, a phenomenan which one would expect during hard times or a housing shortage. To pick up all household and family heads the definition of "adult" will be persons 15 years or older.

Beginning with Tables 8 and 9, in which a certain degree of control of the effects of migrancy on headship is achieved by limiting the analysis to persons born outside of Minnesota only, it is clear first of all that the overall decline in headship in 1895 was not caused by the "doubling up" of migrant families in households. Only

Table 8

Household and Secondary Family Headship, Men and Women Aged 15 and Over Born Outside of Minnesota, By Place of Birth, St. Paul, 1860.

	Place of Birth				
Headship Type	Ireland %	German States %	Other Foreign %	USA %	Total %
Household Head	70.5	65.7	60.1	58.5	63.6
Secondary Family Hd.	1.1	3.3	4.7	4.5	3.3
Non-head	28.4	31.1	35.3	37.0	33.1
Totals	100.0	100.1	100.1	100.0	100.0
N	373	338	258	467	1436

$p<0.01$ (chi^2 at 6 d.f. = 17.324)
Cramer's V = 0.08319

Table 9

Household and Secondary Family Headship, Men and Women Aged 15 and Over Born Outside of Minnesota, By Place of Birth, St. Paul, 1895.

Headship Type	Place of Birth Ireland %	 Germany %	 Other Foreign %	 USA %	 Total %
Household Head	56.1	60.4	53.9	51.4	54.2
Secondary Family Hd.	0	3.3	2.5	5.1	3.4
Non-head	43.9	36.3	43.6	43.6	42.3
Totals	100.0	100.0	100.0	100.1	99.9
N	123	270	597	590	1580

$p < 0.02$ (chi^2 at 6 d.f. = 16.116)
Cramer's V = 0.07141

about 3% of migrant adults headed secondary families in both years.[48] In general, the ethnic differences in rates were statistically significant in both years (i.e. the probability of the sample distributions occuring by chance were less than 1 in 100 in 1860 and less than 2 in 100 in 1895). The strength of association of place of birth and headship was quite weak, however (Cramer's V varies from 0 for no association to +1.0 for perfect association), indicating that other factors besides place of birth affected headship rates.[49]

Keeping in mind the _expected_ ethnic differences based on other studies (Table 1) it is important to note that, contrary to expectations, Irish headship rates were higher than German or U.S.-born rates in 1860, though by 1895 German rates were highest of the three, as expected. Both German and Irish headship rates were higher than the rate of migrant U.S.-born adults in both years indicating that German and Irish adults contributed to housing demand at a higher rate than U.S.-born migrants in St. Paul. The most striking change from 1860 to 1895 was the decline in headship among Irish adults from 70.5% to 56.1%. This decline of -14% contrasts sharply with the more modest declines of -7% for U.S.-born and -5% for the Germans. Why did headship rates among both foreign immigrants and internal migrants in St. Paul decline from 1860 to 1895?

Why were the rates of German and Irish immigrants higher than those of U.S.-born migrants? Why were Irish rates unusually high in 1860? These are the general questions which require explanation.

Age-Sex Structure and Migration Waves

Changes in the age structure of the migrant adult population of St. Paul from 1860 to 1895 are a logical place to begin the search for an explanation of headship trends among migrant adults. Before examining age structure among migrant adults, it is useful first to note changes in age distribution among all adults. As Table 10 indicates, St. Paul's adult population in 1895 reflected the combined effects of two immigration (and internal migration) waves, one in the 1850's and the other in the 1880's; the population of St. Paul in 1860 was essentially composed of the first wave.

Few if any adults aged 15 years or over in St. Paul in 1860 had been born in what was to become Minnesota (the Territory was organized in 1849). The age structure of St. Paul in 1895 had lower proportions of young adults and a much larger proportion in the age group 35-64. If we use St. Paul's age structure in the two years as a guide, we should expect a lower overall headship rate in 1860 because the adult population was concentrated in younger age brackets when the likelihood of being single was higher than in older age groups.

But what of migrant adults (those born outside Minnesota)? With our knowledge of the probable flows of migrants to St. Paul in the 1850's and 1880's, it is reasonable to expect that the age structure of the migratory adult population of St. Paul in 1895 would closely resemble that of the total adult population. The large migrant adult cohort ages 25-34 which had arrived in St. Paul in 1885, for example, would have helped to swell the total adult cohort ages 35-44 in St. Paul in 1895 (this is the case as Table 10 shows). We also know that immigration declined nationally during the economic depression of the mid-1890's, and this is reflected in the lowered proportions of persons aged 15-34 in St. Paul in 1895 (as compared to previous years). Thus, arguing from age structure and probable migration patterns alone, we would expect an increase in household headship among adult migrants to St. Paul in 1895, not a decrease as our data indicates.

To more closely examine the effects of changes in the age composition of the migrant adult population, 1860 - 1895, Tables 11 and 12 provide a breakdown by age, sex and place of birth for the two years. Looking first at the "N" column in both tables it is obvious that, as

Table 10

Age - Sex Distribution of Total Adult Population of St. Paul, 1860 - 1890

Percentage of Total Adult Population

	1860		1880		1890		1895		1900	
Age	M	F	M	F	M	F	M	F	M	F
65+	0.6	0.6	1.1	1.1	1.4	1.5	0.6	1.1	1.9	2.1
55-64	1.2	1.2	2.3	1.5	2.5	2.5	2.4	1.6	2.8	2.6
45-54	3.7	2.4	6.9	5.0	5.1	4.0	9.3	7.0	6.2	4.7
35-44	11.7	8.9	10.2	6.5	10.1	7.0	12.7	9.1	13.1	9.4
25-34	23.5	18.6	17.3	11.5	19.4	15.0	16.7	10.5	14.9	13.4
15-24	11.1	16.5	17.3	19.1	14.4	16.9	13.7	16.4	13.4	15.4
Total %[a]	51.8	48.2	55.2	44.8	52.9	46.9	52.9	47.1	52.3	47.6
Total Adult Population					91,586[b]				111,812[b]	
Sample Size	1436		1899				1945			

a. Totals for some years do not add to 100.0 due to rounding.

b. Excludes persons with "ages unknown."

Sources: Sample data, 1860, 1880, 1895. U. S. Census Bureau, Eleventh Census, 1890, Vol. 1, Population, Part 2, 1[illegible]9; and Twelfth Census, 1900, Vol. 2, Population, Part 2, 343.

Table 11

Household and Secondary Family Headship Rates. All Men and Women Age 15 and Over Born Outside of Minnesota. By Place of Birth. Sex. and Age. St. Paul. 1860

	N	Place of Birth: Ireland %	German States %	Other Foreign %	U. S. %	Total %	Signif. level	Cramer's V
Household Head		70.5	65.7	60.1	58.5	63.6	.003	.08
Males		74.9	63.4	57.1	57.3	62.8	.009	.11
15-34	263	69.6	57.0	40.4	44.9	53.1	.001	.17
35+	203	86.5	78.0	82.8	82.1	82.[illegible]	NS	NS
Females		67.0	66.8	65.7	59.7	64.7	NS	NS
15-34	309	65.0	68.5	60.0	53.7	61.3	.08	.11
35+	138	73.5	69.4	78.8	73.9	73.8	NS	NS
Secondary Family Head		1.1	3.3	4.7	4.5	3.3		
Males		0.6	2.6	4.1	3.8	2.8		
15-34	11	0	2.[illegible]	5.6	1.9	2.[illegible]		
35+	10	1.9	3.4	1.7	7.7	4.0		
Females		1.5	4.[illegible]	5.6	5.[illegible]	3.9		
15-34	19	1.3	3.7	6.7	4.9	3.8		
35+	8	2.0	5.6	3.0	5.8	4.3		

Source: Sample Data.

Table 12

Household and Secondary Family Headship Rates, All Men and Women Age 15 and Over Born Outside of Minnesota, By Place of Birth, Sex, and Age, St. Paul, 1895

		Place of Birth						
	N	Ireland %	Germany %	Other Foreign %	U. S. %	Total %	Signif. level	Cramer's V
Household Head		56.1	60.4	53.9	51.4	54.2	.02	.07
Males								
15-34	143	35.0	42.0	29.9	30.2	32.1	.08	.11
35+	301	59.5	78.7	78.5	67.1	72.5	.02	.14
Females								
15-34	173	28.0	47.2	44.9	41.9	43.1	NS	NS
35+	237	83.3	75.9	76.8	72.6	75.7	NS	NS
Secondary Family Head								
Males								
15-34	10	0	0	1.1	4.7	2.2		
35+	18	0	5.3	2.7	6.7	4.3		
Females								
15-34	13	0	1.4	3.2	4.7	3.2		
35+	13	0	7.4	4.0	4.0	4.2		

Source: Sample data.

expected, the migrant population of St. Paul had "aged" from 1860 to 1895; younger migrants outnumbered older migrants in the earlier year but the situation was reversed by 1895. Within the age and sex groups headship rates had declined substantially in 1895. Among male migrants aged 15-34, for example, 53% were household heads in 1860, but only 32% were heads in 1895. Though the numbers of persons in the "Secondary Family Head" groups of this table are too small to be statistically reliable, one might suggest that little change in the "secondary family headship rate" occurred among migrants from one year to the next, as the proportions in the table seem to indicate.[50] Among all migrant adults the largest declines in household headship from 1860 to 1895 were registered among the younger age group (-21% for males, -18% for females) though the rates for older males also declined. Thus, despite the presumably upward influence of increased proportions of older people, headship rates decreased among migrants by 10% because declines were present across all age-sex groups (except older females).

Given this general decline we turn to the effect of foreign birth.[51] Recalling from Tables 8 and 9 that Irish rates were unusually high in 1860, we note from Tables 11 and 12 that Irish men and women of both young and older ages (except for older females) contributed high headship rates to the ethnic average of the group in 1860 and that truly remarkable declines in headship rates occurred among all adult Irish men and women by 1895 (again, with the exception of older women). Headship among Irish men aged 15-34 decreased by -35%, and among women of the same age, decreased by -37%. Among Germans, by contrast, the decline in headship was slower than the average for all migrants; the rates for younger German men declined -15% (compared to -21% for all young migrant men) and the rates for older German men actually increased (+1%).

The magnitude of the Irish decline in headship rates can also be seen by comparing the U.S.-born group to the Irish. In 1860, Irish men and women of both age groups had higher headship rates than their U.S.-born counterparts; by 1895, older Irish men and especially younger Irish women had lower headship rates than U.S.-born migrants. And as the number of adults among our ethnic age categories suggest, the age distribution of Irish and Germans in 1895 had "aged" in roughly the same manner as the total migrant population, so that Irish and German declines in headship would not be explained by large proportions of younger migrants in the latter year.

To sum up, it seems reasonably clear that changes in age structure do not explain the trend to lower levels of headship among migrants to St. Paul in 1895; if anything the higher average age of the migrant population in 1895 worked in the opposite direction of the trend among all ethnic groups. What does emerge from our analysis of age and sex among ethnic groups, however, are apparent ethnic differences in the rate of decline in headship within specific age and sex groupings. Especially in the younger ages, ethnic differences in the rate of decline in household headship were large and therefore important.[52]

The rapid rate of decline in headship among young Irish men and women and the much slower decline in rates among young Germans compared to both the Irish and the U.S.-born migrants need to be explained by examining other factors besides age structure. Based on the other studies cited earlier, we may propose that the decline in young Irish headship rates reflected the national trend toward delayed marriage in Ireland (which increased from 1860 to 1895), and that the relative standing of Irish, German and U.S.-born migrant groups in St. Paul in 1895 reflected "preferred" levels of headship rates based on cultural norms developed from national demographic experiences. Another reason for ethnic differences in marriage postponement may have been imbalances in the "marriage market" for young people in St. Paul caused by unbalanced sex ratios within ethnic groups (assuming that endogamy rates were high). Economic differences among the groups also may help to explain differences in headship: average differences in occupational level, unemployment, and female labor force participation, for example, would all effect levels of household income and thus the ability to afford separate dwelling units.

Before moving on to consider these other factors, however, it is useful to recall the trend in headship in the intervening years from 1860 to 1895 (see Table 7). Looking at the trend in number of households per 100 adults, the ratios in Table 7 indicate that among all adults ages 20-21 and over, headship rates were lowest in the mid-1880's probably, as we suggested, because of a housing shortage. Thus the constraints of the housing market, both in the total stock of housing available and in the average cost of housing of each type, may also help to explain declines in headship. There may have been a relative abundance of moderately-priced housing in 1860 (hence the high headship rates) but a relative shortage of the sort of low priced housing which most migrants could afford in 1895. This possibility will be explored in the next section, but first we will examine further the ethnic differerences in marriage and economic patterns.

Young Adults and the Marriage Market

As we suggested earlier, there is no simple one-to-one relationship between marriage rates and household headship rates. Single persons may form households as well as the married, and thus we must investigate both the tendency for young adults to postpone marriage and the tendency to postpone household formation before marriage. Beginning with an analysis of the "marriage market" among young adults, we focus first on young men and women of "prime marriage age" (i.e. women aged 20 to 24, men aged 25 to 29). As Tables 13 and 14 indicate, despite a dramatic shift from a shortage of available women in 1860 to a small "oversupply" in 1895, the household headship rates of all men of prime marriage age declined sharply (-29%) and the same lack of correspondence between available women of the same place of birth and household headship of men occurred for all German, Irish, and U.S.-born as well.[53] Among all women of prime marriage age, the decline in household headship was steeper (-37%) than the men, which one might expect given the overall shortage of available men in 1895 (91 per 100 women).

The "marriage market" for the foreign born was further complicated by the high rate of endogamy among both the Irish and Germans. The Census of 1920, for

Table 13

Sex Ratios Compared to Household Headship Rates, All Men and Women of Prime Marriage Age,[a] by Place of Birth, St. Paul, 1860

	Proportion Who Were Household Heads						
	Men and Women		Women		Men		Males per
Place of Birth	%	N	%	N	%	N	100 females
Ireland	69.8	86	65.8	38	72.9	48	126
German States	64.0	89	64.7	34	63.6	55	162
Other Foreign	53.5	43	43.8	16	59.3	27	169
United States	57.5	87	60.0	40	55.3	47	118
All Places of Birth	62.3	305	60.9	128	63.3	177	138

a. Men ages 25-29, women ages 20-24.

Source: Sample data.

Table 14

Sex Ratios Compared to Household Headship Rates, All Men and Women of Prime Marriage Age,[a] by Place of Birth, St. Paul, 1895

	Proportion Who Were Household Heads						
	Men and Women		Women		Men		Males per
Place of birth	%	N	%	N	%	N	100 females
Ireland	31.3	16	18.2	11	60.0	5	45
Germany	31.7	41	23.1	26	46.7	15	58
Other Foreign	29.4	102	28.9	38	29.7	64	168
United States	27.5	189	22.4	107	34.1	82	77
All Places of Birth	28.7	348	23.6	182	34.3	166	91

a. Men ages 25-29, women ages 20-24.

Source: Samp;e data.

example, reported that 61% of Irish-born mothers of children born in that year were married to Irish-born men, and the figure for German-born mothers was 42%.[54] Assuming high rates of endogamy, can we explain the steeper decline in headship rates among Irish men and women as compared to Germans and U.S., based on sex ratios within ethnic groups? As Tables 13 and 14 indicate, the sex ratios for German women aged 20-24 were somewhat more favorable for endogamous marriage than for Irish women of the same age (58 men per 100 women compared to 45), perhaps partly accounting for the higher headship rates of German women. Among German and Irish men aged 25 to 29, sex ratios may have partly accounted for the higher headship rates of Germans by 1895 but, in general, the change in sex ratios from 1860 to 1895 would point in the opposite direction of the trend in headship rates; Irish and German men aged 25-29 should have demonstrated increases in headship because of an increasingly favorable sex ratio.

The assumption of high rates of endogamy among Irish and Germans is more directly examined in Tables 15 and 16. Despite a shortage of available women of the same place of birth in 1860, and a shortage of men of the same place of birth in 1895, Irish and German young people married within their own ethnic group at a high rate.[55] If marriages between first and second generations were taken

Table 15

Ethnic Intermarriage Rates, German and Irish Married Men Aged 15 to 34 With Spouse Present, St. Paul, 1860.

Wife's Place of Birth	Husband's Place of Birth: Ireland %	Husband's Place of Birth: German States %
Ireland	91.0	10.0
German States	0	72.9
Other	9.0	17.1
Totals	100.0	100.0
N	78	70

Source: Sample data.

Table 16

Ethnic Intermarriage Rates, German and Irish Married Women Aged 15 to 34 With Spouse Present, St. Paul, 1895.

Husband's Place of Birth	Wife's Place of Birth: Ireland %	Wife's Place of Birth: Germany %
Ireland	83.2	0
Germany	0	80.0
Other	16.8	20.0
Totals	100.0	100.0
N	6	30

Source: Sample data.

into account, the endogamy rate would be even higher. summarizing our study of the "marriage market" in 1860 and 1895, we have found that the overall decline in household headship among young people in St. Paul cannot be explained simply by the change in sex ratios from an excess of men to an excess of women, though the steeper decline for young women, and the speedier decline of Irish as compared to German headship rates may be partly explained by higher endogamy rates and lower male-to-female rates among the Irish. It is probable also that the higher headship rates of German and Irish as compared to the U.S.-born in 1895 cannot be explained by differences in sex ratios among the young. The U.S.-born had a more favorable sex ratio in prime marriage ages than did the Irish and Germans (see Table 14).

Marriage Postponement and Household Formation

The trend to strikingly lower household headship rates among young Irish women, taken together with a marked shortage of available Irish men for endogamous marriage, seems to suggest that young Irish women ages 15-34 were postponing marriage in 1895 and were also foregoing the formation of separate "singles" households at a higher rate than in 1860. The markedly higher headship rates for German women of the same age in 1895 seems to indicate that they were postponing either marriage or "singles" household formation (or both) at a substantially slower rate than the Irish or any other group in St. Paul (see Table 12).

To examine the relative marital and household status of ethnic young women in 1895, Table 17 provides percentage rates of household headship, marital status, and labor force participation.[56] Though the numbers upon which the percentages were based in each age group are small in our sample, the general shape of the distribution of rates suggests strongly that household headship rates among Irish women were lower than all other groups because young Irish women (ages 15-34) postponed marriage longer.[57] Irish women ages 15-24 had among the highest proportions gainfully occupied and the lowest proportions heading "singles" households of any group of the same age.

German women, by contrast, had high household headship rates because they married earlier and dropped out of the labor force earlier than other groups. A comparison of Irish, German, other Foreign and U.S.-born migrant women aged 25-34 in Table 17 is instructive: Irish women had the lowest marriage and household headship rates at ages 25-34 of any group, German women the highest. Both German and Irish women were less likely to head "singles" households than U.S.-born migrant women, though the rate

Table 17

Household and Secondary Family Headship Rates Compared to Marriage and Labor Force Participation Rates, Migrant Women Age 15 and Over, By Age and Place of Birth, St. Paul, 1895

Place of Birth and Age	N	Household Headship Rate %	Secondary Family Hdshp. Rate %	Primary Individ. Hdshp. Rate %	Married, Spouse Present %	Domestic Service %	Other Labor Force %
Ireland							
15-24	14	14	0	0	14	29	7
25-34	11	46	0	9	36	9	0
35-44	7	100	0	14	86	0	0
45-64	21	91	0	29	62	5	0
65+	8	50	0	50	0	0	0
Germany							
15-24	41	17	2	7	12	27	10
25-34	31	87	0	0	87	3	0
35-44	26	89	4	0	92	0	4
45-64	22	82	9	27	64	0	5
65+	6	0	17	0	17	0	17

continued on next page

Table 17, continued

Place of Birth and Age	N	Household Headship Rate %	Secondary Family Hdshp. Rate %	Primary Individ. Hdshp. Rate %	Married, Spouse Present %	Domestic Service %	Other Labor Force %
Other Foreign							
15-24	69	17	4	3	19	17	12
25-34	87	67	2	5	66	9	9
35-44	55	82	4	6	80	4	6
45-64	35	80	6	20	66	0	6
65+	12	33	0	17	25	8	0
United States							
15-24	69	19	1	1	19	16	19
25-34	79	62	8	15	54	6	13
35-44	70	73	7	9	70	1	11
45-64	43	81	0	19	63	0	7
65+	11	36	0	18	18	0	0

Source: Sample data.

for Irish women was higher than for German women (see the "primary individual headship" column).

Using the rates in Table 17 as a rough guide to the average life cycle pattern of women in St. Paul's ethnic groups in the latter decades of the nineteenth century, we may pause here to describe probably ethnic differences in the <u>timing</u> of marital, employment, and household formation patterns among young migrant women.[58] Between the ages of 15 and 24 about one third of Irish women entered gainful occupations, typically as domestics. After age 25 Irish women postponed marriage longer than women in other groups, and became heads of "singles" households at a higher rate than other foreign born women (though at a lower rate than U.S.-born migrants).

The typical life cycle of young German women in St.Paul was much more familistic than their Irish counterparts. German women ages 15-24, it is true, tended to postpone marriage and entered gainful occupations at the same rate as the Irish, especially domestic service, but between ages 25-34 a far higher proportion of German women married than the Irish (87% vs. 36% in our table). Unlike married or widowed Irish women, who seldom "doubled up" with other families in a household, a few German married and widowed women became "secondary family heads" as well as household heads after marriage.

The "Other Foreign" and "U.S.-born migrant" women in Table 17 represent more hetergeneous groups than the Irish and Germans, but a few comparisons with them help to give perspective. U.S.-born migrant women ages 15-34 entered other gainful occupations besides domestic service (such as mill work) at a higher rate than German or Irish girls and remained in gainful employment in higher proportions at later ages. Both "Other Foreign" and U.S.-born migrant women postponed marriage less at ages 15-24 than either Irish or German girls, but their proportions married at ages 25-34 were midway between Germans and Irish.

A major problem with using the "U.S.-born migrant" group for comparison is that a large proportion of the group were second generation Irish and German women. In 1890, census data shows that 38% of the female workforce in St. Paul were either Germans or Irish of the second generation.[59] By comparing the surnames of U.S.-born migrant women who were apparently single in 1895 with lists of typical Irish and German surnames, a group of second generation Irish and German single women born outside Minnesota was selected and analyzed.[60] Table 18 compares the labor force participation rates of first and second generation single, migrant women in St. Paul in 1895.

The generational and ethnic differences in the timing of labor force participation by single, migrant

Table 18

Labor Force Participation Rates, Single Migrant Women Ages 15 to 34, By Age, Ethnic Group, and Generation, St. Paul, 1895

	Ethnic Generation					
	First Generation			Second Generation		
Ethnic Group and Age	N	Domestic Service %	Other Labor Force %	N	Domestic Service %	Other Labor Force %
Irish	36	14	3	18	11	17
15-24	12	33	8	9	22	33
25-34	7	14	0	5	0	0
German	55	22	11	15	27	20
15-24	36	31	11	5	40	0
25-34	4	25	0	7	29	29
Other Foreign	118	20	18			
15-24	56	21	14			
25-34	30	27	27			
U. S. - born	138	12	25			
15-24	56	20	23			
25-34	36	14	28			
Other Foreign and U S.-born of U.S. parents				239	5	12
15-24				55	13	18
25-34				67	5	12

Source: Sample data.

women indicated by Table 18 suggest the strength of family norms opposing such participation in each ethnic group. The cell sizes in the table are small and subject to large sampling error, but the pattern of employment for single, migrant women is apparently away from domestic service toward other gainful employment in the second generation.

It seems quite probable, then, that family resistance to the employment of single daughters in mills and stores was lessened by the passage of generations in the United States among both German and Irish groups. The first and second generation women represented in this table were both migrants to Minnesota and entered the same local job market at the same ages. For the Irish this trend toward greater employment outside the home was consistent with established patterns in urban areas of Ireland.[61] The broader question of how this generational change was perceived and how cultural norms were verbalized by Germans and Irish in St. Paul will be analyzed in a later chapter.

Looking back over our discussion of the effects of the postponement of marriage and household formation upon Irish and German household headship rates in 1895, we have found that a substantial difference existed in that year in the age-at-marriage patterns of young German and Irish women; Irish women postponed marriage to a later age than any other group, while German women had the highest marriage rate at ages 25-34 of any other group. We have found also that Irish and German women formed separate "singles" households (as reflected in the "primary individual headship rate") less often than U.S.-born migrants.

On balance, it is quite likely that differences in the timing of marriage was responsible for the much more rapid decline in household headship among the Irish as compared to Germans in St. Paul from 1860 to 1895. German women married earlier and more often doubled up with other families in households if necessary, compared to the Irish. The other question dealt with in this section -- the tendency toward low rates of "singles" household formation among single women -- is more difficult to interpret from the data in Table 17. German and Irish women had lower rates of "primary individual headship" at ages 25-34 as compared to U.S.-born migrants, and we may presume that German rates were low because a high proportion of German women were married at those ages. But what explains the apparently low rate of "singles" household formation among Irish women ages

25-34 compared to the U.S. group?[62] A low rate may have been caused by high proportions of Irish women living in the homes of others as domestics. Or the rate may be explained by a tendency for single Irish women to live together in larger groups in "singles" households, compared to U. S. women in "singles" households. The residence patterns of single Irish and German women will be probed in a later chapter; the question of the effect of "singles" household formation rates on overall ethnic differences in household headship rates will be dealt with there.

Ethnic Differences in Income

So far, in an effort to explain the overall decline in household headship rates in St. Paul from 1860 to 1895 and the ethnic differences in headship rates which contributed to that decline, we have examined the effects of changes in the age structure, in the marriage market for young people, and in the postponement of marriage by young women. As a partial control for the effects of migrancy we have confined our ethnic comparisons to those persons born outside the state of Minnesota. Another probable source of ethnic variation in household headship rates was average ethnic differences in household income -- the effect of social class. We have analyzed briefly the tendency in St. Paul for single ethnic women to move increasingly away from domestic service to factory work from first to second generation, and thus toward greater potential for "singles" household formation. The question considered here is the effect of the average occupational level and unemployment status of ethnic working men on their household headship tendencies.[63]

From the standpoint of the economic market for residential dwelling units, economic theory suggests that household headship rates will be affected positively by increases in income and wealth and negatively with increases in the cost of housing.[64] A detailed study of the negative effects of the cost of housing in St. Paul on household headship rates will be done in a later chapter based on housing permit data. In this chapter we will ask whether ethnic differences in household headship rates remain important among men earning their living at the same occupational level or in the same type of industry. Can we account for ethnic differences in headship by controlling for earnings?

Before presenting tables of headship with occupational controls, it is well to recall that the "census year" for 1895, from June, 1894 to May, 1895, coincided with the beginnings of an economic upturn from the "industrial and commercial stagnation that reached its nadir about June, 1894"[65] nationally. Thus the connection between average wages paid at specific occupational levels in St. Paul and the average annual earnings of workmen was complicated by industrial differences in unemployment rates. It is possible that two workmen paid at the same wage rate earned very different amounts per year because unemployment rates differed among the industries where they were employed.

One way to study the effects of unemployment rates on probable annual earnings in specific industries in St. Paul is to use the unemployment data of the 1890 Census. As Table 19 indicates, workmen in white collar jobs in that year reported very little unemployment. In blue collar trades, unemployment rates varied dramatically depending on the type of industry. In the construction industry unemployment was high, probably because the estimated value of building starts declined 32% from 1889 to 1890.[66] Unemployment rates also varied within the industry; tradesmen like brick masons and stone cutters who worked on high cost brick and stone structures were out of work at more than twice the rate of carpenters. The downturn in construction probably also caused the high unemployment rate among unskilled laborers. In sharp contrast, tradesmen in the apparel industry had lower unemployment rates than the average for all male workmen.

Table 19

Industrial Differences in Unemployment Rates in Selected Occupations, All Gainfully Occupied Males Age 10 Years and Over, St. Paul, June 1, 1889 - May 31, 1890

Industry & Occupation	Total Workers (1)	Total employed 6 mos. + (2)	Total employed 6-8 mos. (3)	Adjusted Unemployment Rate (%) (3/2x100)
High White Collar				
Lawyers	476	474	0	0
Officials	453	450	6	1
Physicians	225	224	1	0
Bankers	433	431	3	1
Merchants	2436	2421	13	1
Sub-total	4023	4000	23	1
Low White Collar				
Hotel Keepers	200	198	0	0
Restaur. Keep.	379	377	4	1
Bookkeepers	4831	4780	93	2
Salesmen	866	860	15	2
Comm. Travel.	593	590	2	0
Agents	1425	1414	16	1
Sub-total	8294	8219	130	2
Construction Trades				
Masons	964	914	367	40
Cutters	220	196	68	35
Carpenters	2993	2869	411	14
Painters	1048	1018	140	14
Plumbers	471	459	35	8
Plasterers	259	255	75	29
Sub-total	5955	5711	1096	19
Apparel Trades				
Boot & Shoe	716	703	28	4
Tailors	586	573	26	5
Sub-total	1302	1276	54	4
Laborers	7131	6809	1533	23
All Male Work.	57,817	56,778	3609	6

Building construction in St. Paul declined steadily from 1888 to 1898, though jobbing and manufacturing quickly resumed a steady upward trend in 1895 after the "Panic of 1893".[67] In fact, there is some evidence that the Depression of the 1890's improved the commercial position of jobbers in St. Paul by allowing them to undercut competition from Chicago and Milwaukee.[68] At the Census of 1895, the unemployment rate for blue collar workmen in St. Paul was 23%; the rate for unskilled laborers in 1895 was 28%, and 20% for skilled labor.[69] The white collar unemployment rate was not available from the published summary of the Census of 1895, but due to the overall strength of St. Paul's commercial sector we may assume that the rate was substantially lower than the blue collar rate.

Given these economic circumstances in St. Paul in 1895 we will not be far wrong if we presume that unemployment patterns generally increased the distance between average white and blue collar annual earnings. While wage <u>rates</u> probably did not decline substantially among blue collar workers during the depression,[70] annual <u>earnings</u> especially among workmen in the construction industry probably fell off dramatically. Since our sample size does not allow finer distinctions, we will confine ourselves to a white collar/blue collar dichotomy to represent the social class differential in income and a "primary-secondary" vs. "tertiary" division (i.e. agricultural, extractive, manufacturing, and construction vs. business, professional and government) to represent the major economic sectors.

Keeping in mind the unusual circumstances of 1895, we turn in Tables 20 and 21 to a study of trends in ethnic household headship rates, 1860 to 1895, with controls for probable average annual earnings. To control for the effects of labor force participation, migration, and age we confine the analysis to gainfully occupied men aged 15 to 34 born outside the state of Minnesota in both years. Looking first of all at the statistics for strength of association between place of birth and household headship, we note that, (except in three sectors where sample size produced non-significant results as indicated by "p"), ethnicity does not "wash out" statistically when controlling for income. On the contrary, place of birth is more strongly associated with headship <u>within</u> economic classes than is the case overall and the association seems to be stronger in 1895 than in 1860.[71]

Before examining specific ethnic trends in Tables 20 and 21, it is important to note the startingly different trends for gainfully occupied young men in these tables as compared to the trends for <u>all</u> young men

Table 20

Household and Secondary Family Headship Rates, Migrant Gainfully Occupied Men Ages 15 to 34, By Place of Birth, Occupational Level, and Economic Sector, St. Paul, 1860

Headship Type and Place of Birth	Occupational Level		Economic Sector		Totals	
	White Collar %	Blue Collar %	Primary Secondary %	Tertiary %	Percent	N
Household Head	67.7	54.4	59.5	70.0	58.2	
Ireland	100.0	68.4	79.2	100.0	72.0	77
Germ. States	80.0	54.7	62.8	75.0	60.8	76
Other Foreign	47.1	46.6	50.0	57.1	46.7	35
United States	61.8	39.0	37.0	66.7	50.8	65
Secondary Family Head	3.1	1.6	1.6	3.0	2.1	
Ireland	0	0	0	0	0	0
Germ. States	0	2.1	2.6	0	1.6	2
Other Foreign	5.9	5.2	4.2	0	5.3	4
United States	4.4	0	0	5.3	2.3	3
Significance Level	.05	.01	.01	NS	.01	
Cramer's V	.22	.19	.24	NS	.15	

Source: Sample data.

Table 21

Household and Secondary Family Headship Rates, Migrant Gainfully Occupied Men Ages 15 to 34, By Place of Birth, Occupational Level, and Economic Sector, St. Paul, 1895

Headship Type and Place of Birth	Occupational Level		Economic Sector		Totals	
	White Collar %	Blue Collar %	Primary Secondary %	Tertiary %	Percent	N
Household Head	55.6	55.5	62.0	50.3	55.7	436
Ireland	60.0	54.8	62.5	46.0	56.1	32
Germany	69.4	64.1	64.6	67.3	65.1	84
Other Foreign	63.0	50.9	58.5	50.3	54.9	173
United States	48.6	57.8	66.7	46.6	52.1	147
Secondary Family Head	4.7	2.4	2.0	4.4	3.4	27
Ireland	0	0	0	0	0	0
Germany	2.8	2.2	2.5	2.0	2.3	3
Other Foreign	3.3	1.4	1.3	2.6	1.9	6
United States	6.2	5.9	4.2	6.8	6.4	18
Significance Level	NS	.04	NS	.07	.01	
Cramer's V	NS	.12	NS	.12	.10	

Source: Sample data.

(including those not reporting an occupation) reported in Tables 11 and 12. The household headship rates for young men with occupations declined only 3% while the rate for all young men declined 21% for 1860 to 1895, probably caused by an increase in the age at entry into the labor force for young men during the period.

Turning now to the "blue collar" columns in Tables 20 and 21, where we had predicted a strong depressant effect on headship in 1895 because of high unemployment rates, it is curious to find that headship rates for gainfully-occupied, young migrant men <u>increased</u> during the period in every ethnic group except the Irish (whose household headship rate decreased by -14%). In fact, looking at ethnic household headship trends in all of the economic categories, declines in headship were associated with white collar occupations and the tertiary sector and increases in headship were associated with blue collar occupations and the primary and secondary sectors -- exactly the opposite of what we expected. The only major exception to this pattern was the Irish whose headship rates declined in all sectors.

Of course the underlying fact that higher income produces higher headship rates is born out by our tables; white collar rates are uniformly higher than blue collar rates in both years. What is surprising is the direction of trends within each sector over the period. One possible explanation is that average income differences between white and blue collar workers narrowed from 1860 to 1895, causing the rates to converge, but this interpretation seems to be doubtful in view of the substantial differences in unemployment rates between the two classes suggested by Table 19. What we may have here is a major difference in social class preferences. Despite the economic difficulties of forming separate households, young men in blue collar occupations may have preferred separate household arrangements and sacrificed other consumption items to obtain separate dwelling units. Or it may be that the frontier housing conditions of St. Paul in 1860 provided unusually small opportunities for separate household formation for the working class, a condition which was rectified by the growth of St. Paul's stock of housing.

To discover whether housing conditions in frontier St. Paul in 1860 were especially unfavorable for young blue collar workers we turn to Table 22. The category "$0" or no real estate holdings is especially revealing. A sharp break in the proportions of household heads holding no real estate is apparent between the "Low White Collar" and "Skilled" levels (36% vs. 53%). And it is especially interesting that a lower proportion of Irish household heads were without real estate

Table 22

Real Estate Holdings of Household Heads, By Place of Birth and Occupational Level, St Paul, 1860

Occupation and Value of Real Estate Holding	N	Place of Birth: Ireland %	German States %	Other Foreign %	U. S. %	Total %
High White Collar						
$1501 and over	8	0	16.7	100.0	66.7	47.1
$1 to $1500	3	0	16.7	0	22.2	17.6
$0	6	100.0	66.7	0	11.1	35.3
Low White Collar						
$1501 and over	21	18.2	40.0	28.6	39.3	34.4
$1 to $1500	18	63.6	13.3	28.6	25.0	29.5
$0	22	18.2	46.7	42.9	35.7	36.1
Skilled						
$1501 and over	11	13.3	5.0	5.0	42.9	12.4
$1 to $1500	31	26.7	37.5	35.0	35.7	34.8
$0	47	60.0	57.5	60.0	21.4	52.8

continued on next page

Table 22, continued

	N	Place of Birth Ireland %	German States %	Other Foreign %	U. S. %	Total %
Semi skilled						
$1501 and over	1	0	0	0	20.0	4.8
$1 to $1500	7	50.0	0	33.3	40.0	33.3
$0	13	50.0	100.0	66.7	40.0	61.9
Unskilled						
$1501 and over	1	0	0	0	50.0	2.0
$1 to $1500	13	28.2	16.7	50.0	0	26.5
$0	35	71.8	83.3	50.0	50.0	71.4
Not Gainfully Occupied						
$1501 and over	3	0	50.0	0	28.6	27.3
$1 to $1500	1	0	0	0	14.3	9.1
$0	7	100.0	50.0	100.0	57.1	63.6

Note: The association between place of birth and value of real estate for all heads is significant at the .001 level and the strength of association (Cramer's V) is .27. Among occupational categories, only "Skilled" and "Unskilled" groups were significant at the .05 level, with strength of association between place of birth and value of holding (Cramer's V) at .31 and .51, respectively.

Source: Sample data.

holdings compared to German heads (in every category except "Skilled"), which helps to account for the unusually high Irish household headship rates in 1860 as compared to the Germans (see Table 8)[72]

Whatever the reason for the increases in household headship rates among young, migrant, blue-collar workers from 1860 to 1895, it is clear from Tables 20 and 21 that ethnic patterns could not be "explained away" by controlling for social class. The dramatic Irish decline in headship showed up there as well even in the blue collar sector where other groups registered increases in headship. And as Table 8 suggests, despite low blue collar real estate holding tendencies, Irish blue collar workers in 1860 may have exceeded their German counterparts in forming households in that year because of their greater desire to hold real estate, in a housing market where few structures could be rented because so few had been constructed. By 1895, perhaps largely because of the increasing Irish propensity to postpone marriage, Irish headship rates among young men had declined to a midway position between German and U.S. rates, as we expected from other studies. (Table 1)

Conclusion

The question of ethnic differences in household headship rates as we have dealt with them in this chapter involves two separate issues: how much did ethnic groups differ from each other in the level of household headship rates in each year, and how much different were ethnic *trends* in household headship rates from one year to the next. Limiting our comparisons to migrants to St. Paul from outside Minnesota only, we observed (Tables 8 and 9) that the level of difference among ethnic groups was greater in 1860 than in 1895, and the same pattern was generally true among all age, sex, and income categories (Tables 11,12, 17, 20, 21).

To achieve the more nearly similar household headship rates among ethnic groups in 1895, Irish headship rates declined sharply from an unusually high level in 1860 (compared to Eastern urban areas) to a position midway between German and U.S.-born migrants in 1895. The trends for Irish, German and U.S.-born migrant groups were generally downward from 1860 to 1895, though the pace of the decline varied from rapid for the Irish to quite slow for the Germans. Though the precise level of ethnic difference in household headship rates was affected by demographic and economic factors, in St. Paul Irish and German rates varied from 9% to 22% higher than that of U.S.-born migrants.

An explanation of both the levels of difference in ethnic headship rates and of the differences in the rate of decline of those rates involves cultural, demographic and economic factors. The most powerful reason for the general decline in headship rates for all groups in St. Paul for 1860 to 1895 was probably the strong depressant effect of unemployment during the Depression of the 1890's. Though unemployment information was not available for St. Paul in 1860, it is safe to assume from national trends that unemployment in that year was much less than for 1895 even though both were "trough" years.[73] Oddly enough though, the effect of unemployment was less in the blue collar sector of the workforce than in the white collar, despite the greater unemployment among blue collar workmen. Demographically speaking, the "maturing" of the age-sex structure in St. Paul from the "young" migrant population of the frontier town to the "older" migrant population of the commercial metropolis did not explain the general decline in headship rates, but probably worked in the opposite direction, retarding the downward slide.

Against this background of a general decline in headship rates, the ethnic trends differed considerably, from the rapid descent from unusually high levels among the Irish, to a slower descent at middle levels among the Germans. Here the explanation of differences in rate of decline involves an interaction of cultural and demographic factors. Both Irish and German immigrants strongly preferred mates of the same nationality in St. Paul, but for young women spouses of the same nationality were increasingly scarce from 1860 to 1895 as the sex ratio among young people changed from an excess of males to an excess of females. The result, especially for young Irish women, was an increasing tendency to postpone marriage and separate household formation.

The scarcity of Irish males in the marriage market helps to explain the increased postponement of household formation by Irish women, but it must be remembered that Irish men (especially those in the white collar employment sector) also increasingly postponed the formation of separate households. The explanation for this seems to be primarily cultural; a rising trend toward marriage postponement and permanent celibacy in Ireland during these decades was reflected in a similar cultural norm among young Irish migrants in St. Paul in 1895.

German household formation trends were much slower to change than those of the Irish in St. Paul and reflected to some extent the demographic experience of Prussia during the same decades. E. A. Wrigley found that, though either Catholic affiliation or residence in an industrialized area tended to increase postponement of marriage among Prussian women from 1850 to 1900, in general Prussian women aged 25 to 29 married at a higher rate than women in a similar region of France.[74] This national demographic tendency toward early marriage was reflected among young German women in St. Paul (Table 17) and helps to explain why German household headship rates among young people declined more slowly than those of the Irish or U.S.-born migrants.

If these Irish and German trends in family and household formation were generally true in other cities, the economic implications of the ethnic differences would be important for our understanding of the history of urban growth in the nineteenth century. It would be important to know not only the total amount of net immigration but also the ethnic composition of that immigrant population to correctly assess the influence on levels of demand for housing and other services. In a later chapter we will test this possibility with an ecological comparison of other major American cities.

I have suggested the probable influence of cultural norms upon family and household formation patterns in this chapter, based upon comparisons with what is known about national demographic patterns in Ireland and Germany.

In a later chapter we will investigate the reactions and rationalizations of Irish and German immigrants in St. Paul (and other Midwestern cities) to their ethnic trends in family and household behavior. What we have accomplished in this chapter is to identify the range of group differences in the timing of family and household formation, a range which indicates that German family patterns changed more slowly than those of the Irish, and that early marriage continued to be highly valued for young German immigrants at the end of the century. Our brief foray into generational changes among single women suggests also that both German and Irish families allowed greater freedom to their single daughters by the second generation. These generational changes will be more thoroughly explored in later chapters on housing and occupational patterns.

What we have learned about the internal processes of urban development in the nineteenth century is less clear but a few possibilities can be ventured. The metamorphosis from frontier town to commercial metropolis, typical of Western cities for example, provided a housing market where the Irish impulse to acquire real estate gave them a substantial early advantage over other immigrants at the same income levels. (Table 22) The ability or desire to acquire title to housing was especially important in frontier cities where immigrants directly increased the demand for new housing.

We have also learned that the pattern of only one household per dwelling unit (reflected in the low rates of "secondary family headship") was surprisingly stable during this metamorphosis, despite changing unemployment levels and housing supply. The impetus for single family dwellings reflected by the statement of St. Paul's Chamber of Commerce in 1884 that "very liberal terms" were offered to "persons of small means, mechanics and laborers, to secure a comfortable home of their own in a respectable locality"[75] was especially powerful and successful in frontier cities.[76]

Footnotes

[1]For a recent review of the literature see Rudolph J. Vecoli, "European Americans: From Immigrants to Ethnics," International Migration Review, 6 (Winter, 1972), 403-434.

[2]See for example: William V. Shannon, The American Irish (New York, 1963), 22-23, and Edward M. Levine, The Irish and Irish Politicians: A Study of Cultural and Social Alienation (Notre Dame, Indiana, 1966),146-155

[3]See for example: Claude M. Fuess, Carl Schurz: Reformer, 1829-1906 (New York, 1932), 5-16

[4]Marcus L. Hansen, "The Third Generation in America," Commentary, 14(November, 1952) 493-500.

[5]Leonard Covello, The Social Background of the Italo-American School Child (Leiden, 1967) is an important example.

[6]Virginia Yans McLaughlin's doctoral dissertation, "Like the Fingers of the Hand: The Family and Community Life of First-Generation Italian-Americans in Buffalo, New York, 1880-1930" (State University of New York at Buffalo, 1970) is one of the few recent studies of this kind.

[7]Though ethnic differences are not explored, the possibilities are suggested by studies of the twentieth century setting: Reuben Hill, Family Development in Three Generations (Cambridge, 1970), a study of family consumption decision patterns, and Christopher Jencks, et al., Inequality: A Reassessment of the Effect of Family and Schooling in America (New York, 1972). The family influence on political affiliation in contemporary America is reviewed in R. W. Connell, Political Socialization in the American Family: The Evidence Re-examined," Public Opinion Quarterly, 36 (Fall, 1972, 322-333.

[8]See Charles M. Dollar and Richard J. Jensen, Historian's Guide to Statistics (New York, 1971), Chapter One, and pages 90-124, for a general discussion of these issues in historical research.

[9]See, for example, Kathleen Neils Conzen, "The German Athens: Milwaukee and the Accomodation of its immigrants, 1836-60" (Ph.D. dissertation, University of Wisconsin- Madison, 1972)

[10]Susan E. Bloomgerg, _et al_., "A Census Probe into Nineteenth-Century Family History: Southern Michigan 1850-1880," _Journal of Social History_, 5 (Fall, 1971), 26-45; Frank L. Mott, "Portrait of an American Mill Town: Demographic Response in Mid-nineteenth Century Warren, Rhode Island," _Population Studies_, 26 (March, 1972), 147-157; Daniel J. Walkowitz, "Working Class Women in the Gilded Age: Factory, Community and Family Life Among Cohoes, New York, Cotton Workers," _Journal of Social History_, 5 (Summer, 1972), 464-490; Laurence A. Glasco, "Ethnicity and Social Structure: Irish, German and Native-born of Buffalo, New York, 1850 - 1860," (Ph.D.dissertation, State University of New York at Buffalo, 1973); Barbara Laslett, "Household Structure on an American Frontier: Los Angeles, California, in 1850." _American Journal of Sociology_, 81 (July, 1975), 109-128.

[11]See the Glasco, Laslett and Walkowitz citations above, and Richard Sennett, _Families Against the City; Middle Class Homes of Industrial Chicago, 1872 - 1890_ (Cambridge, 1970), 81-83; John Modell and Tamara K. Hareven, "Urbanization and the Malleable Household: An Examination of Boarding and Lodging in American Families." _Journal of Marriage and the Family_, 35 (August, 1973), 467-479.

[12]See, for example: E. A. Wrigley, _Industrial Growth and Population Change: A Regional Study of the Coalfield Areas of North-West Europe in the Later Nineteenth Century_ (Cambridge, 1961); Robert E. Kennedy, Jr., _The Irish: Emigration, Marriage, and Fertility_ (Berkeley, 1973) and Michael Anderson, _Family Structure in Nineteenth Century Lancashire_ (Cambridge, 1971).

[13]a.Glasco (Buffalo), 167, 171.
b.Rosenwaike (New York City), 80-81
c.Glasco (Buffalo), 34; Mott (Warren,Rhode Island), 153

13(continued)
d. Glasco (Buffalo), 144-145; Mott (Warren), 155. Rosenwaike (New York City), 74
e. Glasco (Buffalo), 190; Walkowitz (Cohoes, New York), 477
f. Glasco (Buffalo), 190; Walkowitz (Cohoes).
g. Glasco (Buffalo), 190
h. Glasco (Buffalo), 190
i. Glasco (Buffalo), 147; Walkowitz (Cohoes), 479.
j. Glasco (Buffalo), 149, 161; Walkowitz (Cohoes) 479.
k. Modell and Hareven (Boston), 471; Glasco (Buffalo), 149, 161; Walkowitz (Cohoes), 479.

14 Kennedy, The Irish, 139-145.

15 Wrigley, Industrial Growth and Population Change, 132-157.

16 David M. Heer, "The Marital Status of Second-Generation Americans," American Sociological Review, 26 (April, 1961), 236, 239.

17 Ibid., 237

18 Sennett, Families Against the City, 98-119

19 Walkowitz, "Working-Class Women in the Gilded Age" 481-482.

20 Elizabeth H. Pleck, "The Two Parent Household: Black Family Structure in Late Nineteenth-Century Boston," Journal of Social History, 6 (Fall, 1972), 1-31; Paul J. Lammermier, "The Urban Black Family of the Nineteenth Century: A study of Black Family Structure in the Ohio Valley, 1850-1880," Journal of Marriage and the Family, 35 (August, 1973), 440-456; Theodore Hershberg, "Free Blacks in Antebellum Philadelphia: A Study of Ex-Slaves Free-Born and Socio-Economic Decline," Journal of Social History, 5 (Winter, 1971-72), 183-209; Frank F. Furstenberg, Jr., Theodore Hershberg and John Modell, "The Origins of the Female Headed Black Family: The Impact of the Urban Experience." Journal of Interdisciplinary History, 6 (Spring, 1975), 211-233; and Walkowitz, "Working-Class Women in the Gilded Age." 479-482

21 Modell and Hareven, "Urbanization and the Malleable Household." 470-472

[22] Anderson, Family Structure, 20-21, 68-78, 99-110, 180.

[23] Richard A. Easterlin, Population, Labor Force, and Long Swings in Economic Growth: The American Experience (New York, 1968), 23

[24] Ibid., 48-49

[25] Anderson, Family Structure, 112-123.

[26] Virginia Y. McLaughlin, "Patterns of Work and Family Organization: Buffalo's Italians," Journal of Interdisciplinary History, 2 (Autumn, 1971), 299-314

[27] Two reviews by Robert Ferber ably survey the economic and some of the interdisciplinary research on household consumption patterns: "Research on Household Behavior," American Economic Review, 52 (March, 1962), 19-63; and "Consumer Economics: A survey," Journal of Economic Literature, 11 (December, 1973), 1303-1342. See also the historical study by Jeffrey G. Williamson, "Consumer Behavior in the Nineteenth Century: Carrol D. Wright's Massachusetts Workers in 1975," Explorations in Entrepreneurial History, 2nd Ser., 4 (Winter, 1967), 98-135.

[28] Tamara K. Hareven, "The Family as Process: The Historical Study of the Family Cycle," Journal of Social History, 7(Spring, 1974), 322-324.

[29] For an example of the study of family trends via the comparison of cross-sectional distributions see Paul C. Glick, American Families (New York, 1957); on the use of cohort comparisons over time see Norman B. Ryder, "The Cohort as a Concept in the Study of Social Change", American Sociological Review 30(1965), 843-861.

[30] See the efforts of the U.S. Census Bureau to project trends in the formation and composition of households to estimate future consumption demand: "Projections of the Number of Households and Families, 1955 and 1960," Current Population Reports,Series P-20, No. 42, December 28, 1952; and "Projections of the Number of Households and Families, 1967 to 1985," Current Population Reports, Series P-25, No. 394, June 6, 1968.

[31] Burnham O. Campbell, Population Change and Building Cycles(Univ. of Illinois, Bureau of Economic and Business Research, Bulletin No. 91, 1966), 118-143.

[32]See appendix for a discussion of the sampling procedure and reliability estimates.

[33]Richard A. Easterlin, Population, Labor Force, and Long Swings in Economic Growth: The American Experience (New York, 1968), 21-36

[34]See, e.g., the remarks on the new urban histories by Charles Glaab in a book review, Journal of American History, 62(December, 1975), 658-660.

[35]Easterlin, Population, 25.

[36]The proportion of all foreign-born persons born in Germany and Ireland in 1860 was 69.7% and in 1890, 50.3%; see Niles Carpenter, Immigrants and Their Children:1920 (Washington, 1927), 79

[37]On the national "waves" of German and Irish immigration (peak years for Germans were 1854 and 1882 and for Irish, 1851 and 1882), see U.S. Immigration Commission Reports(42 vols.; Washington, D.C., 1907-1910), Vol.3, Statistical Review of Immigration, 1820-1910), 14-44. For a review of German immigration to the State of Minnesota, see John C. Massman, "German Immigration to Minnesota, 1850-1890" (Ph.D. thesis, University of Minnesota, 1966), 168-242.

[38]Minnesota Fourth Decennial Census, 1895,Abstract, 45, and U. S. Census Bureau, Census of 1860, Vol. 1, Population, 259. The exact numbers reported were 10,401, 140,292

[39]See for example Sam B. Warner, Jr., Streetcar Suburbs: The Process of Growth in Boston, 1870-1900 (New York, 1962), 67-86

[40]Secretary of State, Minnesota Executive Documents (St. Paul, 1886), Vol. 1,514, and U. S. Census Bureau, Census of 1880, Vol. 1, Population, 451

[41]According to the St. Paul Chamber of Commerce, it was "cheaper to buy than to rent" in St. Paul in 1884 and "nearly every family lives in its own house;" see Annual Report of the St. Paul Chamber of Commerce for the Year Ending Dec. 31, 1884 (St. Paul, 1885), 62

[42]Mildred L. Hartsough, The Twin Cities As a Metropolitan Market (Minneapolis, 1925), 48-71.

[43]U. S. Census Bureau, Census of 1900, Vol. 1, Part 1, Population, 432

[44]As the notes for Table 4 indicate, Hershberg, *et al*. selected only those gainfully occupied adults whose occupations occurred frequently enough to be found in the upper 75% of all occupations reported; though the St.Paul distribution is based on a sample of *all* gainfully occupied workers, the distributions are probably roughly comparable.

[45]Massman, "German Immigration to Minnesota," 169-170, 176-178, 236, provides background on probable German migration paths to Minnesota.

[46]On the theory of intervening opportunities, see: Samuel A. Stouffer, "Intervening Opportunities: A Theory Relating Mobility and Distance," *American Sociological Review*, 5 (December, 1940), 845-867.

[47]Glick, *American Families*, 22. See also the declines in both rural and urban places in Southern Michigan, 1850 to 1890, reported in Bloomberg, *et al*., "A Census Probe into Nineteenth-Century Family History," 30. Mean size of all U. S. households declined from 5.43 in 1790 to 3.05 in 1950.

[48]A separate calculation for all adults regardless of birthplace showed only 3.1% were secondary family heads. Adults born in Minnesota represented 18.8% of the total adult population in 1895.

[49]For a convenient summary of other reasons why the calculated strength of association may differ from the true strength, see Dollar and Jensen, *Historians Guide to Statistics*, 90-104.

[50]The phrase "not statistically reliable" simply means that the numbers of persons within a "cell" of a table are so small that small chance changes in their magnitude make large differences in proportions. The "real" proportion of adult migrants who were secondary heads in the total adult migrant population may or may not have been equal to the sample proportion; our sample size is simply too small to be certain because of the possibility of large chance variations.

[51]Again, cell size among ethnic age and sex groups are too small to be statistically reliable. A "multiple classification analysis" would seem to be the preferred

technique of multivariate analysis here (see B. Laslett, "Household Structure on an American Frontier") because of small sample size. An attempt to use MCA for the 1895 sample with place of birth, sex, age, migratory status, and occupational status as independents proved unhelpful, however; two-way interaction effects among independents were significant at the 0.01 level (see appendix for more complete discussion).

[52]In statistical terms, the control for age increases the strength of association between headship and place of birth. Among males age 15-34, the values of Cramer's V are increased from 0.08 to 0.17 by controlling for age in 1860 and from 0.07 to 0.11 in 1895 ($p < 0.01$ in 1860, $p < 0.08$ in 1895).

[53]Since the ethnic composition of the "Other Foreign" category was quite different in 1860 and 1895, this group will be treated as a residual category in this analysis.

[54]Niles Carpenter, Immigrants and their Children (Washington, 1927), 234.

[55]Obviously, the cell sizes in these tables are unreliably small and the figures are intended only to suggest the direction of the trend, not the precise level. The high rates of endogamy for Irish women, despite severe shortages of Irish men, was found also in Warren, Rhode Island, where 80% of the marriages of Irish women were to Irish men from 1850 to 1879 (Mott, Portrait of an American Mill Town,"155).

[56]Cell sizes in the table are unreliably small in many cases, but I have reported statistics for significance and strength of association anyway because the overall distribution shows a strong apparent association between place of birth and the reported rates. Statistics were calculated on frequencies for the complete tables including residual categories not reported here.

[57]The rate "married, spouse present" of course understates the true proportions ever married, but this is the closest approximation available for the 1895 census data, which did not report marital status directly.

[58]Comparisons of the behavior of age groups in one year of course are not the same as comparing individual or cohort life cycles longitudinally from one census to the next, and this description of ethnic life cycles

assumes that other conditions over the previous decades were the same as those present in 1895 and affected each age group equally. Since this assumption is questionable the descriptions of life cycles must be treated with caution.

[59]U.S. Census Bureau, Twelfth Census, Special Report-Occupations, 712-713

[60]See appendix for more complete discussion of assumptions made about ethnic surnames. Second generation "Other Foreign" were identified as the remainder of single women born in the U.S. with one or both parents of foreign birth. Second generation U.S. women were U.S.-born with both U.S.-born parents. Widows with co-residence children were excluded from the "single" category.

[61]Kennedy, The Irish, 159-163.

[62]The apparent difference in rates may also be due to chance sampling error as a result of small cell sizes.

[63]Social class distinctions must be confined to men because of the lack of a workable indicator of social class standing for women in the census data. Women's occupations cannot serve this purpose because: a) a minority of women were gainfully occupied; b) those who were occupied were mostly confined to young single women; and c) most occupations held by women were in the domestic service category.

[64]Campbell, Population Change and Building Cycles,46

[65]Charles Hoffmann, The Depression of the Nineties: An Economic History (Westport, Conn., 1970), 71-72

[66]St. Paul Chamber of Commerce, Annual Report For the Year Ending December 31, 1890 (St. Paul, 1891), 41

[67]See St. Paul Building Inspector, Report, 1885-1899; St. Paul Chamber of Commerce, Annual Report,1898, 63.

[68]Hartsough, The Twin Cities as a Metropolitan Market, 165-166.

[69]State of Minnesota, Fourth Decennial Census, 1895 Abstract, 280. For calculation of the rate, see Table 19.

[70] Hoffmann, _The Depression of the Nineties_, 254-258, provides national estimates suggesting this.

[71] In 1860, for example, Cramer's V increases from .10 overall to .12 in blue collar jobs, and in 1895 Cramer's V increases from .15 overall to .19 in blue collar jobs. Those sections of the tables where p is $<.05$ are "not significant" statistically, probably because of our small sample size. In general, though, the association between place of birth and headship is stronger in 1895, and more persistent when social class controls are applied, as compared to 1860, though the _level_ of association is quite weak.

[72] This Irish propensity for real estate holdings is consistent with findings in Newburyport, Massachusetts, 1850-1880; see Stephen Thernstrom, _Poverty and Progress; Social Mobility in a Nineteenth Century City_ (New York, 1964), 155-517.

[73] Stanley Lebergott, for example has estimated the national unemployment rate in 1858 at 6% - 8%, compared to 15%+in 1894; see _Manpower in Economic Growth: The American Record Since 1800_ (New York, 1964), 187,522

[74] See footnote no. 15

[75] See footnote no. 41

[76] See Warner, _Streetcar Suburbs_, 67-116, for a discussion of the economic consequences of this impulse in a large Eastern city.

Chapter 2

Ethnicity and Housing in St. Paul: A study of Irish and German Housing Trends, 1860 - 1895

In the first chapter we discovered that the tendency for adults to form households in St. Paul declined between 1860 and 1895 especially among young adults. At the same time, Irish and German household headship rates remained somewhat higher than those of U.S.-born migrants in 1895, though increasing postponement of marriage among the Irish even in white collar occupational levels had reduced Irish headship levels considerably between the two years. The higher headship rates of Irish and German immigrants, even during a period of severe economic distress indicated that adults in these groups contributed more strongly to the demand for separate dwelling units than did U.S.-born migrants.

A plausible explanation of the general trend toward the postponement of household formation may also have been a response to a housing shortage during the Depression of the 1890's. Residential housing construction in St. Paul declined 94% from 1889 to 1894.[1] Rather than "doubling up" households, within existing dwelling units, St. Paul's young adult migrants may have decided to postpone the formation of households until more housing was built in better times.[2] If young adults made this decision in large numbers we should expect to find a larger proportion of young adults living in boarding houses and hotels, and a larger proportion of young lodgers living in private households in 1895 as compared to 1860. One purpose of this chapter is to test this possible explanation.

The very real possibility of achieving this norm for many households existed during the boom years of the 1880's in St. Paul. During the Depression, however, the construction of all housing including low cost single story frame dwellings fell off dramatically and mortgage credit was at least temporarily scarce. The pressure for home ownership among household heads probably shifted to increased demand for the rental or purchase at low cost of the existing single household dwellings of the city.[3] While unmarried persons are likely to find multiple household dwellings acceptable, the demand for single household dwellings is typically much less "elastic" for household heads.[4] Since most single household dwellings even during the Depression, remained in the sales rather than the rental sector of the housing market, the proportion of heads residing in single household dwellings can be considered a rough indicator of "tenure composition," or the proportions of heads who owned, as opposed to rented, their homes.[5]

The study of the types of dwellings in which adult migrants resided in St. Paul, then, is an indirect way of analyzing the sales and rental sectors of the housing market upon the residential decisions of the adult population. By dividing dwellings into the "single household dwellings" and all others and dividing adults into "non-head" and "head" groupings, we can evaluate both major sectors of the housing market, while holding constant the "elasticity of demand" or the consumption preferences of the two adult groups. Within these adult groups, ethnic differences in the proportions living in single household dwellings were likely to reflect ethnic differences in the demand for specific types of dwellings (when age and income are controlled) and thus further clarify the effect of ethnic group characteristics upon the demand for housing in St. Paul. Identifying such major ethnic differences is another purpose of this chapter.

Adults of course did not simply congregate haphazardly into households in response to the availability of dwelling units which they preferred. The household was a mediating device between the housing demands of adults and the supply of available housing space, and the adult <u>composition</u> of households regularly fell into a few definite and rather stable types and usually passed through several well-defined phases of development during the life cycle of adult household members.

Household developmental stages were mostly reflections of the nuclear family life cycle stages of child-bearing, child-launching, and children-absent. But on the margins of this central pattern the household also adapted itself to the social and housing needs of single migrant adults or older widowed or divorced adults by taking in kin or lodgers, either singly or as secondary families.[6] Though relatively rare in the nineteenth century, households composed entirely of unrelated adults also formed with some regularly in some frontier settings.[7] As Modell, Hareven and Barbara Laslett have found, the taking in of lodgers was a specific life cycle phase in the middle-aged years of household heads; taking in extended kin was a function of both life cycle and social class, with wealthy, older heads more likely to reside with non-conjugal kin.[8]

As young unmarried adult migrants entered St. Paul in the nineteenth century they had several housing alternatives. They could reside in hotel rooms, apartments or even in rented houses with other unrelated adults. They could reside as lodgers in private households or boarding houses. Or if they had parents or other relatives in the city they could live with their families. The flow of young unmarried adult migrants into these various residential alternatives was subject to the obvious restraints of income level and housing supply. A further restraint, however, may have existed because of the ethnic origins of the migrants and of the households where space was available. Modell's and Hareven's study of the South End of Boston in 1880 found significant patterns of both ethnic and occupational clustering of lodgers both with respect to heads and with fellow lodgers.[9] To some degree then, the selection of housing for young adults in St. Paul was probably constricted by ethnic associational preferences. This fact is doubly important for immigrants because most immigrant family households were likely to be in early stages of the family life cycle when both the economic need and the available space for lodgers or kin was lacking. Probably finding that many of their countrymen who headed families were reluctant to take them in, we would expect that young unmarried Irish and German migrants would tend to reside in boarding houses, hotels, and in unrelated adult households at higher rates than their fellow native-born migrants, who had a larger supply of private households in which to lodge.

Still another ethnic restraint on the flow of adult migrants into St. Paul's households may have been the residual cultural influence of the stem family systems which characterized both Ireland and Germany in the nineteenth century. The patterns of inheritance in rural Ireland which allowed "only one child in each generation to inherit the family holding, marry, and produce the next generation"[10] typically required that during the early family life cycle stages of the inheriting son, his parents would live in the same household. If economic circumstances permitted, unmarried siblings of the inheriting son would also remain in the household. The desire to maintain a form of the stem family residential pattern contributed to the increasing rate of marriage postponement in Ireland during the latter decades of the nineteenth century.[11]

Of course, the act of immigration often broke up the stem family pattern when parents and siblings were left behind in the journey to America. When siblings or parents of immigrants accompanied them or arrived at later dates, however, it seems reasonable to suggest that living with relatives rather than strangers would have been preferred as the conventional social pattern by the immigrants. When this association was not possible some form of adoptive, substitutive "family," preferrably of the same ethnicity, probably was accepted as a second choice. On the other hand, as Kennedy has suggested,[12] Irish migrants, especially young single women, were likely to be precisely those young adults who reacted to the stem family system of rural Ireland by leaving it, seeking realization of their marital and material aspirations in American and Irish cities.

Since the behavioral results of the persistence of stem family norms among immigrants in St. Paul is at best ambiguous, the matter will be taken up in the next chapter where we study the verbal evidence on immigrant family life. In this chapter we confine ourselves to the expectation that the proportion of first generation Irish and German lodgers living in private households was lower than the proportion for U. S.-born migrant lodgers because fewer households of the same ethnicity and of the appropriate life cycle stage were available to the Irish and Germans. The demand for alternative housing in the multiple household dwelling market was thus increased by Irish and German associational preferences, if the assumption is correct. A study of ethnic differences in the distribution of household types in St. Paul, then, will contribute to our study of the effect of ethnicity on the demand for housing from 1860 to 1895.

Still another dimension of interaction between population and housing is the physical and social effects of crowding people into limited space and low quality housing. A longitudinal study of two matched groups of black families, one in slum housing and the other recently moved into a new housing project in Baltimore, Maryland in 1954 found, for example, that the incidence of certain diseases and the social-psychological behavior of the two matched groups differed significantly and that the difference widened after a period of residence by one of the groups in new housing.[13] During a period of depression such as the 1890's when a sharp slowdown of housing construction probably created crowded conditions in both sales and rental housing markets in St. Paul, it is reasonable to presume that crowding was intensified in low cost rental housing. If the young adult population postponed marriage and demanded more rental housing units than usual for their age group, then conditions seem to have been ideal for the appearance of similar morbidity and social-psychological symptoms of poor housing environment which researchers discovered in the Baltimore study.

This case study of ethnic differences in housing patterns in St. Paul will help to clarify the interaction between ethnic populations and the housing markets of nineteenth century cities by comparing the reactions of two major immigrant groups to the changing social setting of a rapidly growing frontier city as it passed through the worst depression of the nineteenth century near the end of our period. How far did ethnic differences in the proportions living in single household dwellings and in multiple unit dwellings reflect cultural preferences, all else being equal? How much did both the characteristic demographic composition of Irish and German immigrant populations, and their unique household or residence preferences if any, affect the sales and rental sectors of the housing market? What changes in ethnic housing patterns occurred, if any, between first and second generations? What were the likely physical consequences of poor housing among low income members of each ethnic group during the Depression of the 1890's? These are the general questions of this chapter.

Housing Trends of Migrant Adults, 1860 - 1895

Before examining the proportions of adults in St. Paul who resided in single household dwellings (information available only in the 1895 census sample)[14] it is useful to examine the proportions of adults who lived in hotels or boarding houses in both 1860 and 1895. Again in this chapter we will confine comparisons for the most part to adults aged 15 years and older who were born outside of the State of Minnesota. As Tables 23 and 24 indicate, the proportions of migrant adults living in hotels increased by +7% from 1860 to 1895,

Table 23

Percentage Distribution of Residential Dwelling Types, Adults Aged 15 and Over Born Outside Minnesota, By Place of Birth, St. Paul, 1860

	Ireland	German States	Other Foreign	United States	Total
Hotels	0.9	4.2	3.2	3.4	2.9
Boarding Houses[a]	8.8	9.3	9.9	7.0	8.5
Other Dwellings	90.3	86.6	77.0	89.7	88.6
Total Percent[b]	100.0	100.1	100.1	100.1	100.0
N	342	312	222	417	1293[c]

[a]Includes all dwellings which contained one or more households with more than three unrelated lodgers.

[b]Totals do not add to 100.0 because of rounding.

[c]Values missing for two persons in sample.

Source: Sample data.

Table 24

Percentage Distribution of Residential Dwelling Types, Adults Aged 15 and Over Born Outside Minnesota, By Place of Birth, St. Paul, 1895

	Ireland	Germany	Other Foreign	U. S.	Total
Hotels	21.1	5.6	7.9	11.7	9.9
Boarding Houses[a]	8.9	4.4	10.9	8.3	8.7
Multiple Household Dwelling	13.0	15.2	19.9	17.5	17.7
Single Household Dwelling	56.9	74.8	61.3	62.5	63.7
Total Percent[b]	99.9	100.0	100.0	100.0	100.0
N	123	270	597	590	1530

Significance level: 0.001; Cramer's V: 0.10

[a]Includes all dwellings containing households with more than three unrelated lodgers.

[b]Some totals do not add to 100.0 because of rounding.

Source: Sample data.

the proportion living in boarding houses remained the same, and the proportions living in all other dwelling types declined by -7%. By combining the proportions living in boarding houses and hotels in each year as an indicator of trends in the rental sector, it appears that, as we expected from our study of headship trends, a shift toward the rental sector occurred; the proportion of all migrant adults in this group increased from 11% to 19% from 1860 to 1895. The number of renters was, of course, far higher.

Turning to ethnic differences in the general trend toward multiple household housing from 1860 to 1895, we see that the proportions of Irish adults living in boarding houses and hotels increased strongly (+20.3%), proportions of U. S.-born migrants increased more slowly (+9.6%), and proportions of Germans living in hotels and boarding houses actually decreased (-3.5%). Though we have data on residence in single household dwellings only for 1895 it seems likely from Table 24 that German adults moved strongly into single household dwellings at the same time that the Irish were moving into hotels during the period (or at least the Germans failed to move out of single household dwellings at the same rate once the Depression of the 1890's began).

Ethnic Differences Among Non-heads and Heads

One reason why the proportion of German adults living in single household dwellings in 1895 was higher than the corresponding proportions for the Irish and U. S.-born migrants was because of differences in the composition of adult ethnic populations in 1895. As Table 25 shows the German adult migrant population had a substantially smaller proportion of domestics and "unattached lodgers" (19%)[15] compared to the proportions for the Irish (37%) and the U. S.-born (27%). Since most of this group were "unattached lodgers" (domestics made up only 3% of the adult population in 1895), we would expect higher proportions of all Irish and U. S.-born adults to live in multiple-unit housing.

This ethnic difference in the composition of adult populations, however, does not explain all of the ethnic difference in tendency to reside in single household dwellings, as Table 26 indicates. German lodgers and domestics also lived in single household dwellings at more than twice the rate of Irish lodgers and domestics in 1895 (44.2% vs. 17.4%) and at a higher rate than U. S.-born migrant lodgers and domestics (33.5%). Ethnic differences in dwelling type among migrant adults in 1895 were more pronounced among domestics and lodgers than among familially-related adults (though the overall

Table 25

Percentage Distributions of Adult Populations Aged 15 and Over Born Outside of Minnesota, in Categories of Household Relationships, St. Paul, 1860 and 1895

	Ireland		German States		Other Foreign		U. S.		Total		N	
	1860	1895	1860	1895	1860	1895	1860	1895	1860	1895	1860	1895
Domestics and Unattached Lodgers[a]	23	37	26	19	21	29	21	27	23	27	322	430
Co-resident children Age 15+ and Non-conjugal Kin	3	7	3	13	11	11	14	12	8	11	110	179
Heads of Family or of Household	74	56	71	68	68	60	65	61	69	61	975	971
Total Percent	100	100	100	100	100	100	100	100	100	100	1407[d]	1580
N	365	123	334	270	250	597	458	590				

[a]Excludes lodgers who were also members of secondary families.

[b]Conjugally-related children of family heads only.

[c]Includes non-conjugal kin of secondary family heads as well as of primary family heads (i.e. of household heads); secondary family heads were excluded even if related to head of household.

[d]29 missing cases because of missing data.

Source: Sample data.

strength of association between place of birth and residence in single household dwellings was rather weak).[16]

Table 26 also permits us to estimate ethnic differences in the relative contributions of "head" and "non-head" migrant adults to the demand for single household dwellings in St. Paul in 1895. It is clear, first of all, that the demand for such dwellings among Irish and German <u>heads</u> was substantially above average (+9.2% and +7.5%) in 1895. At the same time, the proportion of all Irish adults who were housed in single household dwellings was lower than average (-6.8%), especially among domestics and unattached lodgers (-18.9%). The proportion of all German adults housed in such dwellings, however, was uniformly higher than other groups in all categories of household relationship (with the single exception of heads where Irish heads had a slightly higher proportion). It appears, then, that the demand for single household dwellings among all migrant <u>adults</u> in 1895 was significantly higher among Germans than among Irish or U. S.-born, but after households were formed, both Irish and German <u>household demand</u> for single household dwellings were about equal and significantly higher than demand among the U. S.-born migrant households (by about +10%).

The difference in demand for single household dwellings among heads as opposed to non-heads was, of course,

Table 26

Proportions Living in Single Household Dwellings, Adults Aged 15 and Over Born Outside of Minnesota, By Place of Birth and Relationship to Household Head, St. Paul, 1895

	Ireland	Germany	Other Foreign	U. S.	Total	N
Domestics and Unattached Lodgers	17.4	44.2	41.5	33.5	36.3	430
Co-resident Children Age 15+ and Non-conjugal Kin	62.5	88.6	69.7	80.0	77.1	179
Heads of Family or of Household	82.6	80.9	69.2	72.1	73.4	971
All Migrant Adults	56.9	74.8	61.3	62.5	63.7	1580
N	123	270	597	590		

	Significance levels:	Cramer's V
All Adults:	0.001	0.11
Dom. & Lodgers:	0.02	0.16
Child. & Kin:	NS	NS
Heads:	0.01	0.11

Source: Sample data.

expected since the demand for such housing among heads was less "elastic" (i.e. more strongly preferred). The substantial foreign/native differences in demand <u>among heads</u>, however, could not have been predicted. Occupational differences among foreign and U. S.-born males would point in the opposite direction. For example, among all gainfully occupied male adults aged 15 years and over in 1895, 31.6% of the Irish and 20.3% of the Germans were unskilled laborers, compared to 6.2% for U. S.-born and an overall average of 14.9%.[17]

Among all gainfully occupied household heads in 1895, 28.1% of the Irish heads and 14.1% of the German heads were unskilled laborers, compared to 4.3% for U. S.-born heads and an overall average of 12.2%.[18] Though there probably would be a somewhat higher proportion of unskilled laborers among U. S.-born migrants (as compared to all adults), the difference was not likely to be important since only a small proportion of U. S.-born adults were born in Minnesota.

Despite a lower occupational level (accentuated by the high unemployment rates among unskilled laborers during the Depression), Irish and German heads lived in single household dwellings at a greater rate than the U. S.-born. Among unmarried adults the high proportion of Irish workers who were unskilled laborers perhaps helps to account for the low proportions of Irish lodgers living in single household dwellings; among German lodgers, however, a higher proportion lived in such dwellings than U. S.-born migrant lodgers even though Germans as a group had a lower average occupational level.

As we indicated at the beginning of the chapter, between the demand for dwellings among migrant adults and the supply of such dwellings which they could afford stood the household with its familial restraints on random flows of adults into housing space. To what degree did regularities of household composition and developmental stage account for ethnic differences in the proportions of migrant adults living in single household dwellings? In Table 26 we examine the extremes of restraint and flexibility imposed on the residential choice of adults by the structure of households. At one extreme was the nuclear family household without lodgers or extra kin, where the criterion of household relationship was strictly conjugal. At the other extreme was the aggregation of "unmarried adults"[19] into households where the only criteria of household relationship presumably were the ability to help with rent, same sex (usually), and the same ethnicity (frequently).

As a comparison of Tables 26 and 27 indicates, the interposition of household relationships between demand

Table 27

Proportions Living in Single Household Dwellings, Adults Aged 15 and Over Born Outside of Minnesota, By Place of Birth and Household Type, St. Paul, 1895

Household Type	Ireland	Germany	Other Foreign	U. S.	Total	N
Unrelated Adult Household[a]	31.6	25.0	45.7	47.5	42.5	179
Nuclear Family Only[b]	80.4	80.8	65.0	67.9	71.3	581
Other Types	43.4	75.8	62.8	62.6	63.0	820
All Types	56.9	74.8	61.3	62.5	63.7	1580
N	123	270	597	590		

	Significance levels	Cramer's V
All Adults:	0.001	0.11
Unrel. Adults:	NS	NS
Nuclear:	0.01	0.15
Other:	0.002	0.14

[a]Households containing only unrelated adults, identified by different surnames.

[b]Households containing one nuclear family with no other persons in household.

Source: Sample data.

for and supply of single household dwellings caused little change in ethnic housing differences among heads, but substantially altered the differences among non-heads. Non-head German adults, for example, were much less likely to live in single household dwellings if they were members of an "unmarried adults" household, but non-head Irish adults were <u>more</u> likely to live in such dwellings if they lived in "unmarried adults" households, and the latter tendency was also true among "Other Foreign" and "U. S.-born migrants" living in such households.

This ethnic difference in housing pattern among the members of "unmarried adult" households, especially the deviation of Germans in such households from other groups, calls for more detailed analysis of the sex and occupational levels of the members of such households. Since our sample of such persons was too small to carry out such a study, we can only suggest possible explanations here. Given the strong German tendency to marry early and form separate conjugal households, it may be that those Germans who did form "unmarried adult" households did so only because of dire economic hardship (hence their inability to afford the higher cost of a single household dwelling). The Irish non-head adults, however, with their greater acceptance of postponement of marriage, perhaps more freely formed such households and thus did not suffer the same economic constraints on choice of housing as Germans in the same situation.

The role of sex and age in determining the housing choices of all migrant, non-head adults in 1895 is explored in Table 28. Comparing the ethnic tendencies in housing for all migrant adults (Table 24) with the ethnic tendencies of young, non-head migrants in Table 28, it is clear that, though the latter group as a whole tended to reside in single household dwellings at a lower rate than the former (46.2% vs. 63.7%), the ethnic deviations of the Irish and Germans from overall averages were even more pronounced among the young, non-head group, especially among females.[20] Young German women who were not heads of households or secondary families lived in single household dwellings at a higher rate than other women of like status in St. Paul. Among Irish non-head young women the tendency was markedly in the opposite direction; they lived in such dwellings at half the average rate.

To sum up what we have learned about trends in the contributions of Irish and German adults to the demand for single household dwellings, we have found that the demand of Irish adults as a group for such dwellings very likely declined from 1860 to 1895. A smaller proportion of Irish adults in 1895 were family or household heads; the increased proportions of Irish lodgers moved

Table 28

Proportions Living in Single Household Dwellings, Adults Aged 15 and Over Born Outside of Minnesota who were not Heads of Household or of Family, By Place of Birth and Sex, St. Paul, 1895

	Ireland	Germany	Other Foreign	U. S.	Total	N
Males	27.3	54.3	46.0	44.4	45.5	347
Females	16.7	64.3	47.8	48.5	47.5	181
All	22.2	58.1	46.5	45.8	46.2	528
N	36	74	217	201		

	Significance levels	Cramer's V
All non-heads:	0.01	0.15
Males:	NS	NS
Females:	0.02	0.24

Source: Sample data.

readily into the rental sector of housing, especially into hotels, particularly among young women. In sharp contrast, the overall adult German contribution to demand for single household dwellings probably remained much the same over the period despite a slowly declining rate of headship. This trend occurred in part because non-head German adults in most circumstances lived in single household dwellings at a higher rate than other non-heads (with the exception of Germans in "unmarried adult" households). The German deviation from overall averages, moreover, was not explained by group differences in income since U. S.-born adults had a higher occupational level. The composition of the German adult population also contributed to the overall demand because a lower proportion of German adults were domestics and lodgers (19%) than among any other major group in 1895.

The persistence of German early marriage trends, combined with a stronger propensity among non-head adults to live in single household dwellings than existed among other groups, suggests the influence of German cultural norms upon their demand for housing. At the same time the combination of economic, demographic and cultural factors which encouraged the postponement of marriage among the Irish was also closely related to their declining demand for single household dwellings by 1895.

Though the demand for such dwellings among Irish heads remained high the overall adult demand was substantially less than average in 1895.

Fertility, Family Life Cycle, Migrancy and Income

We have found that the adult composition of households (for nuclear family households) did not alter substantially the levels of demand for single household dwellings among Irish and German heads in 1895. Another dimension of household composition - the effect of family life cycle stage - should also be considered as an influence on demand for the single household dwelling. Because the coding scheme used to aggregate the number of children ages 14 and under in the 1895 sample provided data only for entire households, we must confine our study of the effects of family life cycle stage to single family households only. Since such households represented 77.2% of all households in our sample, however, we will be studying the largest household type. The coding scheme also imposes an age limitation; since the number of children for each household was aggregated only for children under age 15, we will confine our study further to single family households with young female heads aged 15 to 34 who were either married women with spouse present or divorced, separated or widowed mothers with co-resident children.

In Table 29 we discover that the tendency for single family households to reside in single household dwellings did indeed vary with family life cycle stage. Overall, young single family households tended to live in single household dwellings at a higher rate after having their second child than at an earlier developmental stage (73.9% vs. 58.8%). Since the limitations of sample size imposed by the coding scheme produced unreliably small "cell sizes" for Irish and German households we must be cautious in discussing ethnic differences. In general, the family life cycle stage control does not seem to eliminate the greater tendency of Irish and German heads to live in single household dwellings <u>after the birth of the second child</u> as compared to all U. S.-born female heads of single family households.[21]

A more direct way of measuring the <u>economic</u> burden of additional children on household resources is available in the concept of "child-years-of-dependency."[22] Using this method one totals the number of "child-years" during which the presence of each child has placed an additional economic burden on a family, beginning with the date of marriage; if data is available it is also possible to refine the total by adding the years of dependency for children who died and even to reduce the total burden

Table 29

Proportions Living in Single Household Dwellings, Women Aged 15 to 34 Who were Heads[a] of Single Family Households, By Place of Birth, Family Life Cycle Stage,[b] and Child - Years - of - Dependency,[c] St. Paul, 1895

	Ireland[d]	Germany	Other Foreign	U. S.	Total	N
Age						
15 - 24	(100.0)	(100.0)	33.3	52.9	54.8	31
25 - 34	75.0	66.7	66.7	75.8	70.9	148[e]
Family Life Cycle Stage						
1	(100.0)	50.0	42.9	71.0	58.5	65
2	80.0	86.7	72.1	71.2	73.9	115
Child - Years - of Dependency						
Low	80.0	50.0	46.9	75.6	61.7	94
High	100.0	100.0	78.1	66.7	75.6	86
N	6	27	64	83	180	

[a] Includes both married women with spouse present and widowed, divorced, separated or "married, spouse absent" women.

[b] First stage: no children or one child less than five years; second stage: more than one child under age 14.

[c] Values calculated by multiplying number of children age 0 to 4 by 2, number age 5 to 9 by 7, and number age 10 to 14 by 12; "low" values are 6 or less. See footnote no. 22 for further detail.

[d] Irish values and others in parenthesis were based on unreliably small cell sizes.

[e] One missing case because of missing data

because of the "economies of scale" present in child-rearing (such as using the same clothing for two or more children). A more modest adaptation of this method was applied in Table 29[23] where a "high" value for "child-years-of-dependency" indicated that a family had either more children or more closely-spaced children than families with a "low" value. Under conditions of "high" dependency the households lived in single household dwellings at a higher rate, and the ethnic differences (higher Irish and German rates) apparently were preserved.

It is also true, of course, that "child-years-of-dependency" may be a proxy for family life cycle stage; i.e. households with "high" CYD may simply be those at a more advanced stage of family development. Tables 30 and 31 explore ethnic trends in child-spacing patterns with controls for family life cycle stage from 1860 to 1895 in St. Paul. Though the sample size is so small that we can only suggest apparent trends for further testing, it appears that, overall, high levels of child dependency were achieved at <u>later</u> family life cycle stages in 1895 compared to 1860. The proportion of mothers in these samples who attained high rates of child dependency at the third family life cycle stage was higher in 1860 than in 1895 (100% vs.69%).

Table 30

Child Dependency Rates, Mothers Under Age 35 Living in Single Family Households, By Place of Birth and Family Life Cycle Stage,[a] St. Paul, 1860

Child Years of Dependency[b] (CYD)	Ireland	German States	Other Foreign	U. S.	Total	N	Sig.	Cramer's V
High CYD	90.2	68.5	87.5	82.1	82.5		0.02	0.21
Family Life Cycle Stage:								
1	0	0	0	0	0	0	NS	
2	91.8	96.6	94.1	94.9	93.8	137	NS	
3	100.0	100.0	100.0	100.0	100.0	42	NS	
4	50.0	0	62.5	57.1	41.4	24	0.002	0.52
Low CYD	9.8	31.5	12.5	17.9	17.5			
Family Life Cycle Stage:								
1	0	0	0	0	0	0		
2	8.2	3.4	5.9	5.1	6.2	9		
3	0	0	0	0	0	0		
4	50.0	100.0	37.5	42.9	58.6	34		
N	82	54	32	78	246			

[a] Family Life Cycle Stages: (1)no children;(2)one child less than 5 yrs.;(3)more than one child, at least one less than 5 yrs.;(4)one or more children under age 14, none less than 5 yrs.

[b] See Table 29 for definitions.

Table 31

Child Dependency Rates, Mothers Under Age 35 Living in Single Family Households, By Place of Birth and Family Life Cycle Stage,[a] St. Paul, 1895

Child Years of Dependency[b] (CYD)	Ireland	Germany	Other Foreign	U. S.	Total	N
High CYD	16.7	40.7	50.0	49.4	47.8	
Family Life Cycle Stage:						
1	0	0	0	0	0	0
2	0	0	0	0	0	0
3	20.0	69.2	69.4	74.4	68.8	64
4	0	100.0	100,0	100.0	100.0	22
Low CYD	83.3	59.3	50.0	50.6	52.2	
Family Life Cycle Stage:						
1	0	100.0	100.0	100.0	100.0	31
2	100.0	100.0	100.0	100.0	100.0	34
3	80.0	30.8	30.6	25.6	31.2	29
4	0	0	0	0	0	0
N	6	27	64	83	180	

[a]See Table 30 for definition.
[b]See Table 30 for definitions.

This apparent shift to increased spacing of children between the second and third family life cycle stages (i.e. from one pre-school child to two or more) could be predicted because of the Depression of the 1890's. The implication for housing trends is the main concern here and it seems reasonable to conclude that child-spacing was an additional demographic response to economic restraints in the housing market. Families apparently increased the spacing of children because larger family housing was both more difficult to obtain and to pay for, on the average, for young household heads. Foreign born-U. S. born differences in Table 31 are also suggestive; foreign born families apparently delayed bearing second and later children more frequently than U. S. born, suggesting that the economic influence of the Depression on fertility was greatest among the foreign born.

To more precisely evaluate the effects of income losses or lowered income expectations in 1895 upon the tendency for household heads to live in single household dwellings, we turn to a study of male family or household heads born outside of Minnesota (Table 32). Though the number of such heads was too small to produce statistically significant results at the 5% level, the results suggest, at least, that ethnic differences in the proportions of heads living in single household dwellings

Table 32

Proportions Living in Single Household Dwellings, All Men Born Outside of Minnesota Who Were Heads of Households or of Secondary Families, By Place of Birth, Age, Occupational Level, Length of Residence and Months of Employment, St. Paul, 1895

	Ireland[a]	Germany	Other Foreign	U.S.	Total	N
Age (Select)						
25-34	(100.0)	75.0	54.9	60.8	63.2	136
35-44	(50.0)	87.9	78.8	71.4	76.8	168
Occupation						
Blue Collar	73.9	85.2	67.8	72.3	73.5	264[c]
White Collar	88.9	76.9	73.8	69.1	72.5	193
Length of Residence in Minnesota[b]						
5 yrs. or less	0	63.6	54.2	54.8	55.8	77
More than 5 yrs.	78.1	84.0	72.1	74.0	75.6	390[d]
Months Employ. in Prev. Yr.						
0-8	77.8	80.0	67.7	57.7	69.9	136
9-12	80.0	82.8	73.7	73.4	75.6	295[e]
Total Group	78.1	81.5	70.0	69.6	72.7	
N	32	92	180	168	472	

[a]Since the sample of Irish male heads was so small, values which seem to be clearly wrong because of random sampling error were placed in parenthesis.

[b]This variable was reported in the census only for men aged 21 and over; none of the male heads in the sample were less than 21 years.

[c]15 missing cases because of missing data.
[d]5 missing cases because of missing data.
[e]41 missing cases because of missing data.

cannot be "explained away" by income or length of residence. With a couple of exceptions, the levels of ethnic difference observed among all migrant heads in Table 26 remain much the same in all categories of Table 32. Irish and German proportions remain at a substantially higher level than those of U. S.-born migrants with controls for occupational level, length of residence in Minnesota, and months of employment during the previous year.

Generational Differences in Household Composition in 1895

As we found in Chapter 1, a substantial proportion of the "U. S.-born migrant" population of St. Paul in 1895 were second generation Irish and Germans and thus comparisons between Irish and Germans of the first generation with the "U. S.-born migrant" group are partially confounded by the possible persistence of typical ethnic household structures in the U. S.-born group. To examine generational differences[24] in household composition we turn to Table 33. Comparing generations first, it is obvious that second generation household heads more frequently took in non-conjugal kin or lodgers than did the first generation. Since large proportions of the second generation in St. Paul were migrants the generational difference is not simply a proxy for the effect of

Table 33

Household Composition of All Households, By Ethnic Group and Generation of Heads, St. Paul, 1895

Household Composition & Generation	N	Irish	German	Other Foreign	U.S. and Other For.	Totals	Both Generations
<u>Nuclear Family Only</u>							
First	193	68.2	71.6	49.7	-	58.5	50.2
Second	84	32.1	42.9	-	38.2	37.8	
<u>Nuclear with Lodgers</u>[a]							
First	64	13.6	11.6	24.6	-	19.4	21.7
Second	56	35.7	19.0	-	24.3	25.2	
<u>Non-conjugal Kin Present</u>							
First	15	2.3	4.2	5.2	-	4.5	6.0
Second	18	10.7	4.8	-	8.1	8.2	
<u>Unrelated Adults</u>							
First	41	15.9	6.3	14.7	-	12.4	15.9
Second	47	14.3	23.8	-	22.0	21.2	
<u>Others</u>[b]							
First	17	0	6.3	5.8	-	5.2	6.2
Second	17	7.1	9.5	-	7.5	7.7	
N		72	116	191	173	552	

[a] Excludes lodgers who were also members of secondary families.

[b] Multiple family households in which secondary family members had different surnames than household head.

Note: Relationship between ethnic group and household composition is significant at the 0.02 level in the first generation; not significant in second generation.

migrant status. As we observed in Chapter 1, however, the "chain migration" attraction of first and second generation relatives to the same city probably brought together a larger pool of available kin for the second generation households to incorporate as "extended" relatives.

Ethnic differences in the tendency to bring lodgers or extended kin into the household generally were rather small in the first generation. In the second the Irish heads showed a stronger propensity toward bringing in such persons than did the German heads (35.7% vs 19.0% for lodgers and 10.7% vs 4.8% for non-conjugal kin), possibly because the Irish had a proportionately larger pool of such unattached persons of the same ethnicity from which to draw, at least among first generation relatives and lodgers. Given the ethnic associational tendencies which Modell and Hareven found in Boston, it seems likely that Irish households of the second generation adopted themselves to the surplus of Irish lodgers of the first generation by taking in more lodgers than average.

Ethnic differences both between and across generations are also interesting among "unrelated adults only" households. Irish households of this type formed at about the same rate among heads in both generations.

Among the Germans, the proportion of such households strongly increased from first to second generation, from a level substantially below average for the first generation to a level slightly above average in the second. Though other factors were at work also, it is tempting to conclude that second generation German households were unable or unwilling to take in unattached German adults at the same rate as the Irish, leaving the surplus German lodgers to fend for themselves in "singles" households.

In sum, generational differences in household composition both within and across ethnic groups in St. Paul in 1895 seemed to correspond roughly to the demographic composition of the ethnic populations involved. Second generation Irish households took in more lodgers and extra kin because more of such adults were available in their ethnic group compared with other groups.

But what does all of this mean for the housing market in St. Paul in 1895? To study this effect of household composition upon the demand for single household dwellings in each ethnic group and generation, we turn to Table 34. Looking first at the "All Households" row at the bottom of the table we note that, though Irish and German tendencies to live in single household dwellings were still slightly higher in the second generation, ethnic differences have "washed out"

Table 34

Proportion of all Households Residing in Single Household Dwellings,
By Ethnic Group and Generation of Head and Household Composition, St. Paul, 1895

Household Composition & Generation	N	Irish	German	Other Foreign	U. S. and Other For.	Totals	Both Generations
Nuclear Family Only							
First	193	83.3	79.4	65.3	-	73.1	70.4
Second	84	66.7	-	63.6	64.3	64.3	
Nuclear with Lodgers							
First	64	83.3	100.0	76.6	-	81.3	83.3
Second	56	(100.0)	(100.0)	-	81.0	85.7	
Non-conjugal Kin Present							
First	15	(100.0)	(75.0)	(80.0)	-	(80.0)	81.8
Second	18	(66.7)	(100.0)	-	(85.7)	(83.3)	
Unrelated Adults							
First	41	(71.4)	(66.7)	(67.9)	-	68.3	72.7
Second	47	(50.0)	(80.0)	-	(78.9)	76.6	
Others							
First	17	(0)	(66.7)	(54.5)	-	(58.8)	58.8
Second	17	(50.0)	(50.0)	-	(61.5)	(58.8)	
All Households							
First	330	81.8	80.0	68.6	-	73.6	73.6
Second	222	75.0	76.2	-	72.8	73.4	

Note: Relationship between ethnic group and residence for all households was sifnificant at 0.05 level for first generation only.

statistically; i.e. the differences were so slight that the probability of sample error is above acceptable levels.

Since we know that household composition was to some extent a proxy for family life cycle stage in the nineteenth century (i.e. households with lodgers or non-conjugal kin were usually confined to middle-aged heads) we can also control roughly for the age of household heads by looking at the rows "Nuclear Family Plus Lodgers" and "Non-conjugal Kin Present." In these rows the ethnic tendencies for Irish and German heads to reside in single household dwellings seems to be higher than average in both first and second generations, though cell sizes are too small to be more than suggestive. We may speculate then that the strong Irish and German preference for small homes persisted into the second generation only among heads who had arrived at middle stages of the family life cycle and had brought in lodgers or kin to help pay for the cost of home ownership.

Overall, though, the strongest tendency for Irish and German heads to prefer single household dwellings seems to have occurred in the first generation. While some second generation Irish and German heads in 1895 may have gravitated more strongly than average toward such dwellings, our sample of household heads is too small for further analysis of their behavior.

Consequences of Crowded Housing

We have observed in Table 24 that the proportion of Irish adults living in multiple-unit housing in St. Paul in 1895 was higher than average (+6.8%) and the same proportion among German adults was lower than average (-11.1%). Looking only at hotels and boarding houses, the proportions of Irish adults living in such dwellings was also higher than average (+11.4%) and the German proportion lower than average (-8%). In addition to the fact that residents of multiple-unit dwellings lived in closer proximity to other households for structural reasons, it was generally true also that adults were more crowded _within_ the household in multiple-unit dwellings, at least in lower income housing. A housing study of lower income districts near St. Paul's loop in 1917, for example, found that an average of 2.05 adults per bedroom was typical of multiple-unit dwellings, compared to 1.89 adults for single household dwellings.[25] Table 35 suggests also that a mild correlation existed in 1917 between the quality of housing (in the same low income districts) and the degree of crowding; the lower the "condition of repair" the greater the crowding.

Table 35

Average Number of Persons Per Bedroom, Households in Low Income Districts of St. Paul, April 15 - July 1, 1917, By Type of Dwelling and Rank Order of Districts According to "Condition of Repair" of Buildings in District

District Number	Rank Order of "Condition of Repair"[a] of Buildings (High to Low)	Average Number of Persons per Bedroom: Single Household Dwellings	Multiple Household Dwellings
XVI	1	1.68	1.60
IX	2	1.42	1.84
II	3	1.95	2.09
XIV	4	1.87	1.88
X	5	1.61	1.95
XVII	6	1.98	2.20
XII	7	1.84	2.15
XV	8	1.74	2.24
I	9	2.07	2.18
IV	10	1.81	2.01
VIII	11	1.50	1.69
XI	12	2.05	1.98
III	13	2.35	2.13
XVIII	14	2.55	2.74
District Average		1.89	2.05

[a]Districts were ranked by the percentage of buildings inspected in each district which were considered in "good" repair by the inspectors; districts number 15-18 were omitted from the "Condition of Repair" study in the source, p. 20.

Source: Carol Aronovici, _Housing Conditions in the City of St. Paul_(St. Paul, 1917), 17,20.

Shifting our attention to the probable amount of crowding which existed in boarding houses and hotels, it is useful to again refer to the 1917 housing study of St. Paul. In that year, as Table 36 indicates, room rental increased with the size of the structure; the larger the boarding house or hotel, the more expensive its average room rent. Assuming that about the same economic relationship between size and room rented existed in 1895 as in 1917, and that the lower the room rental the poorer the quality of housing, we may infer from the proportions of Irish and German adults living in boarding houses(Table 24) that more Irish than German adults lived in the low quality housing offered by boarding houses.

With this estimate that, on the average, Irish adults lived in housing which was <u>more</u> crowded and of lower quality than average, and German adults lived in <u>less</u> crowded housing than average, we return to the study of the effects of housing quality on health. That study, conducted in Baltimore in 1954, found that especially among children and women under age 35, a crowded urban housing environment increased the incidence of accidents, infections diseases, acute respiratory conditions, digestive and genito-urinary illnesses, and (among adults) circulatory illnesses.[26] We should expect, then, that

Table 36

Percentage Distribution of Room Rents Per Night, Licensed Rooming Houses and Hotels in Low Income Districts of St. Paul, April 15 - July 1, 1917, By Number of Rooms in Unit

Number of Rooms in Unit	Room Rents Per Night ($) 0.50	0.60	0.75	1.00+	Total Percent	N
6 - 10	52	3	15	30	100	33
11 - 20	35	4	19	42	100	356
21 - 30	23	6	21	49	99	295
31+	31	7	15	47	100	783
All Units	31	6	18	46	101	
N	449	91	258	669	1467	

Source: Carol Aronovici, Housing Conditions in the City of St. Paul (St. Paul, 1917), 57; the 90 units studied here represented 60% of the total of 150 such units in the city in 1917.

if we could find data on the incidence of accidents and disease among ethnic groups in St. Paul in 1895, the Irish should show a greater, and the Germans a lesser, than average incidence as a result of group differences in housing environment.

An available substitute for such *morbidity* data is available for St. Paul in 1890 with the *mortality* tables of the Eleventh Census. While it is true that morbidity and mortality data are not equivalent because many diseases seldom result in deaths and the age structure of populations interacts differently with morbidity rates than with mortality rates, still it seems likely that mortality rates would be more closely associated with morbidity rates in 1890 than today because effective medical control of disease had not begun and public health measures were in their infancy. Especially in the area of infectious diseases such as diphtheria, typhoid fever, and tuberculosis, the incidence of deaths from such causes would at least roughly resemble the total incidence of the diseases, in the absence of effective medical counter measures.

This hypothesis is at least partially born out by the data for St. Paul in Tables 37 and 38. The proportions of Irish females who died from infective and parasitic, circulatory, and digestive or genitourinary

Table 37

Percentage Distribution of Diseases and Other Causes of Death in St. Paul, June 1, 1889 - May 31, 1890, By Sex and Ethnic Group

Causes of Death[a]	Ireland	Germany	Other Foreign	U. S.	All	N
	Birthplaces of Mothers of Deceased					
Females						
Infective and parasitic	21	19	17	19	20	202
Diarrheal	6	15	15	11	13	133
Respiratory	10	9	10	7	9	88
Nervous System	10	12	9	14	11	112
Circulatory	6	3	3	5	4	39
Digestive & Genito-urinary	6	1	2	2	2	23
Still Birth	10	9	11	9	10	98
Other & Unknown	32	32	33	32	31	323
All	101	100	100	99	100	
N	124	269	344	281	1018	
Males						
Infective and parasitic	19	13	22	15	17	228
Diarrheal	6	16	14	15	14	170
Respiratory	13	7	10	9	9	116
Nervous System	4	13	9	10	10	118
Circulatory	7	4	5	4	5	60
Digestive & Genito-urinary	5	3	2	4	3	40
Still Birth	16	11	12	16	13	161
Other & Unknown	31	32	25	27	29	349
All	101	99	99	100	100	
N	130	334	416	342	1222	

continued on next page

Table 37, continued

[a]Disease classifications derived from: U. S. Department of Health, Education and Welfare, Public Health Service, National Center for Health Statistics. *Eighth Revision International Classification of Diseases, Adapted for Use in the United States* (Public Health Service Publication No. 1693; 2 vols., Washington, 1968). I, *Tabular List*, xxii-45. All disease categories in the table are equivalent to the major ICDA classes except for "Diarrheal" which is a subclass of "Infective and Parasitic."

Source: U. S. Census Bureau, Eleventh Census. 1890, Vol. 4, *Report on Vital and Social Statistics in the United States*, Part 2, 645 - 647.

Table 38

Percentage Distribution of Ages at Death in St. Paul, June 1, 1889 to May 31, 1890, By Sex and Ethnic Group

	Birthplaces of Mothers of Deceased					
	Ireland	Germany	Other Foreign	U. S.	All	N
Females						
0 - 5	33	61	56	51	53	538
5 - 15	6	11	6	8	8	81
15 - 25	11	7	11	9	9	95
25 - 65	35	17	21	26	23	234
65+	15	4	6	6	6	66
Unknown	0	0	0	0	0	4
All	100	100	100	100	100	
N	124	269	344	281	1018	
Males						
0 - 5	38	64	57	56	56	686
5 - 15	4	5	6	4	5	60
15 - 25	6	4	6	5	5	66
25 - 65	34	19	28	26	26	312
65+	18	9	4	7	7	91
Unknown	0	0	1	1	1	7
All	100	101	102	99	100	
N	130	334	416	342	1222	

Source: U. S. Census Bureau, Eleventh Census, 1890, Vol. 4, Report on Vital and Social Statistics in the United States, Part 2, 644 - 646.

diseases was slightly higher than average and the proportions of German females who died from the same diseases was lower than average. The low incidence of Irish deaths from "Diarrheal" diseases seems to be partially explained by referring to Table 38. Infants under age 5 were most prone to deaths from such diseases, and female infants of those ages represented a much smaller proportion of total female deaths among the Irish (33%) than among the Germans (61%).

Another body of data which provides evidence more directly on the incidence of accidents and disease for a later period is available in the data on "charity seekers" collected for St. Paul in 1910 by the U. S. Immigration Commission.[28] As the proportions of households who reported "accidents or illness" suggests (Table 39), the housing environment of first generation Germans on welfare seems to have been <u>worse</u> than that of first generation Irish or other groups on welfare in 1910. There is a noticeable tendency also in Table 39 for the incidence of accidents or illness to be higher among second generation immigrants than among the first generation, suggesting that the second generation on the average had a lower quality housing environment than the first generation among welfare households in 1910.

Table 39

Percentage Distribution of Reasons for Seeking Charity Payments, Households[a] Receiving Charity in St. Paul, By Ethnic Group and Generation,[b] 1910

Reason for Seeking Charity	Ethnic Group and Generation									
	Irish		German		Other Foreign		U. S.		All	
	First	Sec.	First	Sec.	First	Sec	Sec White	Sec Black	(Percent)	N
Death, Desertion of Incarceration of Breadwinner	4	9	3	14	8	9	6	7	7	60
Accident to or Illness of Breadwinner	11	23	20	23	15	17	20	34	18	158
Accident to or Illness of other Household Members	5	10	14	17	17	12	6	7	12	10
Unemployment of Insufficient Earnings	47	41	56	56	58	56	45	34	52	451
Other Reasons	83	65	47	47	44	50	58	41	53	456
Total Percent[c]	150	148	140	157	142	144	135	123	142	
N (Reasons)	114	116	194	103	380	95	193	36		1231
N (Households)	76	78	139	66	268	66	144	29		866

[a] Only households "reporting complete data" were included.
[b] Second generation was defined as "native-born of foreign father."
[c] Total percentages exceed 100% because some households gave more than one reason for seeking charity.

Source: U. S. Immigration Commission, Reports (42 vols.; Washington, 1907-1910), Immigrants as Charity Seekers, Vol. 35, 960.

Housing Construction in St. Paul, 1857-1899

So far, we have found that Irish adults as a group contributed an increasing share of demand for boarding house and hotel space and German adults a decreasing share of such demand from 1860 to 1895. Among Irish and German households, however, we have found that the demand for single household dwellings for both groups was substantially higher than among the households of U. S.-born migrants in 1895. For St. Paul's migrant adult population as a whole, we have discovered a shift of demand of +7.2% from houses and apartments toward boarding house and hotel rooms between 1860 and 1895. For the migrant *adult* population as a whole in 1895 we have determined that 63.7% resided in single household dwellings, while 73.4% of migrant household *heads* lived in such dwellings. These trends suggest that the rental sector of St. Paul's housing market expanded faster than the sales sector between 1860 and 1895, and that the Irish contributed most to demand for rental housing and the Germans to sales housing by 1895.

Since a city housing inspector's office was not established until 1883 in St. Paul, the record of housing construction before that date must be gleaned from the *Reports* of the St. Paul Chamber of Commerce (beginning in 1867) and from newspaper accounts. A valuable compilation of newspaper reports on building construction in Minnesota has been compiled by the U. S. Works Progress Administration's Historical Records Survey[29] which speeds the task of searching the newspapers.

Following the Panic of 1857 a surge of housing construction apparently occurred in St. Paul. A total of 658 "private buildings" were constructed in 1857 and 1858 at a cost of over a million dollars.[30] A newspaper editor noted during the summer of 1859 that "the cheapness of lumber and wages, in comparison with previous years, have induced many of our citizens, who have become tired of boarding-house and hotel life, to build homes of their own."[31] By the fall of 1860, lumber costs had declined 36%, stone 50%, brick 58%, and construction labor 25% over the corresponding costs in 1856.[32] This apparent surge of single household dwelling construction helps to account for both the high rates of household headship in 1860 noted in Chapter 1 and for the relatively low proportions of adults residing in boarding houses and hotels in 1860 (Table 23).

In Table 40 estimates of dwelling construction for St. Paul are provided for two surges in construction between 1860 and 1884, based primarily on data from the Annual Reports of the St. Paul Chamber of Commerce. Though in the neighborhood of 2800 dwellings were

Table 40

Building Construction in St. Paul, 1867 - 1872, 1880-- 1884

	Total Buildings	Total Dwellings[a]	Total Value of Bldgs.& Improvm. ($000)
1867	343	262	556
1868	361	276	1005
1869	509	389	1396
1870	771	589	1575
1871	832	636	1736
1872	934	714	2346
	. . . .		
1880	729	614	2790
1881	1200	1011	4572
1882	2466	2170	7431
1883	3583	3019	12907
1884	2383	1920	7266
Total, 1867-72	3750	2866	8614
Total, 1880-84	10361	8734	34966

[a]The underlined entries were provided by the sources; other entries in this column are estimates based on the ratio of dwellings to buildings, using the 1868 ratio for 1867-1872 and the average of the ratios for 1882 and 1884 for the later years.

Sources: St. Paul Chamber of Commerce, Annual Reports:(1869),57; (1872), 19; (1881), 6; (1884), 57. Data for 1882 and estimate for 1883 based on Daily Minnesota Tribune, January 1, 1883, cited in W.P.A., Annals of Minnesota, Box # 97.

constructed from 1867 up to the time of the Panic of 1873, the Chamber noted in its report for 1873 that a "pressing necessity of this city" was "the multiplication of dwelling houses to be rented at moderate figures."[33]

Throughout the 1870's and the early 1880's a rapid expansion of hotel room space occurred. Four hotels were constructed during 1868.[34] A survey of major St. Paul hotels in 1873 revealed 650 total rooms.[35] From 1876 to 1883 several large business structures were converted to hotels, large additions were added to existing hotels, and several large new hotels were constructed, culminating in the seven-story, $1,000,000 Hotel Ryan, begun in 1883.[36] By the time of the State Fair in September, 1880, the _Minneapolis Tribune_ estimated that the hotels and boarding houses of St. Paul had sufficient extra space for 2,000 people and with "cots and makeshifts" the number could be expanded to 3,500 people.[37] The _St. Paul Pioneer Press_ boasted in 1878 that St. Paul had "larger and better hotels, and more of them, than any other city of its size in America."[38]

The most fascinating period of housing construction in St. Paul during this period was the early 1880's when the housing market responded to a tremendous surge of population growth, from a total population of 41,400 in 1880 to 111,400 in 1885.[39] As Table 40 indicates, roughly 9,000 dwellings were constructed from 1880 to 1884. Despite the rapid expansion of hotel room space in the late 1870's, the city's housing was overwhelmed by the incoming flood at the beginning of the decade. The St. Paul Daily Globe reported in May, 1881, that "the rush of travel into and through St. Paul, added to the large number of non-residents employed on building improvements, has filled all the cheap hotels in the city to overflowing."[40] A price inflation for goods and provisions prompted the leading hotel proprietors of St. Paul and Minneapolis in 1881 to "advance rates fifty cents per day, to take effect on and after November 15."[41]

Though there was a call for the construction of tenement houses in 1880 "in which to house the hosts of people who are arriving by every train and steamer,"[42] and over $245,000 worth of "tenement blocks" were built in 1882 in response to this demand,[43] most of the new housing constructed during these years apparently were small single household dwellings constructed by their owners. In April, 1882, the St. Paul Daily Globe reported that there were "hundreds, not to say thousands of small dwellings being erected in every part of the city . . . They are the prospective homes of the laboring classes, and while their cost is not so great their value to the city cannot be estimated in dollars and cents."[44] In

1884 the St. Paul Chamber of Commerce noted the "very liberal terms which are offered to persons of small means, mechanics and laborers, to secure a comfortable home of their own."[45] Lots could be purchased in "good, healthy neighborhoods" for "as little as twenty-five dollars cash down, and the balance on long time at low interest", and the seller "will advance lumber and the necessary materials for building, on equally liberal terms."[46] During the furious building season of 1883 in St. Paul, the total value of new building starts were reported to be fourth largest in the United States, after New York, Chicago and Cincinnati.[47]

The year 1883 was the peak year of the "long swing" in housing construction in St. Paul which began in the mid 1870's and ended approximately in 1896 (see Tables 40 and 41). At the same time the rate of household formation noted in Chapter 1 (Table 7) moved <u>inversely</u> to the housing construction swing, declining to a low of about 28 household heads per 100 adults in 1885 and rising to a high of 33 household heads per 100 adults in 1895 (though the latter ratio was still below that of 41 heads/100 adults in 1860). Taken together these trends suggest that the apparent decline in headship rates from 1860 to 1895 discovered in Chapter 1 was not a direct consequence of housing trends. Low rates of "doubling

Table 41

Residential Dwelling Starts in St. Paul, 1885 - 1899

	One and One-and-a-half Story Frame Dwellings			Hotels and Apartment Buildings			Other Dwellings[a]			Totals		
	Number	Value[b] ($000)	Ave. Value ($)	Number	Value ($000)	Ave. Value ($)	Number	Value ($000)	Ave. V. ($)	Number	Value ($ 000)	Ave. ($)
1885	1073	755	704	0	0	0	404	920	2295	1477	1682	.1139
1886	823	668	812	0	0	0	462	1480	3204	1285	2148	1672
1887	904	876	969	0	0	0	587	2317	4159	1461	3193	3185
1888	461	815	1768	0	0	0	718	3397	4731	1179	4212	3573
1889	579	677	1168	1	20	20000	960	4057	4226	1540	4754	3087
1890	388	429	1106	0	0	0	797	3261	4092	1185	3690	3114
1891												
1892	150	145	966	0	0	0	197	1022	5188	347	1167	3363
1893												
1894	70	51	730	0	0	0	78	506	6482	148	557	3764
1895	72	55	761	0	0	0	76	426	5616	148	481	3250
1896	64	51	792	1	15	15000	74	307	4149	139	373	2683
1897	76	67	884	5	100	19900	78	213	2731	159	380	2390
1898	78	77	986	2	100	50000	92	285	3098	172	462	2686
1899	124	120	971	3	43	14433	140	627	4479	267	790	2959

continued on next page

Table 41, continued

[a]Excluding multi-purpose structures such as "stores and dwellings."

[b]Estimated value by owners when obtaining housing permits; actual value of completed structures probably more than 50% higher (see <u>Report</u> for 1885, p. 218).

Source: St. Paul, <u>Annual Report of the Inspector of Buildings</u>, in St. Paul, <u>Annual Reports of the City Officers and City Boards</u> (St. Paul, 1886-1900).

Table 42

Comparison of Residential Dwelling Starts, Urban Areas of Ohio, Total United States Production, and St. Paul, Minnesota, 1885 - 1899

	Ohio Urban Areas		St. Paul		United States	
	Thousands of Units	Index (1885=100)	Thousands of Units	Index (1885=100)	Thousands of Units	Index (1885=100)
1885	5.840	100	1.477	100	267	100
1886	5.033	86	1.285	87	278	104
1887	8.342	143	1.461	99	326	122
1888	8.397	152	1.179	80	320	120
1889	8.259	141	1.540	104	368	138
1890			1.185	80	278	104
1891					252	94
1892			0.347	23	323	121
1893					226	85
1894			0.148	10	225	84
1895			0.148	10	262	98
1896			0.139	9	218	82
1897			0.159	10	247	93
1898			0.172	12	222	83
1899			0.267	17	239	90

Source: Table 41 and Manuel Gottlieb, *Estimates of Residential Building, United States, 1840-1939* (National Bureau of Economic Research, Technical Paper No. 17; New York, 1964), 61-62, [illegible].

up" among households in both 1860 and 1895 indicate that a housing shortage was not a serious problem in those years, though we may surmise that the rate of "doubling up" by secondary families in 1885 was higher than the rates in either 1860 or 1895.

Though the total number of dwelling units in St. Paul's housing market in 1895 may have been roughly equal to the demand for separate quarters, the "tenure composition," or ratio of rental to sales units, had apparently changed considerably from 1860 to 1895. As Table 41 indicates, the decline of residential dwelling starts among low cost one and one-and-a-half-story frame dwellings was steeper than the overall decline from 1885 to 1896. Small homes of this type declined both absolutely and relatively, from 73% of dwelling starts in 1885 to 46% of starts in 1896. When the housing industry began to revive in 1896, the construction of hotels and apartment buildings was a substantial part of that revival until 1899. The housing construction depression thus apparently imposed a shift in the tenure composition of housing supply.

The severity of the depression in housing construction in St. Paul can be estimated by referring to Table 42. Compared to housing starts in urban areas of Ohio (dominated by Cleveland and Cincinnati) and in the entire nation after 1885, St. Paul's dwelling starts fell off at a much steeper pace in the late 1880's. Part of the reason for the steeper pace of St. Paul's decline may be indicated by examining the "average value" columns of Table 41. Unit cost of small frame dwellings increased 151% from 1885 to 1888 while the cost of more expensive dwellings increased by 106% during the same period.

Another factor effecting the steep rate of decline in single household dwelling construction in St. Paul was the relatively high proportions of young adults who postponed marriage in St. Paul compared to other cities. Compared to other cities within its region in 1890, St. Paul had the highest "proportions single" among men and women of prime marriage ages (see Table 43). Since single young adults tended to move more readily into rental quarters than families, the demand for small homes in St. Paul was not as strong among young adults as in other cities in the region.

On balance, then, we can say that Irish and German households increased the demand for single household dwellings in the "sales" sector at a higher rate than the households of migrant U.S.-born households, and thus very likely contributed more than their expected share to the building booms of the early 1870's and early 1880's, assuming that ethnic propensities to prefer such

Table 43

Proportions of Adults Never Married,
By Age Group and Sex, Six Midwestern Cities, 1900.

	Males, Age 25-29	Females, Age 20-24	Females, Age 25-29
Chicago	53	60	32
Kansas City	52	56	30
Milwaukee	45	62	32
Minneapolis	59	67	38
St. Louis	53	61	35
St. Paul	66	71	42

Source: U. S. Census Bureau, Twelfth Census, 1900, Vol. 2, <u>Population</u>, Part 2, 314-343.

dwellings were fairly constant.

Of course, both Irish and Germans were a relatively small part of the total demand for housing in St. Paul in 1895(and as we have seen, the demand for small homes was somewhat <u>less</u> than average among second generation Irish and Germans). Still the ethnic tendencies toward household headship and home ownership documented in Chapters 1 and 2 for St. Paul provide a more general hypothesis for testing in other cities.

German and Irish Home Ownership in Other Areas, 1890

We have suggested in the analysis above that the decline in levels of residence in single household dwellings in St. Paul from 1860 to 1895 was accompanied by a similar decline in the level of home ownership in St. Paul in 1895. Fortunately, a study of home ownership at the Eleventh U. S. Census of 1890 was made which allows us to compare exact levels of home ownership in St. Paul with other cities and to assess the effects of city size and regional differences on levels of Irish and German homeownership.[48] Table 44, based on this report, reveals that at the end of the boom decade of immigration and housing construction in the 1880's, St. Paul and Milwaukee (a city with high proportions of Germans) had the highest proportions of home ownership among six major cities in

Table 44

Percentage Distribution of Tenure Classes, Households in Six Midwestern Cities, 1890

	Renting	Owning		
		All	Free	Incumbered
Chicago	71	29	16	12
Kansas City	77	23	12	11
Milwaukee	58	42	23	19
Minneapolis	69	31	14	17
St. Louis	80	20	15	5
St. Paul	60	40	20	20
Average for All U.S. Cities With 100,000 Population +	77	23	14	9

Source: U. S. Census Bureau, Eleventh Census, 1890, Vol. 13, Report on Farms and Homes, 32.

the West North Central region. Compared to an average of 23% home ownership among heads in all cities in the United States of 100,000 population or more, St. Paul had a 40% homeownership proportion in 1890. The proportion of heads who owned their homes free and clear in St. Paul was also among the highest among cities of the West North Central region.

Though a breakdown of home ownership proportions was not provided for specific ethnic groups in St. Paul, an ethnic breakdown was provided for cities of various sizes and regions as groups. Table 45 indicates that both regional and urban-size factors affected Irish and German home ownership rates in 1890. Among all U. S. cities of 50,000 to 250,000 population, (which would include St. Paul), Germans and Irish heads owned homes at higher rates than average, though the advantage was especially pronounced among the Germans (+3% for Irish, and +14% for Germans). In cities over 250,000 population, ethnic differences declined and converged sharply, though even in such cities the German homeownership proportion was 5% higher than average.

Regionally, Table 45 also indicates that residence in the North Central region increased home ownership levels above national averages. Though ethnic differences were not reported for cities of middle size in the

Table 45

Proportions of Household Heads Owning Homes in Urban Areas, United States and the North Central Region[a] By Place of Birth and Population of Cities, 1890

Place of Birth	United States			North Central Region	
	All	All Cities 50,000 to 250,000	All Cities 250,000 +	All	All Cities 250,000+[b]
Germany	43	45	26	53	34
Ireland	36	34	20	52	32
Scandanavia	42	30	21	46	26
United States	41	27	20	45	21
All	39	31	21	47	27

[a]"North Central" includes: Ohio, Indiana, Illinois, Michigan, Wisconsin, Minnesota, Iowa, Missouri, North and South Dakota, Nebraska, and Kansas.

[b]These proportions were calculated by adding totals for: Chicago, Cinncinati, Cleveland, and St. Louis.

Source: U. S. Census Bureau, Eleventh Census, 1890, Vol. 13, _Report on Farms and Homes_, 191, 197, 598-599.

North Central region, the ethnic proportions for cities of more than 250,000 also reflect the substantial regional advantage of home ownership for Irish and German heads. The urban-size and regional differences in overall levels of homeownership probably were caused chiefly by economics; homes were cheaper out West and in medium-sized cities.[49] The ethnic variations _within_ regions and cities of specified sizes are more difficult to explain.

Conclusions

We have found that between 1860 and 1895 Irish and German immigrant populations interacted with St. Paul's housing market in a complex process which involved economic, demographic and cultural factors. Our study of housing construction trends and household headship rates (from Chapter 1) has indicated that an overall shortage of separate dwelling units was not a serious problem in either 1860 or 1895, though a shift in the tenure composition of available housing toward the rental sector was evident in 1895. Using residence in a single household dwelling as an indicator of the home ownership trend among migrant adults (both heads and non-heads) we have found that two general trends were occurring: household heads as a proportion of all migrant adults were shrinking in relation to "unattached" lodgers, and though household heads as a group continued to prefer single household dwellings, a larger proportion of all migrants were lodging in the multi-unit dwellings of the rental sector in 1895 as compared to 1860.

Within these overall trends among migrants, Irish and German demographic and cultural differences interacted with the housing market to maintain a high level of German concentration in the single household dwelling sector but decreased the Irish component in that sector below average in 1895. Though both German and Irish heads continued to reside in single household dwellings at a rate substantially above average in 1895, the large increase in the proportion of Irish adults who were lodgers (and their lower tendency to live in single household dwellings compared to lodgers in other groups) tended to decrease sharply the total adult Irish demand for single household dwellings. German adults, on the other hand, contained proportionately more heads than average, and German lodgers, as a group, tended to live more frequently in single household dwellings than the lodgers of any other group.

These ethnic deviations from the average for all migrant adults, moreover apparently cannot be "explained away" when controlling for other factors; the levels of Irish and German residence in single household dwellings remained roughly the same (or increased) when controlling for age, sex, family life cycle stage, child-spacing patterns, occupational level, length of residence in the state, and months of unemployment in the previous year (Tables 28, 29,32).

Though a sharp drop in the construction of small homes after 1883 and the lowered income expectations of the Depression of the 1890's may have contributed to the decisions to postpone marriage and to live in rental housing among young adults in 1895, we have seen that characteristic ethnic cultural norms may help to explain the pattern. Irish young adults postponed marriage and household headship at greater rates than average for migrants, perhaps reflecting the persistence their national demographic experience in the late nineteenth century. And the uniformly high rates of residence in single household dwellings (and in home ownership) among German adults, and the unusually low proportions of unattached German lodgers in 1895, suggest strong cultural norms toward early marriage, single family residence, and home ownership in St. Paul. As we have found in a national study of home ownership in 1890, the relative levels of Irish, German, and U. S.-born rates were borne out nationally as well.

As for ethnic differences in household composition, and the effects of such differences on housing trends, the evidence suggests that Germans of both first and second generation were more strongly inclined to the strictly nuclear pattern than either the Irish or U. S.-born. This very likely was simply a demographic response to the relative proportions of lodgers within each ethnic group, however; since lodgers tended to associate with heads of the same ethnicity, German households had relatively fewer lodgers to house than did Irish or U. S. households. Our study of the residential patterns of households also indicated that the strong German and Irish tendency toward residing in single household dwellings in the first generation may have decreased substantially by the second generation, except among middle-aged heads.

We also investigated the physical consequences for the immigrants of ethnic differences in the degree of crowding into housing space from 1890 to 1910. We found evidence that the higher than average degree of crowding among the Irish and the lower than average crowding among the Germans affected mortality rates in the predicted direction among women in 1890, and the greater crowding typical of the second generation also affected disease rates in the predicted direction among welfare families in 1910. In general, greater crowding increased the incidence of accidents, and fatal respiratory, circulatory, digestive and genitourinary diseases.

Though the overall economic effect of Irish and German headship and home ownership tendencies in St. Paul were relatively minor toward the end of the century because Irish and German adults represented only 25% of total migrant adults in 1895 (compared to 51% in 1860), the ethnic tendencies toward headship postponement and toward home ownership which we have documented in St. Paul have a wider significance for all those cities, particularly in the West North Central region, where Irish and German immigrants represented a substantial proportion of population. Not only total Irish and German proportions of adult population but (in the case of the Irish) the timing of arrival of immigrants have a direct bearing on total consumption demand. Cities such as Milwaukee where German immigration was large tended to have more households (per 100 adults) and more home ownership, we would argue, at least partially because of cultural norms about family formation and the ownership of homes.

In both Chapters 1 and 2 we have relied on demographic comparisons of the behavior of Irish and German immigrants, both with trends in Europe and in other cities of the United States, to deduce apparent cultural norms. In the next chapter we will turn to the writings of the immigrants themselves, in St. Paul and other areas, to see whether the "norms" which we have identified demographically were actually verbalized in the documents which have been preserved. Did the Irish perceive that their family formation patterns were changing? Did the Germans verbalize their apparently strong attachment to early marriage and home ownership? How did both groups evaluate marriage and housing opportunities in the latter decades of the nineteenth century in the Midwest? These are the issues of the following chapter.

Footnotes

[1]See Tables 41 and 42.

[2]The choice of marriage postponement rather than secondary family formation is supported by the facts that headship declined most sharply among young adults and secondary family headship (in both 1860 and in 1895) was at a low level of about 3% of adult population.

[3]This shift is demonstrated by comparing statements of the St. Paul Chamber of Commerce in 1884 during the building boom with the observations of the St. Paul Pioneer Press editor in 1892 after the housing construction downtown; in the former year the Chamber could say that "nearly every family lives in its own house," but by May 1, 1892, "in the language of the rental agencies more people will move today than at any other time in the history of the city . . . For the past month the agents have been swamped with applications for houses" (St. Paul Chamber of Commerce, Annual Report, 1884, 62; and St. Paul Pioneer Press, May 1, 1892)

[4]Burnham O. Campbell, Population Change and Building Cycles (Univ. of Illinois, Bureau of Economic and Business Research, Bulletin No. 91, 1966), 16-19, 98-103, provides an historical view of the relation between the age composition of adult population and tenure rates at the national level, 1870 to the present.

[5]Of course, hundreds of single household dwellings in St. Paul were converted from sales to rental housing during the Depression as indicated by a report of the St. Paul Pioneer Press on May 1, 1872, when the editors stated that "some of the big rental agencies have disposed of several hundred houses and claim that the demand is still heavy." Campbell argues, however, that the conversion of houses from the sales to rental sectors was a slow "filtering down" process related to the age and condition of the structures (Campbell, Population Change and Building Cycles, 39-40); in any case, home ownership was almost certainly higher in the single unit sector than in the multiple unit sector because of the large stock created by the boom in small homes construction in St. Paul during the previous decade.

[6]See the discussion in John Modell and Tamara K. Hareven, "Urbanization and the Malleable Household: An Examination of Boarding and Lodging in American Families," Journal of Marriage and the Family, 35 (August, 1973), 467-479.

[7]Barbara Laslett, for example, found that 15.5% of all households in Los Angeles in 1850 were composed of unrelated persons: "Household Structure of an American Frontier: Los Angeles, California in 1850," American Journal of Sociology, 81 (July, 1975), 116. In 1895 in St. Paul, the proportion varied from 12.4% in the first generation to 21.2% in the second (see Table 33). This was not a universal frontier or urban pattern, however; Modell found that half of the frontier counties of Indiana in 1820 contained 10% or less of all households with more than two adults aged 26 or over, and the proportion did not vary regularly with density of population: "Family and Fertility on the Indiana Frontier, 1820," American Quarterly,23, (December, 1971), 620,622-623.

[8]Modell and Hareven, "Urbanization and the Malleable Household," 470-478; Laslett, "Household Structure on an American Frontier," 123-125.

[9]Modell and Hareven, "Urbanization and the Malleable Household," 476-477.

[10]Robert E. Kennedy, Jr., The Irish: Emigration, Marriage and Fertility (Berkeley, 1973), 151.

[11]Ibid., 153-163

[12]Ibid., 163-172, 211

[13]Daniel M. Wilner, et al, The Housing Environment and Family Life; A Longitudinal Study of the Effects of Housing on Morbidity and Mental Health (Baltimore, 1962).

[14]"Single household dwellings" were identified in the 1895 census manuscript schedules by comparing the street addresses of the households selected in the sample; if addresses were the same as adjacent households the residence type was considered "multiple" and if not the same, then "single". This coding procedure was not possible in 1860 because addresses were not provided in the schedules; in addition, the city directories

revealed that most dwellings at this early stage did not have numbered addresses but rather were identified as being situated between two intersections. "Boarding house" households were identified in both years as those which contained more than three unrelated lodgers; "hotels" were so labelled in the schedules. See appendix for further discussion.

[15]"Unattached lodgers" refers to all adults who were unrelated to the head of household as indicated by surnames (whether living in private households, boarding houses, or hotels), _except_ those who were also members of secondary families in a household or who were domestic employees of the household head.

[16]In statistical terms, the strength of association measured by Cramer's V was higher among domestics and lodgers (.16) than among all migrant adults (.11) or among migrant heads of family or household (.11).

[17]Sample data: see appendix for complete distributions.

[18]Sample data; see appendix for complete distributions.

[19]By "unmarried" I mean all adults who fell _outside_ the categories of "married, spouse present" or of "single parent with co-resident children," the only two marital categories which could be identified precisely in the 1895 census data. The "unmarried" group thus included divorced and separated persons and childless widows and widowers as well as the strictly "single".

[20]The strength of association between place of birth and single household dwelling residence in Table 28 (measured by Cramer's V) increase from .15 overall to .24 for females only.

[21]We have not further confined the U. S.-born women heads to those born outside Minnesota because sample size was already so small that such a control would probably be meaningless anyway.

[22]Allan Schnaiberg, "The Concept and Measurement of Child Dependency: An Approach to Family Formation Analysis," _Population Studies_, 27 (March, 1973), 69-84

[23]Since dates of marriage were unavailable and children under 15 were aggregated into 5-year age groups, a "CYD" rate for each single family household was calculated by multiplying the number of children in each age category by a constant representing the average age for that category (with a downward adjustment from the numerical mean to compensate for the effects of mortality).

[24]See appendix for a description of the methods used for identifying members of the second generation based on surnames; widows for divorced female heads could not be assigned properly because of lack of information on their maiden names, but they represent a small proportion of household heads in Table 33.

[25]Carol Aronovici, Housing Conditions in the City of Saint Paul (St. Paul, 1917), 17.

[26]Wilner, et al, The Housing Environment and Family Life, 104-114.

[27]The "Diarrheal" category also has been separated from the "Infections and Parasitic" class for this analysis because these illnesses were identified by a symptom common in areas with high levels of public water contamination.

[28]U. S. Immigration Commission, Reports (42 vols., Washington, 1907-1910), Immigrants as Charity Seekers, Vol. 35, 960.

[29]"Annals of Minnesota in Historical Records Survey, U. S. Work Projects Administration, Minnesota Papers, 1939-1942, (Manuscripts Division, Minnesota Historical Society), Boxes 96, 97 and 100; hereafter cited as W. P. A., Annals.

[30]Daily Minnesotian (St. Paul), April 28, 1859, cited in W.P.A., Annals, Box #96.

[31]Pioneer and Democrat (St. Paul), August 11, 1859, cited in W.P.A., Annals, Box #96.

[32]Ibid., (1868), 12.

[33]St. Paul Chamber of Commerce, Annual Reports (1873), 37.

[34] *Ibid.*, (1868), 12.

[35] *St. Paul Daily Pioneer Press*, September 20, 1873, cited in W.P.A., *Annals*, Box #100.

[36] *Ibid.*, January 14, 1876; February 9, 1876; January 10, 1877; June 17, 1877; November 3, 1877; July 19, 1878. *St. Paul Daily Globe*, September 3, 1878; January 10, 1880; May 7, 1881; December 31, 1891; all cited in W.P.A. *Annals*, Box #100. *Daily Minnesota Tribune*, August 4,1883, cited in W.P.A *Annals*,Box #97.

[37] *Minneapolis Tribune*, September 5, 1880, cited in W.P.A. *Annals*, Box #100.

[38] *St. Paul Pioneer Press*, July 19, 1878, cited in W.P.A. *Annals*, Box #100

[39] Secretary of State, *Minnesota Executive Documents*(St. Paul, 1886), Vol. 1, 514, and U. S. Census Bureau, Tenth Census, 1880, Vol 1, *Population*, 451.

[40] *St. Paul Daily Globe*, May 7, 1881, cited in W.P.A., *Annals*, Box #100.

[41] *Ibid.*, November 9, 1881

[42] *Ibid.*, July 31, 1881.

[43] *Ibid.*, April 10 and April 23, 1882.

[44] *Ibid.*, April 23, 1882.

[45] St. Paul Chamber of Commerce, *Annual Reports*, 1884, 62.

[46] *Ibid.*

[47] Stillwater Gazette, October 17, 1883, cited in W.P.A., *Annals*, Box #97

[48] U. S. Census Bureau, Eleventh Census, 1890, Vol. 13, *Report on Farms and Homes* (Washington, 1896).

[49] *Ibid.*, 73-82.

Chapter 3

Family Values and the Urban Economy: Ethnic Differences Among Irish and German Immigrants in the Midwest, 1860 - 1900

Why did Irish and German immigrants to the cities of the Midwest in the nineteenth century differ in their attitudes toward family formation and home ownership? What major cultural values[1] characterized the two immigrant groups and what role did the immigrant family play in socializing[2] its members to assume these values, especially in those areas of family formation and housing preference which we analyzed in Chapters One and Two? This chapter will address these questions but its purpose is primarily exploratory. Very little scholarly work on the cultural values of Irish and German immigrant families is available and thus the initial problem is to find an appropriate method of investigating them with the surviving historical documents to the nineteenth century. Some of the chapter will be taken up with a consideration of the historical importance of a systematic study of ethnic[3] subcultural values at the family level. A method of investigating family values will be proposed. The secondary historical and sociological literature on Irish and German families will be evaluated from the perspective of this proposed method. Finally, an analysis of Irish and German cultural values toward family formation, family relationships, and home ownership will be included, drawn from a limited selection of nineteenth century sources in the urban Midwest.

For the most part, the scholarly research on nineteenth century American immigrant groups has attempted to trace the formation and adaptations of ethnic subsocieties[4] either at the institutional or the individual levels of analysis. With the use of the abundant and relatively accessible immigrant press, historians have documented the emergence of the complex network of clubs, beer gardens, theaters, churches, synagogue and parochial schools which characterized the urban German communities.[5] The newspaper sources have revealed a similar pattern of ethnic institutional growth among the parish schools and academies, parish benevolent societies, saloons and occasional Fenian societies of the urban Catholic Irish.[6] Studies at the individual level have taken the forms either of biographies of prominent persons or of analyses of such individual attributes as occupational level and mobility, residential location and mobility, wealthholding, organizational officeholding and religious affiliation.[7] Ecological studies (based on aggregations of individual attributes for townships, wards, and counties) have analyzed ethnic voting behavior and residential segregation patterns.[8]

While it is true that some attributes such as intermarriage rates and residential location have provided indirect information on family and household behavior, the interpretation of results typically has produced generalizations about _individuals_ who shared the same ethnic origin. Until the recent revival of interest in primary groups such as family, friends, kin and neighborhood, these intervening levels of ethnic group life in the nineteenth century virtually have been ignored in the literature.[9] In so doing, historians have been unable to explain satisfactorily the _process_ of cultural adaptation[10] undergone by immigrant groups in nineteenth century America. The rise and decline of ethnic institutions, or the increasing proportions of individuals who intermarried, moved to the suburbs, or rose to white collar occupations has indicated apparent _results_ of cultural adaptaion, but the process which these indicators purportedly measure has been hinted at only vaguely. There is reason to believe that small, face-to-face groups, especially the family, were the crucial social arenas in which ethnic values were applied and modified, but actual study at this level has been sparse, perhaps in the mistaken belief that sources did not exist for such research.[11]

Another serious limitation of the literature on the nineteenth century immigration is the lack of an adequate conception of the socialization process over the life cycle. Cultural values are inculcated in the care of infants, the rearing of children, and in the degree and kind of association with parents, peers and kin during adolescence.[12] The values learned in childhood and youth may be maintained or modified by the kind and quality of personal associations during adulthood. In the case of nineteenth century ethnic sub-cultures (Particularly in urban settings where direct competition with competing sub-cultural values occurred) a close linkage of these stages, and smooth passage from one to the other, became paramount concerns for immigrants who valued their cultural identity.[13] When competing values and institutions threatened to upset the socialization process strenuous efforts were made to maintain it through separate ethnic institutions such as schools and clubs, or through "normative" exhortations in press and pulpit. The timing and nature of the several stages of this process, the connections among them, and the results of serious disruption of one or more of the stages of ethnic socialization is a central theme of ethnic history, yet the question has not been explicitly studied from a systematic, developmental perspective.[14]

In the first two chapters we have isolated specific foreign places of birth as a significant independent variable affecting the rate at which German and Irish immigrants formed households and resided in single household dwellings (and, by implication, owned homes) in St. Paul. Merely isolating "place of birth" as an independent demographic variable, however, does not explain why immigrants of the same origins had the observed demographic and economic tendencies, why the strength of these tendencies varied from one ethnic group to another, and why changes in these tendencies occurred (all else being equal) at different rates among the groups.

Our demographic analysis has cleared the way for a discussion of the cultural values underlying these tendencies by showing that differences in marriage rates during young adulthood and ethnic associational preferences affected headship and residential patterns. By examining the families under the stress of an economic depression with appropriate controls for age, income and other factors, we have identified the range of influence of purely demographic and economic factors on ethnic family patterns. What remains to be done is an investigation of the consciously expressed cultural values of the Irish and Germans regarding family behavior and home ownership, and a study of the socialization process by which these values were transmitted and maintained, with emphasis (for the sake of balance) on the family's role in this process.

Explicitly stated, the hypothesis of this chapter is that the "place of birth" of Irish and German immigrants was (all else being equal) a significant, independent factor in explaining household formation and home ownership trends in St. Paul because place of birth was typically associated with ethnic cultural values, and that the ethnic family had an indispensable role in the socialization process by which these values were implanted in succeeding generations. While recognizing that values expressing "ideal" behavior may not conform to actual or even "expected" behavior, (and that some cultural values may be only implicit or unconscious and thus never expressed in written form), we will assume that when verbally expressed cultural value statements coincided with actual behavior of group members, the behavior was at least partially "caused" by adherence to a cultural value.[15] We will also assume that the national cultural backgrounds of Irish and German immigrants were sufficiently homogeneous that group values were recognizably similar wherever immigrants settled in the urban Midwest throughout the nineteenth century.[16]

A Method for the Study of Ethnic Values

If previous studies of nineteenth century ethnic groups in the United States have not focused on cultural values at the family level and have not conceived of the ethnic socialization process as a developmental whole, to be studied systematically, what method of research can be used to accomplish such a study? At least five elements of a satisfactory method can be identified: a comparative approach, a multiple-level conception of subcultures as wholes, a conception of subcultural change through time, the identification of a manageable number of measurable subcultural characteristics, and the replication of results with several types of sources. We will briefly explain these elements and then evaluate the secondary historical literature on Irish and German groups in the United States with these elements as a yardstick.

Perhaps nothing is easier to do than to call for comparative historical study, and few of the historian's tasks are more difficult to accomplish successfully. The usual purpose of comparative history is to vary the setting in which an historical process occurred to discover whether changes in setting produced differences in behavior. Another possibility is to compare somewhat dissimilar groups in one setting to see whether the same setting produced similarities in behavior. Some characteristic of the social setting is presumed to cause differences (or similarities) in response, and this presumption is tested historically by examining comparable units in several settings (or somewhat unlike units in the same setting). Ideally the units of analysis should be identical in all respects except for the element of behavior which is presumed to vary because of the social setting.[17]

In Chapters One and Two we have applied a form of comparison in a single setting by selecting comparable subgroups from the major ethnic groups of St. Paul (such as young, employed men born outside Minnesota) and comparing their tendencies to form separate households and live in single household dwellings. The surviving documents for the study of verbal expressions of ethnic family values, however, are not available in sufficient quantity in one city to allow this sort of strict control for internal variations of values among subgroups (such as the young and the old or the middle and lower classes).

The limitations of verbal family sources seem to require that ethnic family documents from several similar cities (preferrably of about the same size and in the same economic region) be combined and compared to provide some indication of the strength of values among internal subgroups of ethnic populations. In effect, to permit the study of internal variations in family values within ethnic groups this approach calls for shifting the geographic level of analysis to the region (with urban/rural controls). If internal comparisons among lower and middle class German values were not possible in a single city, for example, sources from several similar cities might allow such a study. Obviously, the level of rigor in obtaining strictly comparable units of analysis will be lower for this kind of analysis than for demographic work, but the intrinsic historical importance of cultural study makes the effort worth the risks.

Another important element for the effective study of ethnic values is a conception of subcultures as multi-layered but unified systems. In a summary of the pitfalls of "national character" studies from a sociologist's point of view, Alex Inkeles has pointed out that many such studies have assumed that infant and childhood experiences were the major factors in shaping adult personality, ignoring intervening life experiences.[18]

If ethnic subcultural values are to be explained with reference to the socialization process which produced them, then a study should be made of each of the successive stages of socialization over the life cycle, and of the linkages among them. It may be, for example, that the decline of membership in ethnic clubs and societies (with which much of the secondary literature deals) was simply an indication of the replacement of one form of institutional reinforcement of the socialization process with another at a particular life cycle stage, rather than an index of the decline of ethnic values generally. To fully test this possibility would require an analysis over historical time of all of the important forms of interpersonal association within ethnic groups at each life cycle stage.

Another familiar topic in the literature, the question of the survival of ethnic values among members of the group who apparently dissociated themselves from all institutional contact with the group, would also benefit from a wholistic understanding of the ethnic subculture. It might be true, for example, that some measurable ethnic behavioral tendencies learned in childhood and youth persisted into adulthood even among members of the second generation who removed themselves completely from ethnic institutional affairs. Ethnic subsocieties thus would encompass all persons of specific national origin who at any time in their lives were exposed to the ethnic socialization process, and ethnic subcultural values would range along a continuum, with variation from "modal" values depending upon length and quality of personal exposure to ethnic socialization.[19]

Another important element for the study of values among ethnic groups is an explicit conception of the ways in which social interaction with environment produced changes in subcultural values over a period of time. The parochial schools and benevolent associations established by Irish and German immigrants adapted their cultural patterns to the American environment at the institutional level. But what of the primary group level - family, kin, friends, neighbors, work-mates? What adjustments in conduct and values occurred in family life when some of the institutional supports for traditional family behavior were altered or removed in America (such as the land inheritance system of rural Ireland)? When family behavior in America began to diverge from cultural values learned in Europe, how were such gaps perceived and dealt with? What new forms of family and kin relationships were developed to meet the conditions of the new environment yet still reflect to a degree the older cultural values?

Michael Anderson's study of urban migrants in Preston, England in the nineteenth century (many of them from rural Ireland) has provided an intriguing conception of cultural adaptation over time at the family and kinship level. Anderson postulates that values remained stable among migrants to Preston at those points where the new social environment made conformity to the values advantageous to those who applied them. An example of such stability discovered by Anderson was the presence of mothers of working wives living in as babysitters of their grandchildren. This role for grandmothers was in effect an adaptation of the rural stem family pattern based on a different but quite functional economic task.[20]

When the new social environment made the application of learned values disadvantageous to those who applied them, Anderson argues that the equilibrium of values and actions was destabilized until, over time, either values slowly altered to accommodate changes in conduct or environing conditions changed once again to be supportive of the values. An example of the destabilized pattern found in Preston was the tendency for teenage children to leave home earlier or to assume a more independent relationship with parents because of the availability of employment at the factories, often at nearly the same wages as their parents earned. Since income opportunities no longer depended upon the inheritance of parental farmland, the dependent social role toward parents assumed by teenagers and young adults in rural society was no longer advantageous.[21]

Other factors in the nineteenth century urban environment, however, tended to counteract the tendency for children to free themselves from parents. The lack of bureaucratized forms of insurance or welfare systems, for example, often meant that family or kin were the only dependable source of help in time of personal financial crisis.[22] On balance, Anderson concludes that the kinship system of rural areas was maintained and even enhanced in some ways in Preston because kinship ties were found to be advantageous.[23]

The process of cultural adaptation proposed by Anderson need not be thought of necessarily as rapid, unilinear, or completely dependent on environmental conditions. Kinship relations, for example, very likely affected patterns of job recruitment independently in early industrial settings by introducing an intervening layer of supervision and responsibility between workmen and factory supervisors. The process of adaptation was probably not a mere shedding of values but more likely a transformation of them to fit new circumstances. Moreover, cultural adaptation at one level of social interaction may have only subtly, if at all, affected values at other levels.

One advantage of making explicit the important causes and paths of value changes over time is that source materials may be exploited more fully. Having a prior conception of how and why change occurs acts as a sensitizer to the possible avenues of explanation available in the sources. The prior conception one adopts, moreover, need not necessarily act as in intellectual straightjacket. Other sources and paths of change may very well appear in the analysis and alter one's overall view of the process.[24]

Still another important element for the study of ethnic values is the identification of a manageable number of indicators of subcultural values which can be followed continuously over time in the verbal source materials. Both comparative study and the analysis of trends through time require that only a few important explicit values be chosen, in order to ensure comparability of the items to be studied. Usually the verbal sources themselves will report explicitly only a limited number of values with sufficient frequency to allow subgroup comparisons and trend analysis.[25]

An important hazard of this approach is to avoid the pitfalls of ethnic stereotyping into which "national character" studies have sometimes fallen. Frederick C. Luebke's recent book on German-Americans during the World War I period, for example, has described the appearance of pseudo-scientific studies of ethnic group "traits" at the turn of the century as part of a national drive toward Anglo-American conformity and immigration restriction.[26] German-Americans were influenced by stereotypical perceptions of their "traits' by others and tended in some degree to internalize these perceptions of themselves by others.[27] Thus the task of identifying German-American values is confounded not only by the unusual degree of internal variation in the group but also by the effects of external conceptions of their "traits" by others.

The pitfalls of the earlier studies can be avoided by careful attention to the comparability of sources used. For example, an effort should be made to identify the religious social class, and political backgrounds of editors when using newspaper sources. Rather than seeking stereotypical "traits" presumed to be universally present in all members of ethnic groups, subcultural values could be viewed as varying within a certain range along a continuum of values as a result of cultural and social factors, rather than through biological inheritance as presumed by the earlier analysts. The intrinsic importance, despite the hazards, of studying the values which members of ethnic groups themselves applied to their own behavior is implicitly recognized in most of the historical literature, though the reputation of much of the earlier work on the subject has contributed to scholarly reluctance to analyze specific ethnic values.[28]

A final element of a satisfactory method for studying ethnic values is the replication of research results with several types of sources. Zubrzycki, for example, has pointed out that demographic study of immigrant populations is needed to discover the extent to which primary group relationships could be built anew given the composition of the immigrant population.[29] We should not be surprised to find that few stem families existed among immigrants if only a small proportion of the total group consisted of grandparents. A study of explicit statements of ethnic values about stem family relationships would be more informative (and the frequency or character of such statements partially explained) if the demographic possibilities for putting the values into action were known in advance.

Among verbal sources also, the value statements reported in newspapers, for example, could be usefully compared with those in personal letters. The pressures upon newspaper editors to conform to the sort of popular opinion which would build subscription lists may have led to a form of distortion which would not appear in personal communications. Errors in interpreting value statements by the researcher might also be discovered by using more than one form of verbal source.[30]

Review of the Secondary Literature

We have noted that the scholarly literature on German and Irish immigrants and their children in the United States often has ignored cultural values at the family level and has not studied systematically the socialization process within ethnic groups (especially the early developmental stages of the life cycle). To some extent, the secondary literature has incorporated the five elements of a method for the study of ethnic values which we have outlined above. The extensive descriptions of trends in the institutional life of ethnic groups and the evaluations of inter-group conflict within and without the groups also provides a larger pattern of cultural adaption over time into which new studies of ethnic family life may be placed. Before examining the primary sources on Irish and German ethnic family life in nineteenth century Midwestern cities, we will evaluate the secondary literature from the viewpoint of the elements of method proposed in the previous section.

A comparative approach to the history of the Irish and German immigration and settlement in the nineteenth century has been applied in a few instances to the institutional life of ethnic groups in specific cities, comparing adaptations to the American urban environment.[31] Comparisons of the social and geographic mobility, residential segregation, and voting patterns of the Irish and Germans in the same city (or in some cases in several cities, wards, precincts or counties) have provided information on ethnic behavior at the individual adult level.[32] The family formation patterns of Germans and Irish in the same city have been studied demographically in a few cases.[33] Only rarely have efforts been made to compare Irish and German family values in a single setting,[34] and no comparative studies of Irish and German family socialization patterns exist for the nineteenth century.[35]

The historical literature on the Irish and Germans occasionally has made passing reference to family-related matters from which a tentative view of apparent family values and processes can be gleaned and the linkages between family and other ethnic institutions suggested.

Among the Irish, the strength of inter-generational kinship ties, even when kin were residing far apart, has been noted. Return trips and frequent dispatches of money and other aid to relatives in Ireland, for example, were found among the Irish in Lawrence, Massachusetts.[36] Other historians have used descriptions of rural family life in Ireland in the nineteenth century to suggest the strength of immigrant family loyalty learned in the stem family system.[37] Research conducted in the twentieth century on rural families in Ireland and on Irish-American families in the United States indicates the persistence in both locations of strong inter-generational family relationships.[38]

If parent-child relationships remained strong among Irish families in passage from rural Ireland to American cities, the distribution of relative authority among family members apparently changed under the stresses of the new urban environment. Children, especially adolescent girls who left rural Ireland in increasing relative numbers during the century to take up domestic service or mill work in American cities, gained new independence from parental authority.[39] The active home management and child-rearing role of the Irish wife in rural Ireland apparently was enhanced under the pressures of poverty, unemployment and the relatively high rates of mortality, drunkenness, and incarceration of Irish husbands in American cities.[40]

The secondary literature on the real estage ownership tendencies of Irish immigrant families is sparse but suggestive. Several arguments have been advanced to explain the fact that the Irish, of mostly rural origins, settled in high proportions in American cities, avoiding opportunities to purchase low-priced farmland in the American West. The reluctance of the Irish to reside in isolated farm districts away from social life, the stark poverty of the "famine generation" of immigrants who were unable to purchase even cheap land and had been conditioned by poverty to expect only a bare subsistence from life, and the oppression of landlords in Ireland which made the farm a symbol of insecurity - all have been put forward to explain the avoidance of farming in the United States.[41]

As we noted in Chapter Two, once the Irish arrived in American cities the levels of home ownership by Irish heads of household were higher than average except in the largest cities on the Eastern seaboard. Despite the low average level of income, there is some evidence that savings, however modest, were highly valued by Irish laboring families.[42] A network of Irish building and loan societies closely tied to the Catholic parish emerged which assisted families to invest savings in the purchase of modest homes.[43] One author has argued that property ownership among urban laboring families involved financial sacrifices of other goods (such as education of children) and did not reflect necessarily a substantial upward step in social mobility during the nineteenth century.[44]

The secondary historical literature on the Irish also contains suggestive clues about the linkages between the family socialization process and the adult "modal personality" which family and parish life tended to produce among the urban Catholic Irish. Writing from the viewpoint of their own Irish ethnic background as well as from the nineteenth century sources, George Potter and William V. Shannon have described the high level of sociability within the tight network of home, church and saloon, and the "warm, gregarious, communal style of life that bred strong family and neighborhood loyalties and permitted the avowal of strong passions".[45] The warm-hearted sentimentality, the deeply-held loyalties and animosities, the devotedly religious yet romantic outlook, the love of wit and display of personality which most often impressed observers (and the Irish themselves) as somehow "typical" of the Irish character provide important clues for more systematic research on the distribution of these personality characteristics in the ethnic population.[46] Shannon argues that even novelist F. Scott Fitzgerald subtly reflected his Irish Catholic upbringing; his novels revealed that in contrast to non-Irish novelists he was a "romantic about the possibilities of experience and a moralist about the consequences of it" despite his "lace-curtain" background and relative estrangement from Irish institutional life.[47]

Recent sociological research, based both on national survey data and on "participant-observation," indicates that a high level of warmth in family relationships is still a "modal personality" characteristic among Irish-Americans. Greeley's survey data from the late 1960's revealed that among adult men, for attitudes reflecting warmth in family relationships (such as time spent with children, amount of hugging and kissing of children, and time spent with wife) Irish Catholics ranked highest or nearly highest among eight of the largest white ethnic groups with controls for social class.[48] Ellen Horgan Biddle's recent sociological report on her youth in a Massachusetts Irish parish suggests that the close social connections among family, kin and parish, and the sentimentality and warmth of Irish social relationships, has persisted in the twentieth century at least among those Irish who remain closely tied to parish life.[49]

Overall, the secondary literature provides clues about the early stages of the subcultural socialization process and about the close links among family, kin, and the social and religious institutions of the parish for the urban Irish. Further research is needed to explore these linkages and to place them in the larger contexts of both Irish subcultural institutions and the interaction of the Irish with the larger urban society.

Recent scholarly work on the German immigrants by American scholars provides even fewer leads than the literature on the Irish regarding family values and socialization processes though a few apparent tendencies appear. Among Germans who settled on farms in the Midwest, the strong inter-generational ties typical of the stem family system tended to persist; bride-choice by parents and close association between the families of mature children and their aged parents continued in the American rural setting.[50] German rural settlements tended to be stable and to expand with each generation as sons took up additional holdings near their fathers' farms.[51] A clue that a strong patriarchal role in the socialization process was valued is the fact that German Catholic elementary schools typically employed only male lay teachers until the end of the nineteenth century.[52]

We have noted the higher than average home ownership tendencies of urban German-Americans in Chapter Two(Table 45). German building and loan associations and small savings banks were also typical institutions in urban German-American communities.[53] Both of these behavior patterns suggest that savings, investment and property accumulation were culturally valued by German immigrants, and the recent work on the social history of "hometowns" in Germany during the nineteenth century provides a probable explanation of this. About a quarter of the population in German states in the mid-nineteenth century lived in small "hometowns", (midway in size between peasant villages and cities) and the percentage was especially high in Bavaria, Baden, Wurttemberg and nearby areas where emigration was heaviest.[54] Reacting against the growing, rootless laboring population created by industrialization in the southwestern German states, centers of middle class, hometownsmen strength imposed legal restrictions on hometown citizenship, guild membership, and the right to marry, limiting access only to persons possessing property.[55] Thus the possession of property became the cornerstone for the defense of the entire communal way of life which the hometownsmen feared they were losing at mid-century.[56] We should not be surprised then if a strong concern with the status which property represented in marriage, family and social life appeared also among the largely artisan class from southwestern German states who settled in Midwestern American cities during the 1850's.

Another feature of the subcultural socialization process for many German-Americans was the maintenance of language within the family, the German parochial school, and the German language class which flourished for a time in the public schools. Though German Jews after the 1880's moved increasingly away from involvement in the cultural institutions of the Germans, the immigrant generation spoke a mixture of German, Hebrew and Yiddish in the home and used both English and German in their newspapers.[56] Secular Germans or "club Germans" also cultivated the German language in their homes and societies.[57] In the late 1880's, however, an external attack on the teaching of German in schools began; German was soon eliminated in the lower elementary grades of public schools and legally restricted to only a few subjects in the parochial Lutheran schools of Illinois and Wisconsin.[58] The desire for autonomous German parishes and separate German clerical associations among German Catholics was curbed by pressure from the Irish-dominated American Catholic hierarchy.[59]

What was the effect of this disruption of language maintenance efforts on the socialization process? Heinz Kloss has argued that a complex set of factors, including density of German settlement, religious policies, as well as external social attitudes by other groups led to a widely diverse response varying from complete rejection of German ethnic identity in the second generation to cultural persistence to the present.[60] A complete study of the question surely will include the German family. It seems clear that, given the strong importance attached to language maintenance (especially among Lutherans and Catholics) and the primary role of the family in passing on language to successive generations, the German socialization process involved close links between the family and other ethnic institutions.

It is especially risky to consider the question of "modal personality" characteristics which the German-American socialization process produced in America because of the highly diverse nature of the German immigration. Close study is likely to produce several "modal personalities" corresponding to the religious, regional, social class and other subdivisions of the group. German-American spokesmen themselves, however, have noted certain broad tendencies despite their internal differences which we will consider briefly. Albert B. Faust's early history of German-Americans published in 1909, for example, argued that "respect for the law, honesty, and promptness in the discharge of business obligations, dogged persistence, industry, and economy" were typical German traits.[61]

Frederick Luebke has argued that these "traits" were simply elements of an American stereotype of Germans developed because of lack of understanding of their sociological rather than cultural causes.[62] Nearly all of the elements listed by Faust could be tested at both the verbal and overt behavioral levels with controls for sociological factors.[63] Because such attitudes have economic consequences and, (in view of current sociological research on the connections between family socialization and such attitudes), because they provide indirect information about family life, it seems unjustified to dismiss them out of hand as unworthy of scholarly study.[64] The oversimplifications and "explanations" of these attitudes by earlier pseudo-scientific studies can be avoided as we have argued above.

On balance we can say that the secondary literature on German and Irish immigrants and their children provides some indication of the multiple levels of the subcultural socialization process in the nineteenth century. Comparing the apparent subcultural systems of both groups it seems clear that sharply different national experiences in Europe produced important group differences in American cities. The German immigrants as a group had more distinct subgroups than the Irish though their concern for German language maintenance linked the socialization processes of each faction together until the late 1880's. Both German and Irish immigrants brought elements of patriarchal stem family behavior with them to America, and intergenerational ties remained close; among the urban Catholic Irish, however, greater authority for wives and independence for children seemed to characterize the cultural adaptation process. Both Germans and Irish created a network of building associations in American cities to assist with the purchase of homes and purchased homes at above average frequency. German values about property, however, especially among the middle class artisans from southwestern German states, apparently had a more central place in marriage and family life and ethnic identity than among the Irish. The avoidance of farming despite opportunities for cheap land suggests an ambivalent attitude toward the importance of real property ownership among the Irish.

So far we have found that the secondary literature has applied the comparative method to Irish and German ethnic history to some degree and has provided suggestive clues about the interconnections of the levels and stages of the ethnic socialization process. What of the other elements for the study of ethnic family values - a conception of cultural change, identification of cultural values, and replication?

Since only passing attention has been given to family matters, no explicit conception of cultural adaptation at the family level has been used. When the problem of cultural change in the family has been considered some notion of interaction between subculture and larger society has been employed. In Lawrence, Massachusetts between 1845 and 1912, for example, Cole found trends in age at marriage, degree of endogamy, and fertility which led him to argue that family life conformed to an "immigrant cycle"; as increasing security and prosperity replaced early years of insecurity, the immigrant depended less on the family and was less eager to "protect his family from the unfriendly city."[65]

As we have indicated, the identification of ethnic values at family level (or at any level of ethnic subculture) has been avoided completely, dismissed as stereotyping, or briefly speculated upon without substantial evidence. Indicators of family values about "social distance" from other groups (such as intermarriage rates and residential segregation indices) and values about family formation and dissolution (age at-marriage, fertility, female-headedness, divorce) have not been pursued serially through time for the Irish and Germans though some "cross-sectional" studies at single points in time exist. Basic work on the family values of these important nineteenth century immigrant groups really has not begun, though opportunities for comparative replicative study of trends over time are available.

Explorations in the Primary Sources

Before examining the family values and socialization patterns of Irish and German groups in the primary verbal sources we will raise several knotty problems of interpretation. As we stated earlier in the chapter our study of the primary sources will assume that when verbal statements of values coincided with actual conduct measured by other means, the verbal statements expressed actual values which at least partially caused the observed conduct.[66] Much of the primary verbal source material contains statements which only implicitly express values; can this more indirect reflection of values be used? Statements exist which appear to conflict with actual conduct; do such discrepancies provide valid evidence of the process of value changes over time? Finally, it is a common sense axiom of historical interpretation that statements of value were less likely to be distorted by self-interest if they were expressed incidentally to some other purpose; hence, "normative" prescriptions about how families ought to behave (e.g. in child-rearing manuals or sermons) were less likely to reflect actual standards of conduct than off-hand remarks contained in personal letters. Should the latter axiom prompt us to give greater weight to casual remarks in personal letters than to published advice in newspapers?

All of these interpretative issues will emerge in our analysis of the primary sources but the difficulties they pose will not be considered at length here because of the tentative, exploratory purpose of this study: we will ask only whether widespread verbal evidence exists in a variety of sources to support the view that ethnic subcultural values affected the family formation and home ownership behavior of Irish and Germans in Midwestern cities in the same direction as the demographic trends which we have measured in St. Paul. We will examine both explicitly stated and implicitly suggested value statements in personal letters, newspapers and contemporary novels, written by first or second generation Irish or Germans in urban areas of the Midwest in the late nineteenth century. A thorough consideration of these interpretive problems, it seems to me, can only be done within the context of a larger more systematic investigation.[67]

With this limited purpose in mind we turn first to the question of the stem family in the primary sources. Among the Germans several indications of the preservation of stem family values in the American urban setting appear in personal letters, immigrant newspaper columns and novels authored by members of the ethnic group. The extensive personal correspondence of the Frank and Kerler families, of Lutheran persuasion, who settled in Milwaukee and its rural environs in the 1850's and 1860's (after immigrating from Dietlingen, Baden and Bavaria, reveals the continuing deference paid to aging parents left behind in Europe, the continuation of strong parental roles in mate selection, the preservation of the formal written marriage contract and the dowry, and the naming of children after kin - all indicative of the patriarchal, stem family values of the German "home towns" from which they had come.[68]

A characteristic exhange of letters among Henry and August Frank with their father in Dietlingen in 1852 suggests the strength of these patterns. The Frank brothers had settled originally on a farm along the Titibawasee River in Saginaw County, Michigan in 1850, a property apparently purchased with shares from August Frank, his brother-in-law Edward Barck, and August's father John H. Frank (a Lutheran pastor who had remained in Dietlingen, Baden). When August married the daughter of John Kerler, (a German immigrant farmer from Greenfield, Wisconsin near Milwaukee), in 1852, he moved to Milwaukee and with his father-in-law's aid became a partner in a hardware and drygoods firm with a Milwaukee merchant. On July 22, 1852 Henry (on the family farm in

Michigan) wrote to his brother August in Milwaukee with the following plan:

> According to father's last letter, it is certain that they will surely come in 1854. It seems as though they have a longing for America. While I weigh all reservations which you have always expressed that we are not yet able to provide for them, the difficulties do not seem so great to me, since you and Sopie have attained a worry-free existence. . . . If you and father plan on leaving your share as fixed capital, I will become yours and father's tenant. I would put the farm into such condition that our dear parents will find house, yard and field in good order and could move right into the haven for their old days.[69]

In the same month August wrote to his father in Dietlingen:

> I am enclosing the letter from Henry so that you can give your own opinion of Henry's plan. I answered him that I considered it as most natural to wait with a division until the parents come. . . I wrote to him that if father would take over the farm, it would be taken for granted that Henry would stay with him and take over the farm. [70]

The plans for the immigration of the Frank parents from Germany did not materialize; in 1854 father Frank wrote that he and mother Frank would not be coming in that year because they had used the money saved for passage to America to provide a dowry for daughter Mathilde in Germany.[71]

Other examples of the strong influcence of father Frank on his children in America abound in the extensive correspondence of the family. In 1853, father Frank wrote to Henry advising him: "Remain single or make an attempt to get Veronica's sister for your wife. Her name is Regina and she has 8,000 dollars."[72] To his son August in the same year he wrote: "You have thought it out well, giving your sons the names of both grandfathers and I thank you for such piety. Your son is the first of our grandchildren who bears the name of Frank. May the name always remain honored".[73]

The strong ties between parents remaining in Germany and their immigrant children in America were reflected also in the case of Wenzel Petram, who migrated from Tetschen, Germany in 1849 as a young, single man. Working first as a dry goods clerk in Lockport, New York, for three years, he then married a local German girl and purchased a farm near Lockport. In 1855, he and his new wife moved to Minneapolis where he rented a shop and opened a retail and wholesale grocery, hardware, and farm supply business, remaining there until his retirement. Throughout the period 1849 to 1890 he maintained a regular correspondence with Johann and Theresia Pompe, his aunt and uncle who had raised him and remained in Germany. The Pompe's assisted Petram financially in 1852 when he bought his farm in New York, and their extensive correspondence with Petram reflected very similar stem family values as we have observed in the Frank-Kerler letters.[74]

The strength of parent-child ties among adult immigrants in America with parents who had remained in Germany is the theme of an important German-American novel, The Hyphenated Family : An American Saga, by Hermann Hagedorn. Based on real life recollections and family letters of his own German-American family in Brooklyn, dating from his birth in the early 1880's, Hagedorn traced the tragic consequences for their family of his father's domination by a strong-willed grandmother who remained in Germany. Grandmother Hagedorn's "four-thousand mile finger was in every pie. The clothes the children wore, the food they ate, their schooling, their friends, nothing was too large, nothing too small, to call forth her minatory injunctions."[75]

Irish family letters seem to have been preserved only rarely from the nineteenth century in the Midwest, though the extensive correspondence of the family of Ignatius Donnelly (a second generation Irish politician who spent much of his adult life in St. Paul) provides some insight about kinship and family values. Ignatius, for example, assisted his sister Eleanor by helping make her poetry known.[76] He also recommended his nephew John to Bishop John Ireland of St. Paul for a job at

Graceville, Minnesota.[77]

The Catholic Irish press in the Midwest was more plentiful as a source of commentary on Irish family life than family letters though the "normative" prouncements of Catholic family ideals in the Irish press cannot be taken to be actual values since they often took the form of advice or remonstrance rather than of description and affirmation. The loosening fabric of the patriarchal stem family of rural Ireland in the American urban environment seem to be reflected by the fact that pronouncements about family life in the Irish press usually took the form of criticism rather than praise throughout the century. The editor of the Irish Standard of Minneapolis, for example, in an article about "female employment" in 1888 decried the fact that "thousands and tens of thousands of girls and boys in the cities seek employment who are not under the necessity of supporting themselves, but who lighten the burden of the parents a little. . .by glutting the market with their labor at any price they can get."[78]

As more single Irish women continued to immigrate and enter the workforce in the urban Midwest at the end of the century, the Irish Standard editors continued to criticize family trends. "Why is it that Catholic girls very often marry non-Catholics, or do not marry at all?" asked the editors in an article headlined "God Help the

Boys" in 1889.[79] Noticing increasing "coquetry and flirtation" among girls, the editors warned that "the spirit of absorbing everyone's notice and attention, and feeling wronged by their being paid to anyone else, is a very dangerous one."[80] In 1896, the Standard's columns carried advice that "when women undertake to occupy what heretofore has been almost exclusively a field for men's activity, they should not try to make their work just like the men's. It should be invested with the feminine soul."[81] In 1900 the Standard reported a sermon by Rev. J. M. Cleary of St. Charles Catholic Church warning working girls of "The Wickedness of Winerooms" where "inexperienced girls, foolish girls - of whom the number seems to be legion - reckless girls, wayward and wicked girls are easily enticed for no good or noble purpose."[82]

Similar criticisms and advice appeared in the Irish Catholic Citizen of Milwaukee in the 1890's. Noting that a "Catholic gentleman of thirty-three, worth $75,000" had advertised for a wife in the "secular papers" the Milwaukee paper declared that "no Catholic gentleman would care to risk his chances of earthly happiness with a young woman so devoid of maidenly modesty and discretion as to open such a correspondence with an utter stranger."[83] In the same year the Milwaukee Catholic Citizen warned that "one of the great inconsistencies of the stenographic age is the way in which it regards the circumstances which force a girl to remain in a back office from eight o'clock in the morning till six in the evening in the company of a man whose morals are not what they should be".[84] In 1894 the paper noted that the "newest feature of eastern life is the bachelor girl. This is a girl who is educated, energetic, independent and enterprising, and who does not believe that a woman's sole aim and purpose in life is to marry."[85]

At the same time that the Irish editors in Minneapolis and Milwaukee were criticizing trends among single Irish women they also began to endorse women's employment, including married women's employment, by the century's end. In 1890 the *Irish Standard* carried a report of a speech by Bishop Spaulding of Peoria on "Women's Rights," noting that "in the freer and wider ranges of thought of this New World, women have developed other aspirations" and that "there is an ever-increasing number who desire to live an independent life, and in doing so have equal opportunities" and declared that "we believe with Bishop Spaulding that the time has come to give women larger opportunities".[86] In 1903 the *Standard* praised those wives who "in this inspiring age have done their duty to the fullest," who have "managed the household, worked in the factory or the store, spoke on the lecture platform, or written for the press."[87] The *Standard's* columns in 1904 cited a department store manager's claim that Catholic training made a Catholic girl a better employee and that her "store life" made her "no stranger to domestic science or to social requirements".[88] Reflecting the growing influence of the Irish wife in the family, however, the *Standard* noted disapprovingly in 1903 that "fully one-half of the married men are the most abject cowards where a wife is concerned. They will do anything for the sake of peace".[89]

Similar recognition of changing employment and authority patterns in the Irish family appeared in the Milwaukee paper as well. In 1894 the *Catholic Citizen* quoted Cardinal Gibbons approvingly on the subject of the "increasing activity of women in the higher occupations," declaring that "especially are women physicians desirable for women and children".[90] Husbands, in a list of "Don'ts", were advised not to think of their wives as servants or to "imagine you are a superior person".[91]

The tenor of German-American newspapers in the Midwest usually was critical of the family patterns of Americans rather than of German-Americans. German family values were defended with the implicit assumption that they were essentially stable, though some difficulties with maintaining the pattern in the second generation were admitted. The editors of the Illinois Staats Zeitung of Chicago, a "Forty-Eighter" paper, in an editorial on "American Family Life" in 1888 criticized the "modes of living and habits of life of the American family" which were "aimed at emancipation of the woman from the house or home." The "kitchen barely exists for the American woman, while it is a source of continual worry for the German woman," argued the editors; the American menu was usually only "beefsteak and salad" which was "prepared in five minutes". The editorial concluded that "in every nook and corner" of American family life was a "lack of that mutual spiritual support, which makes a truly married life possible".[92] The same paper also noted in 1888 that the "frequent unhappy marriage in America" was "due to a lack of dowry. Both sexes enter marriage with the same outrageous frivolity and thoughtlessness. Neither . . . has seriously considered whether they are able or not to conduct a home and rear children".[93]

Another Chicago paper, the Abendpost, a commercially successful, middle-of-the-road paper which refrained from the politically reformist stance of the Illinois Staats Zeitung,[94] adopted much the same attitude toward German and "American" family life. An article on "German versus American Child Training" published in 1891, for example, took issue with an exponent of "American" child training practices who had argued in an English-language paper that the "principles of democracy" were applied in America to child rearing, unlike the "very conservative training methods" prevalent in England and Germany. On the contrary, declared the Abendpost editors, "Children who do not respect their parents and teachers, obstinately refuse to obey rules and regulations, behave unruly and shamelessly in the presence of guests, are not any more the product of our free institutions as, for instance, the Ward-Politicians or the tobacco-spitters." Criticizing the "American" husband who was "too eager to leave the care of the children "to the wife", the editors concluded that "where the husband is in reality the 'head of the house' and the wife not too strong mentally, but motherly and truly feminine, there the children are well trained, obedient and modest".[95]

Though a middle-of-the-road paper like the Abendpost relfected the widespread, culturally-based rejection of the women's suffrage movement among German-Americans in the nineteenth century,[96] the socialist paper Arbeiter-Zeitung carried at least one article by a feminist calling not only for access to the vote and jobs but for a new more independent personal identity for women.[97] Other signs of deviations from the German pattern were reported among second generation children in Chicago. In 1874 the *Staats Zeitung* admitted that "it cannot be denied that in many German homes the children grow up without any supervision and that boys and girls become loafers of the worst type".[98] Blaming parents who sent children to work in factories and who became objects of ridicule by their children for not learning English, the editors called for the maintenance of German language among second generation children to retain the family bond of a common mother tongue.[99] Overall, though, the German-American press in Chicago took the stance of defending German-American family values taken to be identical to those in Germany, from invidious comparisons with other groups, quite unlike the self-criticism of Irish family trends reported in the Irish press of Minneapolis and Milwaukee during the same period.

Summing up our study of family values among Irish and German groups in Midwestern cities in the nineteenth century, the sources *apparently* indicate that such values remained fairly strong among the Germans but underwent important modifications among the Irish in response to the urban conditions of female immigration and employment. Within these broad trends in family values, we next consider ethnic values about family formation and home ownership. What do the verbal sources reveal about age at-marriage, fertility, and property among the Irish and

German immigrants and their children?

There was some indication in the Irish newspapers of St. Paul, Minneapolis, and Milwaukee in the nineteenth century that postponement of marriage was regarded uneasily from the point of view of Catholic family ideals. As early as 1889 the Irish Standard of Minneapolis noted the tendency for Catholic girls to marry non-Catholics or "not marry at all".[100] In 1890 a report in the same paper noted that while the "destiny of the vast majority is to be wives and mothers" there was an "ever increasing number who desire to live independent lives".[101] The exhortations against the evils of winerooms for young women which we have noted in the Standard may be taken as a sign of concern about the newly-independent ways of working women. In both the Irish-dominated Northwestern Chronicle of St. Paul and the Irish Standard of Minneapolis at the turn of the century, reports of increasing attention to providing low cost "Homes for Young Women" and explicit condemnations of "those who give up marriage and the joy of a family for the barren and fruitless pleasures of the clubhouse and the bachelor apartment" revealed the anxiety felt by local custodians of Catholic family values about the Irish marriage postponement trends.[102]

Though I found no direct discussion of the proper age for marriage in the German sources, there were strong statements endorsing matrimony in the letters of the Kerler and Frank families. Father Frank, for example, writing to congratulate his son August on his marriage in 1852, wrote:

> Your letter has given us inexpressible joy. You have found your ideal - I would say with the Turners - a fresh, pious, free, young, joyous, Christian and honest virgin, whose heart has turned to you in love. You are again in your accustomed business with a dear wife at your side who dries your sweat and helps bear your burdens.[103]

Like the Irish Catholics, German Lutherans also valued several children in the family. One German Lutheran immigrant in St. Louis, for example, reporting on his visit to a German Lutheran pastor near St. Louis, noted that the pastor praised him for having six children because "the more children, the more there are to read the Lord's Prayer" and it was "easier to feed 12 children here in this country than two in Germany".[104]

Turning finally to the question of family values about property and home ownership, the primary sources consulted tended to substantiate the ethnic differences suggested by our review of the secondary materials. Among the German Lutheran families of the Frank-Kerler letters, the close connection of patriarchal influence on mate selection, the bridal dowry, the formal marriage contract listing the properties of each partner, and the firm insistence on a substantial financial base for matrimony - all of these tendencies appeared among both urban and rural members of the kinship network. Some of the provisions of the "Marriage Agreement between August Frank and Veronica Kerler" in 1852 are worth quoting:

> II. The bride will bring as a dowry the customary amount of $300 and an additional $1430.69, partly in cash and partly invested in mortgages, the income of which:
>
> III. The bridegroom accepts, and also adds $500.
>
> IV. This combined property shall be used to carry on business and a joint ownership established, so that the husband is entitled to the use of this money, but may not dispose of it without the wife's consent. [105]

The agreement was signed by the bride's father, John Kerler, by the bride's two brothers, and by the bride and groom at the bride's family home in Greenfield, Wisconsin. Other references in the correspondence to the place and importance of the dowry,[106] to the importance of land ownership for sons before they married,[107] and of the importance of mutual contributions of property to the marriage,[108] occur as well.

Besides its importance as a firm foundation for matrimony, the possibilities of investment in property also influenced the choice of residential location and of occupational choice by members of the Frank-Kerler families. A sharp entrepreneurial eye for the main chance, whether it be in farming, a skilled trade, or commerce, characterized the Franks and Kerlers in the Milwaukee area and the Wenzel Petram family in Minneapolis. In a letter dated November, 1849, for example, John Kerler reported on his arrival in the Milwaukee area as a new immigrant: "I preferred farming, because I was convinced that a longer stay and knowledge of the locality were needed before starting a business . . . I found considerable differences in locations and soil . . . The more and more promising prospects for the future induced me to settle here with my family, especially as the price of land was steadily increasing".[109] August Frank also invested first in farmland in Michigan before settling in Milwaukee as a merchant with the aid of his father-in-law, John Kerler.[110] As we have noted previously, Wenzel Petram was successively a dry goods clerk in Lockport, New York, a farmer near Lockport, and a grocery and hardware merchant in Minneapolis. While these few instances do not establish a pattern they conform to other evidence about the importance of property investment in the lives of German-Americans and suggest the flexibility with which they responded to good investment opportunities wherever they occurred.

For the Irish, I have found very few direct or indirect statements about values attached to property ownership in the sources consulted. The Ignatius Donnelly papers included much correspondence about property matters, beginning with Donnelly's participation in immigrant building associations in Philadelphia as a legal consultant, and his promotion along with John Nininger of a speculative townsite in Minnesota optimistically called "Nininger City".[111] Donnelly was a second generation Irish-American, however, and it would be useful to consider first generation Irish family values as well. As we have indicated previously we were unable to locate first generation Irish letters, but some indirect information on immigrant property values are provided by Archbishop John Ireland's various projects for settling Irish immigrants on farm and urban land in Minnesota.

As a young priest, John Ireland became the first president of the Minnesota Irish Emigration Society organized in 1864.[112] In a brochure addressed to prospective emigrants in Ireland printed by the Society in 1869, the Irish were encouraged to come to Minnesota and settle on farm land under the Homestead Act rather than crowding into tenements in the big cities: "the occupation that will raise the emigrant, who comes from the rural districts of Ireland, who has no professions, trade or business calling, who must live by the labor of his hands, is agriculture, the tilling of his own land".[113] After his elevation to bishop in 1875, Ireland made an agreement with the Northern Pacific Railroad to reserve 75,000 acres of Railroad lands in Swift County on which he proposed to settle 2,000 Catholic families.[114] The necessity of capital for successful farming in Minnesota prevented poor Irish immigrants from taking advantage of this arrangement, though some Irish-Americans who had previous experience as farmers in other areas of the United States did in fact settle there.[115]

Some signs of the close connection between Irish home ownership and the Catholic Church which Dennis Clark found in Philadelphia also appeared in St. Paul. In 1885 at the height of the building boom, for example, the "Home Building Society" whose officers were John Dowlan, T. A. Prendergast, and Edward McNamee, met monthly in the Catholic Block on East Third Street.[116] In 1894 during the Depression the Northwestern Chronicle, a Catholic newspsper published in St. Paul at the behest of Archbishop Ireland, urged Catholics to buy lots at low depression prices in "College Place" near St. Thomas College. The paper argued that real estate was the "most stable of all investments" and that Catholic families could save money on their son's college education by living near the school.[117]

The bits of evidence which we have gathered on the Irish attitude toward property and home ownership are not strictly comparable with the evidence presented above on German Lutheran attitudes and are presented here mainly to show the sorts of indirect verbal evidence which might be used in a more systematic study of the question with the nineteenth century sources. The bits of evidence are consistent, however, with the hypothesis derived from the secondary literature, namely that - mainly by force of economic circumstances in Ireland - the connections among matrimony, land and property ownership which characterized the Germans were not present in the same strength among Irish immigrants.

Taking an overall view of the verbal evidence from the primary sources, we can say that verbal evidence does exist for the nineteenth century in a variety of ethnic sources in several Midwestern urban areas which supports the view that cultural values underlay the demographic trends measured in Chapters One and Two. German family patterns were perceived to be stable at least among first generation immigrants, while Irish spokesmen expressed both alarm and signs of cultural adaptation to the loosening of family relationships and, apparently, the increasing postponement of marriage by Irish young people at the end of the century. Home ownership and property ownership generally, we have found, were closely bound to German marriage values (at least among German Lutherans) while the legacy of poverty among most immigrant Irish families made such a close linkage difficult, at least in the earliest stages of married life.

Conclusions

In the first two chapters we found demographic evidence for St. Paul between 1860 and 1895 that Irish immigrants postponed marriage at higher rates than other migrant groups and that both German and Irish immigrants who were heads of household moved into single household dwellings at higher rates than U.S.-born migrant heads. After examining several alternative demographic and economic explanations of these marital and housing tendencies, we concluded that "place of birth" remained a significant independent factor in explaining these group trends.

Was "place of birth" a significant factor in these demographic trends in St. Paul because ethnic subcultural values about family formation and family dwelling place existed which influenced this observed behavior? In an attempt to answer this question in this chapter we have reviewed the secondary literature on Irish and German ethnic family values and socialization processes and we have examined a few primary verbal sources of several types from St. Paul, Minneapolis, Milwaukee and Chicago, assuming that if ethnic subcultural values existed among St. Paul's Irish and Germans they would have appeared also in other Midwestern centers of Irish and German immigration.

We have found some evidence in these primary sources that the Irish pattern of marriage postponement was perceived by Irish spokesmen, that cultural adaptation to this pattern occurred in the form of an increasingly positive attitude toward the employment of young women and the beginning of "homes for young women" to provide continuity of ethnic influence on the socialization process, and that the process of adaptation occurred despite anxiety that marriage postponement violated Catholic family values (expressed in the Irish-related newspapers of both St. Paul and Minneapolis). The employment of young women in American cities, coupled with the fact that many of them had separated themselves from parental control by immigration, contributed to a pattern of loosening authority in the Irish family which was recognized, criticized, but implicitly accepted as an established new state of affairs by Irish-American spokesmen.

Among the German families and ethnic newspapers which we examined a quite different pattern of strong and apparently stable patriarchal authority was maintained after immigration to Midwestern cities. Patriarchal German family values were defended from the criticism of the English-language American press by both secular and religiously-oriented German-American editors in Chicago throughout the century. Traditional patriarchal stem family values in mate selection, the dowry, land ownership and child naming practices clearly influenced the behavior of those German Lutheran families in Milwaukee, St. Louis and Minneapolis for which we found family letter collections. Though concern about the failure of the second generation to learn the German language and thus to move away from the socialization process of the group was expressed, the overall impression is one of relative stability of patriarchal authority and inter-generational influence among the urban Germans. This general impression coincides with the demographic trends of the Germans in St. Paul, whose household headship trends showed least change compared to other migrant groups, and with the secondary literature on German families.

On the question of home ownership which we explored demographically in Chapter Two, the verbal evidence also confirmed our hunches derived from these trends and from the secondary literature that property ownership was closely linked to German values about matrimony and family responsibilities, helping to account for the unusually high levels of German home ownership in Midwestern cities. We found very little direct discussion of home ownership as a value in the Irish sources, though the linkages between the Catholic parish, the Irish building society, and the Irish family which has been found in Philadelphia was also present to some degree in St. Paul. From force of poorer circumstances both in Europe and, at least immediately in the American urban setting, the Irish were less able to associate home ownership with marriage in the rural stem family tradition.

This survey of a few of the primary source materials on Irish and American families in Midwestern cities in the late nineteenth century demonstrates the possibilities of family study with the verbal sources but does not meet the standards of a rigorous comparative research design which we outlined earlier in the chapter. Among the Germans, for example, we have used the family letters only of Lutherans and were unable to locate Irish family letters except for the Donnelly family. Though the Irish newspapers from St. Paul, Minneapolis and Milwaukee were reasonably comparable, the variety available among the German papers was only slightly represented by the

Chicago press.[118] Though we have attempted to control our selection of materials for the effects of regional economic development and rural/urban residence by confining our sources to those of Midwestern cities in the late nineteenth century, the ideal design would control also for variation among such cities. Likewise, though we have pointed out the ways in which changes in family behavior prompted an adaptive institutional and ideational response by the Irish Catholic subculture (homes for young women under Catholic auspices, for example) and explored the close relationship between patriarchal authority, matrimony, and property ownership among German Lutherans, we have only scratched the surface of the multiple levels of the ethnic subcultures, the linkages among them, and the adaptive process through which they passed.

We have discovered, however, that a more extensive, systematic study of these values is possible if more sources of several types are brought together on a regional basis so that more rigorous comparisons of ethnic subgroups can be made. We have shown that the identification of only two cultural values (age at marriage and home ownership) has helped to organize bits of evidence from several kinds of sources around important central themes with wide implications for subcultural structure and adaptation. More careful specification of these and other central family values could make a larger study much more profitable. A larger study would also permit the explicit testing of theoretical propositions of family value change (such as those developed by Michael Anderson).[119]

If a larger study of family values and behavior should confirm the demographic and value trends found here, the implications are far-reaching indeed. If the propensities to marry early, to form separate households and to own homes at high rates were partly caused by cultural values inculcated at the primary group level in the family among the Germans, then family socialization of cultural values played an important, and hitherto ignored, role in economic consumption levels wherever German immigration was large. Not only in the demand for housing but in all those durable goods and household services associated with the formation of new households, the German influence on total demand would have been disproportionately high compared to their total numbers. Politically speaking, the perception by other groups of the Germans' apparently innate advantages in such economic matters may have helped to fuel the anti-German sentiments of the World War I era.

If the Irish population of other American cities

exhibited similar values about family authority and female employment which we found in the verbal sources are confirmed by a larger study of the Irish family, we should expect to find a lesser influence of rural stem family values upon economic activity in American cities. Though Irish household heads exhibited a high propensity to own homes and to live in single household dwellings after households were formed, the lower overall group demand for sales housing created by marriage postponement would effectively lower the total consumption demand of the group.

The question of the cultural effects of female employment opportunities upon family relationships has emerged in this chapter as a crucial dimension in the study of cultural adaptation among the Irish. Our study of the apparently strong and stable patriarchal authority structure of the German-American family also suggests the possibility that German fathers strongly influenced career choices of their sons. To evaluate these issues, and the broader question of the existence of and economic effects of ethnic occupational preferences and socialization patterns, we turn again in the next chapter to our case study of St. Paul.

Footnotes, Chapter 3

[1]The concepts of culture and cultural values in this chapter are based on Robert F. Berkhofer, Jr., *A Behavioral Approach to Historical Analysis* (New York, 1969), Chapter 4. "Culture" or "group-derived ideation" is defined as a mental construct of the observer after analyzing both the internal states and external behavior of a group of actors (pp. 84-85). Technically speaking, when the group of actors are the population of a complex modern nation (or of a linguistically related group of small, contiguous states as in the case of the German states before 1871) the word "culture" applies only to aspects of ideational and behavioral conformity shared by all members of the national population, while "subculture" describes the "group-derived ideation" of ethnic or other minorities (pp.86-88). "Cultural values" are "standards by which objects and objectives are judged according to an interpersonal process of ranking" (p.101).

[2]By "socialization" I mean all of the learning processes, both deliberate and unplanned, by which the beliefs, values, and social roles of a culture or society are transmitted from one generation to another. For a further discussion of the term, see the section on "Socialization" in David L. Sills, ed., *International Encyclopedia of the Social Sciences* (17 vols.; New York, 1968), vol. 14, 534-562.

[3]The term "ethnic group" is used here and throughout the dissertation to mean persons born in a specific foreign country and their immediate offspring. The term has been defined elsewhere more broadly as "any group which is defined or set off by race, religion, or national origin, or some combination of these categories" whose members share "through historical circumstances, a sense of people-hood" by Milton Gordon in *Assimilation in American Life* (New York, 1964), 27. Since we are considering only immigrants and their children here, it is not necessary to consider the question of ethnic values in later generations or other groups' values.

[4]The term "subsociety" here simply means the associational life of members of an ethnic group, regardless of the further subdivisions created by religion, social class or geographical factors. Gordon (*Assimilation in American Life*, 47-48), has labelled the smaller sub-divisions themselves as "subsocieties"; I have not followed that use of the term here for the sake of simplicity.

[5]See for example: Guido Dobbert, "The Disintegrating of an Immigrant Community: The Cincinnati Germans, 1870 - 1920" (Ph. D. disseration, University of Chicago, 1965); Sister Audrey Olson, "The Nature of an Immigrant Community: St. Louis Germans, 1850 - 1920," Missouri Historical Review 66 (April, 1972), 342-359; John Fredrick Nau, The German People of New Orleans, 1850 - 1900 (Leiden, 1958); and Kathleen Neils Congen, "The German Athens; Milwaukee and the Acculturation of its Immigrants 1836 - 60" (Ph.D. dissertation, University of Wisconsin-Madison, 1972). See also portions of: Robert Ernst, Immigrant Life in New York City, 1825 - 1863 (New York, 1949); Oscar Handlin, Boston's Immigrants (Cambridge, 1959); Donald B. Cole, Immigrant City: Laurence, Massachusetts, Chapel Hill, 1963).

[6]See, for example, Dennis Clark, The Irish in Philadelphia: Ten Generations of Urban Experience (Philadelphia, 1973); Earl F. Niehaus, The Irish in New Orleans, 1800 - 1860 (Baton Rouge, 1965); and portions of the works by Ernst, Hanklin and Cole cited above.

[7]Examples of biographies of nineteenth century Irish and German immigrants include: Claude Fuess, Carl Shurz, Reformer, 1829 - 1906 (New York, 1932); and Josphine Phelan, The Ardent Exile: The Life and Times of D'Arcy McGee (Toronto, 1951). On the occupational mobility of immigrants the most prominent work is Stephan Thernstrom, The Other Bostonians: Poverty and Progress in the American Metropolis, 1880 - 1970 (Cambridge, 1973). Recent examples of studies of residential mobility, wealthholding, officeholding and religious affiliation based on collective portraits of individual level data include: Howard P. Chudacoff, Mobile Americans: Residential and Social Mobility in Omaha, 1880 - 1920(New York, 1972); See Soltow, Patterns of Wealthholding in Wisconsin Since 1850(Madison, 1971); Dean R. Esslinger, Immigrants and the City: Ethnicity and Mobility in a Nineteenth-Century Midwestern Community (Port Washington, N.Y., 1975); and Frederick C. Luebke, Immigrants and Politics: The Germans of Nebraska, 1880 - 1900 (Lincoln, 1969).

[8]For a recent review of the literature on ethnocultural factors in the analysis of electoral returns, see Richard McCormick

On residential segregation, see Stanley Lieberson, Ethnic Patterns in American Cities(New York, 1963), and Otis Dudley Duncan and Stanley Lieberson, "Ethnic Segretation and Assimilation," American Journal of Sociology 64 (January, 1959), 364-374.

[9]For a sociological review of the older literature on primary groups among immigrants(represented by W. I. Thomas, Florian Znaniecki, and Robert Park) and a call for a new focus on the small group level, see Jerzy Zubrzycki, "Sociological Methods for the Study of Immigrant Adjustment," Migration, 1 (October-December, 1961), 51-56. Recent examples of published work on ethnic families include: Virgina Yans McLaughlin, Patterns of Work and Family Organization: Buffalo's Italians," Journal of Interdisciplinary History, 2 (Autumn, 1971), 299-314: and Charles H. Mindel and Robert W. Habenstein, Ethnic Families in America (New York, 1976).

[10]I am using the term "cultural adaptation to describe the process of cultural change which occurred as a result of interaction between ethnic groups and their social and cultural environments in the United States. Though the word "adaptation" implies change I am not making deterministic assumptions about the paths, speed, or outcomes of the process in the nineteenth century. For a sociological view of the competing research assumptions about the process in the twentieth century, see Gordon, Assimilation in American Life. The implications of the competing assumptions about cultural adaptation for historical research are explained in Rudolph J. Vecoli, "Ethnicity: A Neglected Dimension of American History," in Herbert J. Bass, ed., The State of American History Chicago, 1970), 70-88.

[11]A beginning has been made by Ellen Horgan Biddle's recently published chapter on "The American Catholic Irish Family" in Mindel and Habenstein, Ethnic Families in America, which suggestively describes topics and sources for both historical and contemporaty research on family and parish life. Though the importance of parish life has been long recognized in the historical literature on the Irish, the inerconnecting of family and kin with the parish have not been explored in the way Biddle's study begins to do.

[12]See Appendix A for a review of the interdisciplinary literature on the family's role in the socialization process.

[13]The parochial school systems and(in the case of the Germans) language maintenance efforts in the public schools were major examples of the institutional expression of this ethnic concern in the nineteenth century. See Heinz Kloss, "German-American Language Maintenance Efforts" in Joshua A. Fishman, ed., Language Loyalty in the United States (The Hague, 1966), 206-252, and Clark, The Irish in Philadelphia, 88-105.

[14]By using the words "systematic" and "developmental" I mean to imply the organzation of all aspects of ethnic socialization into a whole and the study of the resulting system on two dimensions of time: the life cycle and historical change. For a concise discussion of the implications of such an approach for historians, see Berkhofer, A Behavioral Approach, 169-187. On the importance of studying both the developmental and historical dimensions of change over time, see John Modell, "Levels of Change Over Time," Historical Methods Newsletter, 8 (September, 1975), 116-127.

[15]On the use of Clyde Kluchohn's "tripartite division of all behavioral regularities into actual, expected, and ideal" and other strategies for dealing with the disjunction between words and deeds in the past, see Berkhofer, A Behavioral Approach, 100 and passim. A recent example of historical research on the causes and consequences of gaps between normative expressions and actual behavior at the family level, see Michael Anderson, Family Structure in Nineteenth Century Lancashire (Cambridge, Eng., 1971), 5-16, 86-98, 170-179.

[16]By confining the study of sources to groups with the same national origins in large Midwestern cities in the late nineteenth century, we are in effect roughly controlling for the factors of rural/urban and regional residence(see Gordon's discussion of the significance of these factors in Assimilation in American Life, 39-51).

[17]See Berkhofer, A Behavioral Approach, 252-253, for a somewhat narrower definition of comparative history.

[18]"Some Sociological Observations on Culture and Personality Studies," in Clyde Kluckhohn and Henry A. Murray, eds., Personality in Nature, Society and Culture 2d ed,: New York, 1969), 581

[19]For a discussion of the "modal personality" concept in the historical study of cultures, see John Demos, "Developmental Perspectives on the History of Childhood," Journal of Interdisciplinary History, 2(Autumn, 1971), 315-327. The persistence of ethnic family values among second and later Irish and German generations in America is suggested by the results of a national public opinion survey reported in Andrew Greeley, That Most Distressful Nation: The Taming of the American Irish (Chicago, 1972), 144-177.

[20]Anderson's conception of the adaptation of family values over time is explained in Family Structure in Nineteenth Century Lancashire, 5-16; the use of grandmothers as "baby minders" is explained on pp.141-144.

[21]Ibid., 123-132

[22]Ibid., 136-161

[23]Ibid., 170-171

[24]Anderson's work, for example, is an example of the novel application of insights from exchange theory to explain empirical findings which did not fit an older conception of family change (see his "Introduction", 1-4). On the variety of conceptions of cultural change over time which are available to the student of cultures, see Anthony F. C. Wallace, Culture and Personality (2d. ed.; New York, 1970), 183-199.

[25]For an example of trend analysis using only explicitly stated values reported by historical sources, see Herman K. Lantz, et al., "Pre-industrial Patterns in the Colonial Family in America: A Content Analysis of Colonial Magazines," American Sociological Review, 33 (June, 1968), 413-426. On the necessity of selecting a manageable list of values to be compared or traced over time, see Inkeles, "Some Sociological Observations on Culture and Personality Studies," 578-579.

[26]Bonds of Loyalty: German Americans and World War I (Dekalb, Ill., 1974), 63-66.

[27]Ibid., 66-67, 77-78

[28]Luebke's recent book, for example, emphasizes the critical importance of the German-American perception of their own cultural heritage and values (and the stereo-

typical view of Anglo-Americans of those values) in producing the "explosive mix" of competing ethnic chauvinisms which led to suppression of the German element during World War I (pp. 77-78), On the danger of "knowing too much" about ethnic values and their relative rankings in American society, see Daniel P. Moynihan's foreword to Greeley's That Most Distressful Nation, x.

29"Sociological Methods for the Study of Immigrant Adjustment," 57-58.

30A thorough discussion of the advantages to be gained by replication of results is Norman K. Denzin, The Research Act: A Theoretical Introduction to Sociological Methods (Chicago, 1970), 297-313. Denzin advocates replication not only with different types of data but with different observers, methods and theories as well.

31Examples are: Ernst, Immigrant Life in New York City; Handlin, Boston's Immigrants; and Cole, Immigrant City. See also Rudolph J. Vecoli, The People of New Jersey (New York, 1965), 66-172, on Newark and other cities.

32Irish and German comparisons in the same city are present in: Clyde Griffen, "Workers Divided: The Effect of Craft and Ethnic Differences in Poughkeepsie, New York, 1850-1880," in Stephan Thernstrom and Richard Sennett, Nineteenth-Century Cities: Essays in the New Urban History (New Haven, 1969), 49-97; Conzen, "The German Athens;" Laurence A. Glasco, "Ethnicity and Social Structure: Irish, German, and Native-born of Buffalo, New York, 1850-1860" (Ph D. thesis, State University of New York at Buffalo, 1973); and John M. Allswang, A House for All Peoples, 1890-1936 (Lexington, Kty., 1971). Broader comparisons in several settings are present in the studies of ethnic voting behavior: see McCormick.

33See the citations for Table 1 in Chapter 1.

34The only example I have found for the nineteenth century period is Cole, Immigrant City, 99-112.

35Greeley's comparative work on twentieth century Irish and German ethnic socialization patterns is available in: That Most Distressful Nation, 145-165.

[36]Cole, Immigrant City, 99-100.

[37]William V. Shannon, The American Irish (New York, 1963), 22-23, and George Potter, To the Golden Door: The Story of the Irish in Ireland and America (Boston, 1960), 87, 89-90.

[38]Conrad M. Arensberg, The Irish Countryman: An Anthropological Study (Gloucester, Mass., 1959); Arensberg and Solon T. Kimball, Family and Community in Ireland (Gloucester, Mass., 1961); Andrew Greeley and Peter H. Rossi, The Education of Catholic Americans (Chicago, 1966), 89-96; and Greeley, That Most Distressful Nation, 95-98. See also Edward M. Levine's description of the ties between inter-generational relationships and political recruitment among Irish politicians and administrators in Chicago in The Irish and Irish Politicians: A Study of Cultural and Social Alienation (Notre Dame, Ind., 1966), 146-155.

[39]The emigration of young Irish women and their employment in American cities is evaluated in Robert E. Kennedy, Jr., The Irish: Emigration, Marriage, and Fertility (Berkeley, 1973), 76-85, 167-172; Potter, To the Golden Door, 513-517; and Daniel J. Walkowitz, "Working-Class Women in the Gilded Age: Factory, Community and Family Life Among Cohoes, New York, Cotton Workers," Journal of Social History,5 (Summer, 1972), 464-482.

[40]See Potter, To the Golden Door, 89-90 on the Irish wife in rural Ireland in the nineteenth century: William V. Shannon, The American Irish, 37-38; and Walkowitz, "Working-Class Women in the Gilded Age," 479-482; and Vecoli, The People of New Jersey,105-106, all discuss the destabilizing pressures of the urban environment on the Irish family in the nineteenth century. Greeley, in That Most Distressful Nation, 98-101, argues that the tradition of the "Irish matriarch" in Irish-American life and literature was a consequence of the urban environment in both Ireland and the United States.

[41]Potter, To the Golden Door, 171-172, 509-513; James P. Shannon, Catholic Colonization on the Western Frontier (New Haven, 1957), 28; Clark, The Irish in Philadelphia, 38-40.

[42]Potter, To the Golden Door, 512-513; Clark, The Irish in Philadelphia, 54-56.

[43]On the Irish building and loan societies see Clark, The Irish in Philadelphia,57-60. Thernstrom, Poverty and Progress, 125-131, provides a general account of laborers and savings banks in Massachusetts during the same period. Irish property-owning levels in nineteenth century cities are reported in Thernstrom, Poverty and Progress, 155-156; Esslinger, Immigrants and the City, 93-99; and Soltow, Patterns of Wealthholding, 40, 89-104. See also Chapter Two, Table 45.

[44]Thernstrom, Poverty and Progress, 157

[45]William V. Shannon, The American Irish, 34-35; see also Potter, To the Golden Door, 87, 171-172.

[46]These aspects of personality are noted throughout the secondary literature; see, e.g., Wittke, The Irish in America, 236, 246, 253; Potter, To the Golden Door, 83,102,171-172; Sister M. Justille McDonald, History of the Irish in Wisconsin in the Nineteenth Century (Washington, D.C., 1954), 250-253.

[47]William V. Shannon, The American Irish, 241

[48]Greeley, That Most Distressful Nation, 164-165

[49]Biddle, "The American Catholic Irish Family," 103-121.

[50]Frederick C. Luebke, Immigrants and Politics: The Germans of Nebraska, 1880-1900 (Lincoln, 1969), 30-31.

[51]Terry G. Jordan, German Seed in Texas Soil: Immigrant Farmers in Nineteenth-Century Texas (Austin, 1966), 115-117; and Marian Deininger and Douglas Marshall, "A Study of Land Ownership by Ethnic Groups from Frontier Times to the Present in a Marginal Farming Area in Minnesota," Land Economics, 31(November, 1955), 351-361.

[52]Philip Gleason, The Conservative Reformers: German-American Catholics and the Social Order (Notre Dame, Ind., 1968), 50.

[53]Ernst, Immigrant Life in New York City, 132; Dieter Cunz, The Maryland Germans: A History (Princeton, 1948), 347; Handlin, Boston's Immigrants, 67; Bayrd Still, Milwaukee: The History of a City (Madison, 1948) 341;

Klaus Wust, The Virginia Germans (Charlottesville,1969), 241; John F. Nau, The German People of New Orleans, 1850-1900 (Leiden, 1958), 58. In St. Paul in 1885 (near the peak of the residential building boom), German surnames appear among the officers of 18 of the 37 building societies listed in the Polk's St. Paul City Directory for that year, including two societies named the "German-American Building Association" and the "Germania Loan and Building Association" which held its meeting at the Germania Bank (pp 76-79).

[54] Mack Walker, German Home Towns: Community, State, and General Estate, 1648-1871 (Ithaca, N.Y., 1971), 30-33.

[55] Ibid.,390-404. See also: John Knodel, "Law, Marriage, and Illegitimacy in Nineteenth-Century Germany," Population Studies, 20 (1966-1967), 279-294; and Edward Shorter, "Middle-Class Anxiety in the German Revolution of 1848," Journal of Social History 2(Spring, 1969), 189-215. The latter study of middle-class values is based on an analysis of 656 essays on the question of the "material distress of the population" written by home-townsmen leaders from Bavaria in 1848.

[56] Eric E. Hirshler, ed., Jews from Germany in the United States (New York, 1955), 42-55, 114-116; Rudolph Glanz, Studies in Judaica Americana (New York, 1970), 232-248; Carl Wittke, The German-Language Press in America (Lexington, Kty., 1957), 185.

[57] Luebke, Bonds of Loyalty, 42-44

[58] Heinz Kloss, "German-American Language Maintenance Efforts," in Joshua Fishman, ed., Language Loyalty in the United States (The Hague, 1966), 236-237.

[59] Colman J. Barry, The Catholic Church and German Americans (Milwaukee, 1953), 131-236. On the Americanizing stance of Irish members of the hierarchy see also Rudolph J. Vecoli, "Prelates and Peasants: Italian Immigrants and the Catholic Church," Journal of Social History, 2(Spring, 1969), 217-268.

[60] Kloss,"German-American Language Maintenance Efforts." 206-212. See a case study of German accomodation to the attack on German language training in the public schools of St. Louis in Selwyn K. Troen, The Public and the Schools: Shaping the St. Louis System, 1838-1920 (Columbia, Mo., 1975), 55-78.

[61]The German Element in the United States (2 vols.; Boston, 1909), II 465-475.

[62]Bonds of Loyalty, 47-51, 59-67.

[63]Local criminal records, business credit reports, savings and property records, as well as a tremendous file of German-American newspapers exist for the nineteenth century which could be linked to information about German religious, regional and social class divisions found in the membership lists of religious bodies and the manuscript census materials.

[64]See Appendix A for a review of the sociological literature relating family socialization patterns to economic and political attitudes. Jordan's study of German farmers in Texas provides documentation of the economic consequences for farming of the German cultural attitudes in German Seed in Texas Soil, 192-203.

[65]Cole, Immigrant City, 112. Cole's statistics on marriage and fertility rates lack proper controls for the population at risk, however, and his argument that age at marriage declined and fertility increased when immigrants felt most "insecure" is only speculation.

[66]In a recent article on the existence of "values" in child-rearing manuals Jay Mechling has argued that verbal expressions of values should be considered only as verbal behavior and that "pure" values can be discovered only be examining overt child-rearing behavior; this objection loses force, however, when both overt behavior and verbal statements coincide, all else being equal: "Advice to Historians on Advice to Mothers," Journal of Social History, 9(Fall, 1975), 54.

[67]For useful suggestions on how such a study might proceed, see Anderson, Family Structure in Nineteenth Century Lancashire, 20-21, 180.

[68]Harry H. Anderson, ed., German-American Pioneers in Wisconsin and Michigan: The Frank-Kerler Letters, 1849-1864(Milwaukee, 1971), 87, 91, 125,143,171,191, 225, 251, 255. The letters were translated into English by Margaret Wolff.

[69]Henry Frank at Titibawassee, Michigan to August Frank at Milwaukee, Wisconsin, July 22, 1852, in Anderson, ed., German-American Pioneers, 141-142.

[70] August Frank at Milwaukee to John H. Frank at Dietlingen, July, 1852, in Anderson, ed., German-American Pioneers, 142-143.

[71] John H. Frank at Dietlingen to his children in and around Milwaukee, January 9, 1854, in Anderson, ed., German-American Pioneers, 191

[72] John H. Frank at Dietlingen to Henry Frank at Titibawasee, March 2, 1853, in Anderson, ed., German-American Pioneers, 191.

[73] John H. Frank at Dietlingen to August, Veronica, and John Henry at Milwaukee, August 17, 1853, in Anderson, ed., German-American Pioneers, 225

[74] "Letters of Wenzel Petram Translated from the German, 1849-1890," in Wenzel Petram Papers, Manuscripts Division, Minnesota Historical Society. The financial assistance of the Pompe's was indicated in: Wenzel Petram at Lockport, New York to Johann and Theresia Pompe at Tetschen, November, 1852.

[75] Hagedorn, The Hypenated Family: An American Saga (New York, 1960), 44.

[76] Eleanor C. Donnelly at Philadelphia to Ignatius Donnelly in Minnesota, November 17, 1856, in Ignatius Donnelly Papers, microfilm copy, Roll 2, Manuscripts Division, Minnesota Historical Society. See also Martin Ridge, Ignatius Donnelly: The Portrait of a Politician (Chicago, 1962), 9.

[77] John L. Donnelly at Donnelly, Minnesota, to Ignatius Donnelly, April 29, 1880, Donnelly Papers, Roll 65.

[78] Irish Standard (Minneapolis), October 13, 1888.

[79] Ibid.,August 10, 1889.

[80] Ibid., December 7, 1889

[81] Ibid., April 23, 1896.

[82] Ibid., March 10, 1900.

[83] Catholic Citizen (Milwaukee), September 23, 1893

[84]Ibid., October 14, 1893.

[85]Ibid., February 3, 1894

[86]Ibid., August 2, 1890.

[87]Ibid., November 14, 1903.

[88]Ibid., February 13, 1904.

[89]Ibid., May 30, 1903

[90]Catholic Citizen, February 10, 1894.

[91]Ibid., December 23, 1893

[92]Illinois Staats Zeitung (Chicago), May 23, 1888, translated into English in the Chicago Foreign Language Press Survey, microfilm copy deposited at the Immigration History Research Center, University of Minnesota, Roll 13.

[93]Ibid., May 9, 1888.

[94]Wittke, The German-Language Press in America,204.

[95]Abendpost(Chicago), September 8, 1891, in the Chicago Foreign Language Press Survey, Roll 13.

[96]Ibid.,April 21, 1894 and November 7, 1895.

[97]Arbeiter-Zeitung (Chicago).

[98]Illinois Staats Zeitung, May 18, 1874, in the Chicago Foreign Language Press Survey, Roll 13.

[99]Ibid.

[100]Irish Standard,August 10, 1889.

[101]Ibid., August 2, 1890

[102]Northwestern Chronicle (St. Paul), May 4, 1894 and June 7, 1895; Irish Standard(Minneapolis), January 23, 1904.

[103]John H. Frank at Dietlingen to August Frank at Milwaukee, August 6, 1852, in Anderson, ed., German-American Pioneers, 149.

[104] Johann W. Tubbesing at St. Louis to his brothers" in Red Wing, Minnesota, January 23, 1853, in Tubbesing Papers, Manuscripts Division, Minnesota Historical Society.

[105] Anderson, ed., German-American Pioneers, 124

[106] Ibid., 125, 171, 251

[107] Ibid., 91

[108] Ibid., 153.

[109] John Kerler at Milwaukee to Mag. Consultant Kerler in Memmingen, Bavaria, November, 1849, in ibid., 125-126

[110] August Frank at Greenfield to his parents at Dietlingen, July 4, 1852, in ibid.,125-126.

[111] These activities are summarized in Ridge, Ignatius Donnelly, 13-27.

[112] Shannon, Catholic Colonization, 44

[113] Address of the Minnesota Irish Emigration Convention Held in the City of Saint Paul, Minnesota, January 20th, 1869, to the People of Ireland (St. Paul, 1869), 2.

[114] Shannon, Catholic Colonization, 46

[115] Ibid.,131-133, 150-153.

[116] Polk's St. Paul City Directory for 1885, 77.

[117] Northwestern Chronicle (St. Paul), March 23, 1894. On Archbishop Ireland's influence on the paper and its essentially Irish outlook, see: Stanley J. Maslowski, "Minnesota's First Catholic Newspaper, the Northwestern Chronicle, A survey of its History and Content, 1866-1894" (unpublished disseration, St. Paul Seminary, 1963), 10.

[118] For a complete listing see Karl J. R. Arndt and May E. Olson, comps., German-American Newspspers and Periodicals, 1732-1955 (2d rev. ed.).

[119] See Appendix B for a more developed proposal for further study, using content analysis techniques.

Chapter 4

Ethnicity and Occupations in St. Paul: A Study of Opportunities, Resources and Values, 1860 - 1900

The study of occupational mobility has emerged as a prominent topic of concern among students of the nineteenth century American city. Beginning with Stephan Thernstrom's study of Newburyport, Massachusetts published in 1964, a spate of local studies have examined the movements of workers up and down skill levels and, occasionally, from one industry or employer to another or from one generation to the next.[1] Partly because the chief source of data for these studies - the manuscript schedules of federal and state censuses - report place of birth and sometimes places of parental birth, nearly all have compared the mobility paths or occupational distributions of the most numerous immigrant workers, Irish and Germans, to the native born. The conclusion usually drawn is that both the differences in the distribution of immigrants among occupations and in their tendency to move upward or downward among skill levels were the largely involuntaty results of prior circumstances at the time of immigration.[2] Because most Irish immigrants were unskilled laborers and most Germans were skilled craftsmen when both groups immigrated to the United States, it is not surprising to discover that each group then congregated in corresponding occupational sectors of the urban workforce after their arrival. Nor is it surprising to find that unskilled Irish immigrants moved upward occupationally at slower rates than Germans or the native born, given their initial handicaps. Regardless of what occupations Irish and Germans might have preferred, the differences in their careers in the American workforce were largely the result of circumstances upon their entry.

The study of the occupational careers of the <u>second</u> generation of Irish and German immigrants in America, however, is a much more complex problem conceptually than the study of the immigrant generation's careers. On the one hand, immigrant families, after a period of residence in the United States, became part of networks of mutual aid which assisted their offspring to find places in factories, industries or trades where they or their countrymen or neighbors had established a beachhead.[3] The economic resources of immigrant familes of even the humblest origins usually allowed sons and daughters to stand on parental shoulders educationally, to extend their range of occupational options to some degree. Cultural preferences about work - the complex of values about preferred types of work, about the importance of expensive education for work, or the importance of upward mobility in the context of competing values such as family stability- all these had an opportunity to influence the second generation's choices.[4] Though little is yet known about the process of family socialization for careers among immigrant families in the nineteenth century (or among the native born for that matter), it is reasonable to assume that each ethnic group in some ways socialized their children differently and that ethnic differences in occupational career patterns may have reflected this family influence.

On the other hand, once we assume that the American urban setting allowed significant room for career decisions based upon preference for the second generation, the dynamic nature of the urban occupational marketplace must be considered. The structure of occupational opportunities varied markedly from one decade to the next or from one region of the country to another during the years of rapid population growth and industrial development between 1860 and 1900. The "long swing" cycle of both urban population growth and immigration which we have noted previously affected these opportunities, especially in the construction and local service industries most sensitive to population fluctuations. Short term business cycles, sometimes accompanied by massive industrial layoffs or widespread business failures at their low points, added further complications. The process of industrialization itself, exemplified by the expansion of heavy "producers goods" manufacturing, added a slower but decisive element of change. Though a relatively small proportion of urban workers were actually employed in the "producers goods" sector where mechanization and mass production were most advanced, the overall structure of the urban workforce shifted perceptibly; lower proportions of unskilled laborers and higher proportions of semi-skilled manufacturing operatives characterized the national urban workforce by 1900.[5]

Regional differences in development were another element of complexity in the structure of opportunity confronting second generation workers. The urban-industrial heartland expanded strongly from the Northeast into the Great Lakes region in the late nineteenth century, but the workforces of urban places on the fringes of this heartland also responded slowly and indirectly to this expansion. The boots, shoes, clothing and machinery produced by mass production techniques undercut much of the business of local handcraftsmen in the urban fringe. Though a few factories emerged on the fringe, most manufacturing establishments remained small and the trade sectors remained strong or even grew in relative size by 1900. While the engine of urban-industrial development influenced the opportunities of nearly all urban workers in the nineteenth century, the effect was smaller and more indirect in places like St. Paul, Minnesota.[6]

These elements of change in the urban occupational marketplace impinged upon the occupational careers of both first and second generation Irish and German workers, of course, but the problem of accounting for these dynamic factors is crucial when career decisions based upon preference are being studied. Depending upon locality and timing, the opportunity to prepare for and to choose a preferred occupation or career may or may not have existed. If we assume that second generation immigrants had greater freedom than the first to make voluntary decisions about their careers based upon ethnic values or by making use of ethnic aid networks, we must then account for the limits which structural change in the marketplace placed upon the range of that freedom. It would do no good, for example, for a young Irish worker to prefer a job as a construction contractor or even to make use of his Irish contacts in the industry if the bottom had fallen out of the construction market. The problem of analysis, then, is to identify those economic conditions and moments in time where career decisions based on ethnic preferences or resources might be observed, and then to assess the relative significance of ethnicity as an influence on such decisions. The range of voluntary career choice for first generation immigrants also should be examined as a basis of comparison for the actions of the second.

A Strategy for the Historical Study of Occupational Decisions

The basic question of this chapter is to determine the degree to which ethnicity affected the occupational decisions of first and second generation Irish and German workers in St. Paul between 1860 and 1895. By "ethnicity" we refer to the exercise of either cultural preferences about occupations learned primarily through family socialization in childhood and early adolescence, or the use of ethnic resources which facilitated the placement of workers of specific ethnic backgrounds in particular occupations or industries. These elements are to be distinguished from ethnic circumstance at the time of migration (e.g. the fact that most Irishmen arrived as unskilled laborers) which were "given" characteristics of ethnic workmen, at least as far as the American scene was concerned. The argument here is that, while the careers of the first generation in America may have been channelled largely by their prior circumstances at the time of immigration, the second generation was allowed more freedom to choose (all else being equal) preferred career paths, and we are most likely to discover cultural factors at work in their choices.

Did identity as an Irishman or a German (all else being equal) cause significant differences in preferences for certain occupations? Did membership in an ethnic resource network (be it fraternal association, trade union, sports club, kinfolk, family or simply friends) help to smooth the way into certain distinctive occupations? To answer these questions we will:

a) summarize what is known about ethnic differences in occupational distributions at the national level during the nineteenth century;

b) suggest possible cultural sources for the existence of ethnic differences in occupational distributions especially in the second generation;

c) analyze Irish and German occupational distributions (first and second generations separately) in St. Paul, 1860 to 1895, looking first for purely demographic and economic explanations of those differences with census "cross-sections" in both year;

d) if ethnic differences in occupational patterns existed independently of such demographic and economic conditions, determine the role of <u>family</u> socialization by tracing the careers of sons during a period of prosperity (1880 - 1885) and during a period of depression (1895 - 1900), looking for patterns which reflected expected cultural preferences (all else being equal);

e) examine verbal expressions of ethnic values about occupational choices found in ethnic newspapers, personal papers and other sources, asking whether verbal statements of value coincided with actual conduct in the workforce and with our previous assessment of the <u>expected</u> occupational values of each ethnic group.

This rather round about procedure is necessary, it seems to me, to cope with the complex set of forces and motives which impinged on the occupational decisions of immigrants and their children in the nineteenth century. Since we are unable to survey the workers themselves to discover which options they considered and what motivated them to choose as they did, we are forced to assess their options indirectly and to find those moments of decision when cultural identity seemed to be the most reasonable explanation of their observed behavior.

Irish and German Occupations in Nineteenth Century America

We have already hinted at the distinctiveness of the occupational distributions of Irish and German immigrants. In Table 46 the "relative concentrations" of the two groups in selected occupations is displayed for both St. Paul and the United States generally. The "relative concentrations" are a fraction calculated by dividing the proportion of all workmen in that occupation and multiplying the result by 100; thus, any amount exceeding 100 is the degree of "excess" ethnic concentration in a particular occupation. At the national level in 1880 and 1890, the Irish were concentrated most highly in unskilled labor, civil service, and transportation. In the same years, Germans were concentrated most highly in trade, manufacturing and construction.

The relative concentrations of the Irish and Germans in St. Paul, however, were somewhat different from national concentrations, probably reflecting the newness and "urban fringe" location of the town and the personal

Table 46

Relative Concentrations in Selected Occupations, Irish and German Immigrants[a] in the United States and in St. Paul, Minnesota, 1880 and 1890

	1880				1890			
	Germans		Irish		Germans		Irish	
	U. S.	St. Paul	U. S.	St. Paul	U. S.	St. Paul	U. S.	St. Paul
Construction								
Carpenters, Joiners	126	144	73	70	106	113	57	34
Painters, Glaziers, Varnishers					109	77	67	52
Painters, Varnishers	123	94	91	50				
Transportation								
Officials of R. R.	23		51					
Employees of R. R.	64		172					
Off. & Employ. of R. R.		56	130					
Steam R. R. employ.					70	37	206	138
Draymen	113	131	245	130	96	110	183	130
Manufacturing								
Printers		50		40				
Printers & related[b]	73		75		66	71	52	34
Cigar Makers	347		26					
Cigar Makers & Tobacco Workers		263		10				
Tobacco & Cigar operatives					251	245	21	11

[a]Entries for 1880 are for both men and women age 10+, though only 64 women of all places of birth were listed for the selected occupations. Entries for 1890 are for males only, age 10+.

[b]Includes lithographers and stereotypers in 1880; engravers, bookbinders and pressmen in 1890.

Source: E. P. Hutchinson, Immigrants and their Children

- continued -

Table 46, continued

	1880				1890			
	Germans		Irish		Germans		Irish	
	U. S.	St. Paul	U. S.	St. Paul	U. S.	St. Paul	U. S.	St. Paul
Service and Trade								
Officials of Gov.	63		149		42	32	103	254
Employ. of Gov.	65		150					
Off. & Emp. of Gov.		56		160				
Watchmen, policemen, Detectives					101	85	356	406
Traders & Dealers		156		50				
Boots & Shoes	269		136					
Cigars & Tob.	337		65					
Clothing	482		57					
Dry Goods	199		74					
Produce	130		107					
Merchants & Dealers					139		84	
Merchants, Dealers, Peddlers						113		56
Clerks in stores	78			56				
Clerks & related[c]		69		20				
Bookkeepers & Accts.					57		43	
Bookkeepers & Clks.						43		54
Commercial Travellers						43	39	38
Laborers	98	106	237	220	126	124	274	204

[c]Includes salesmen and accountants in stores.
Sources: U. S. Census Bureau

circumstances of each group. Neither the Germans nor the Irish, for example, capitalized on the strength of the wholesale and retail trade sectors of St. Paul's booming commercial economy during the 1880's: relative concentrations in selected occupations of the trade sector in every case are lower than national ethnic concentrations. Germans in St. Paul also were more heavily concentrated in occupations related to "frontier-building" - the construction, local transportation, and unskilled labor sectors - than was the case for their countrymen at the national level. The stronger concentrations of the Irish in civil service positions in St. Paul (compared to the national Irish standard) is also interesting, and may reflect the greater "openness" of the frontier political structure to penetration by the Irish, compared to more established structures in the large Eastern cities where Irish populations were concentrated.[7]

The general picture which emerges of the Germans from Table 46 is that of an immigrant group taking its place in the occupational structure in accord with involuntary circumstances: i.e., their own skills and experiences upon immigration, and the opportunities available at their destination. The particular occupations in which the Irish immigrants concentrated require additional explanation. Why did the Irish enter public service or steam railroad jobs far more strongly than the Germans, whose average occupational skill level was higher? Why was the concentration of Irish in political office in 1890 higher than average and far higher than one would expect given the average level of education smong Irish immigrants?

In part, Irish occupations can be explained by circumstances alone: lacking a skilled trade such as many Germans had, Irish workers moved into low status service occupations like watchmen or semi-skilled positions in railroad gangs or car shops. Germans probably avoided these slots because they had skills which brought greater remuneration in other sectors. Many of the Irish "officials of government" may have been of the local variety, holding offices which required no special formal education or wealth to achieve. Still, the ethnic specialization in this sector is striking and requires further explanation apart from economic circumstances.[8]

The occupational distributions of both first and second generation Irish and Germans at the national level in 1900 are displayed in Table 47. An important point about the difference between generations in this table is the progress of second generation Irishmen out of the heavy concentration in unskilled labor of their fathers

Table 47

Relative Concentrations in Selected Occupations in the United States, Irish and German Ethnic Groups, by Generation in the United States, 1900

	Germans			Irish		
	First Gen.	Second Gen.	Diff.	First Gen.	Second Gen.	Diff.
Construction						
Carpenters, Joiners	119	95	-24	71	66	-5
Printers, Glaziers, Varnishers	117	138	+21	67	22	+55
Transportation						
Steam R.R. Employees	60	75	+15	177	178	+1
Draymen	101	125	+24	191	204	+13
Manufacturing						
Printers & related	72	189	+117	63	199	+136
Tobacco & Cigar Operatives	234	241	+7	22	86	+64
Service and Trade						
Merchants & Dealers, Retail	148	130	-18	82	81	-1
Bookkeepers & Accts.	61	153	+92	47	142	+95
Laborers	106	78	-28	231	06	-125

and into manufacturing and bookkeeping. Second generation Irish concentrations in printing exceeded the second generation Germans and nearly matched them in bookkeeping. Was the relative rate of this intergenerational movement out of laboring higher than we would expect, given the status of the immigrant generation? Only comparative studies of similar groups in several national settings could answer that question, but at least with respect to the Germans, the progress of the second generation Irish seems quite high.

In sum, Tables 46 and 47 provide suggestive clues not only about the occupations which German and Irish immigrants assumed involuntarily in America as a result of circumstance, but about the possible role of ethnicity in the voluntary occupational decisions of the first and especially the second generations. Germans of both generations were concentrated heavily in manufacturing and in related commercial establishments. The Irish second generation advanced strongly out of the heavy concentrations of the first generations in unskilled labor and into manufacturing and low white collar business positions. Ethnic "specializations" were maintained by the second generation in some cases (notably, the Germans in manufacturing and the Irish in transportation), suggesting that some combination of ethnic preference or ethnic resources were at work.

Ethnic Occupational Values and Resources: An Hypothesis

Our review of ethnic occupational concentrations provides an indirect source of information about the possible role of ethnicity in the occupational careers of Irish and German immigrants in the nineteenth century. Ideally, we should like to know directly what cultural values about occupations were taught by the immigrants to their children in America. Very little study on this question has been done, in part no doubt because of the scarcity of original source materials for the nineteenth century. We may glean some insight about what to expect on this issue from the work of Andrew Greeley on the family values of twentieth-century white ethnic groups in America. Assuming that ethnic cultural values were passed on by the ethnic family in some recognizable form to the third and fourth generations, the research by Greeley and his associates at the National Opinion Research Center in the 1960's can provide a "forward baseline" for predicting such values in earlier generations. Greeley's national surveys found that with controls for social class: a) Irish Catholic men had more egalitarian child-rearing attitudes than either

German Catholic or German Protestant men; b) for attitudes reflecting warmth in family relationships (time spent with children, amount of hugging and kissing of children, time spent with wife), Irish Catholic men ranked higher than German Catholic or German Protestant men; c) among the middle class, young adult Irish Catholics who had left home visited parents more frequently than did German Catholics or German Protestants.[9]

Though Greeley's findings identify ethnic family patterns generally, rather than occupational values, other recent sociological research has demonstrated that the occupational preferences of adolescent boys and young men are influenced by the occupations of their fathers.[10] Such preferences of fathers as the amount of autonomy allowed by a job, the relative importance of either inter-personal satisfactions or financial rewards, and the amount of social interaction (as contrasted to work with ideas or objects) involved in work have been found to influence the preferences of sons.[11] Though several major studies have indicated that father's attitudes are closely associated with actual conditions where they work (and, thus, occupational position accounts for occupational preferences),[12] it should be recalled that Greeley's survey of ethnic preferences applied controls for both religion and social class. Irish and

German family patterns remained significant <u>within</u> social class categories. Since Irish Catholic fathers in Greeley's survey emphasized autonomy (i.e. equalitarian child-rearing preferences) and sociability more strongly than German Catholic or German Protestant men apart from social class differences, it seems reasonable to conclude that these <u>ethnic</u> preferences helped to shape similar occupational preferences in their sons. We should expect to find, for example, that the son of an Irish manual worker would try to find a job offering more social interaction than his father's job because of ethnic preferences for sociability. German sons of manual workers, on the other hand, would have lesser preferences for such work because of lesser ethnic emphasis on sociability in their families.

This presumption about Irish and German occupational values in the 1960's seems to fit some of the nineteenth century occupational patterns of Tables 46 and 47. While we are not arguing that contemporary sociological research can be applied directly to an earlier period, such comparisons are useful for interpreting historical materials. We find, for example, that the Irish were strongly concentrated in service occupations such as policeman and governmental officials, which we would expect given the Greeley data on the value placed on warm social interaction in the Irish family. Second generation Germans maintained the heavy concentrations of their fathers in manufacturing occupations, a pattern we might have predicted given Greeley's data on German family values. For the sake of argument (and with due caution about the changes which separate the late 19th from the mid-20th centuries) we propose that German and Irish family socialization patterns regarding autonomy and the importance of social interaction have remained reasonably stable for the past century in America, and that Irish sons in the nineteenth century preferred work which allowed greater social interaction with people and greater personal autonomy than did German sons.

The other aspect of ethnicity which affected occupational placement in the nineteenth century - the use of ethnic resource networks to gain information about jobs and assistance in obtaining them - also is a little-studied topic. We know, for example, that Germans dominated trade unions in those crafts where they were concentrated in American cities, but union membership remained only a small fraction of the manufacturing labor force in the nineteenth century.[13] Studies of apprenticeship training in the late decades of the century indicate that most young men entered the trades informally without apprenticeships supervised by the unions.[14]

Contemporary studies of the Irish in politics gives some insight for the "specialization" of the Irish workforce. Kinship and friendship networks are closely integrated with the political recruitment process in cities like Chicago where the Irish dominate grass roots political organizations.[15] One persuasive study by Terry Nichols Clark of the Irish and political patronage expenditures in 51 American cities, 1880 - 1968, found that high proportions of Irish residents in a city consistently predicted high governmental expenditure levels and held that Irish resources for obtaining political jobs was a plausible explanation for this pattern. Among the ethnic resources which the Irish brought to politics, Clark maintained, was a strong sense of "non-ideological particularism" which influenced the Irish to "lean more toward personal contacts for guidance than toward the values and norms" which are present in all social situations. This "Irish Ethic," together with strong patterns of trust, loyalty and sociability among ethnic group members, helped to sustain the Irish patronage machine.[16]

It is reasonable to conclude from Clark's study that Irish resources also facilitated occupational placement in other sectors of Irish concentration such as construction and transportation, but that Irish resources were likely to be strongest in occupations which offered greatest opportunity for the exercise of ethnic occupational values. In the case of the Irish this probably included both the public service and the steam railroad companies (which were large enough to include many low status white collar supervisory positions). Though we lack a similar study of German resources, we know that Germans at least dominated the handcraft trade unions. Though union membership did not include all workers in manufacturing, we propose that German resources were strong in manufacturing both because of the circumstances of their previous training upon immigration and because of ethnic family values favoring such work.

Occupational Opportunities in St. Paul

Before examining empirically the degree to which ethnicity seems to have affected the voluntary occupational decisions of Irish and Germans in St. Paul, it is well to examine the range of occupational options which ethnic workmen faced in the city from 1860 to 1895. Ethnic occupational distributions in St. Paul likely can be traced in part to the structure of employment in the city. Since this structure changed in both cyclical and linear fashion between 1860 and 1895, we turn first to an analysis of changes in the industrial composition of the workforce. As Table 48 indicates, the long term "linear"

Table 48

Percentage Distribution of Gainfully Occupied Workers[a] Among Major Occupational Sectors, St. Paul, Minnesota, 1860 - 1900

	1860	1880	1884	1890	1895	1900
Construction	13	8	12	10	9	6
Labor	17	17	-	12	13	9
Trade	19	19	-	20	25	25
Wholesale		(11)[b]	(13)	-	-	-
Retail	-	(8)				
Transportation	8	13	-	9	13	10
Manufacturing	18	23	22	14	17	23
Services	25	20	-	35	23	27
Total Percent	100	100	-	100	100	100
N		17,809	46,200[c]	57,817		70,954
Sample Size	778				1,062	

[a]Male and female workers age 10+ for 1880, 1890 and 1900; age 15+ for 1860 and 1895.
[b]Percentage based on total number of workers in wholesale trade reported for 1879 in St. Paul Chamber of Commerce, Reports, 1879, p. 5.

changes in employment accompanying the maturation of St. Paul's economy between 1860 and 1900 were: a) declines in construction (-7%) and unskilled labor (-8%); and b) increases in trade (9+6%) and manufacturing (+4%). Little change was registered between 1860 and 1900 in the proportion of the workforce in transportation or local services. Thus, we would _expect_ to find fewer workmen of all ethnic groups in construction and unskilled labor sectors and more workmen in the trade and manufacturing sectors at the end of this period, simply as a result of the maturation of St. Paul's frontier economy.

The cyclic fluctuations of employment in St. Paul during the period 1860 to 1900 are also suggested by Table 48. Cyclic "shrinkages" in the proportion of workmen employed in a sector were most severe in manufacturing (-9% from 1884 to 1890) and in services (-12% from 1890 to 1895). Such temporary "shrinkages" were less severe in transportation (-4% from 1880 to 1890). As for trade, construction and unskilled labor sectors, Table 48 shows no important cyclic effects apart from the long term trends in these sectors, except for a minor increase in construction in 1884, though such effects may have appeared between the years shown in the table.

Another way of looking at trends in St. Paul's economy during these years is to study annual changes in the

gross production values of the wholesale trade, manufacturing, and construction sectors reported for most years by the St. Paul Chamber of Commerce. As Tables 49 and 50 indicate, the gross value of product grew most rapidly in manufacturing (+647%) from 1879 to 1895, with a more moderate rate of growth in wholesale trade(+321%) and a slower growth in construction (+192%) during the same period. These long trends in product values, however, were affected by differences in price trends in each sector as shown in Table 51. Wholesale and manufacturing prices decreased while construction prices increased. Thus, the decline in gross product value in construction tends to understate the decline in actual construction work (which tailed off drastically in the 1890's as we have seen in Chapter 2) and to overstate the actual increases of work in the wholesale and manufacturing sectors.

The cyclic patterns of St. Paul's economy can be seen clearly in Tables 49 and 50. The construction industry followed a "long swing" pattern from 1879 to 1894, with twin peaks in 1883 and 1888 and troughs during the mid-seventies and mid-nineties. Wholesale product values reflected very little cyclic fluctuation, though a few temporary "shrinkages" appear in the manufacturing series in 1882-83 and 1885-86. More "shrinkages" probably

Table 49

Production Values of Wholesale Trade, Manufacturing, and Construction in St. Paul, 1869 to 1899

	Millions of 1879 Dollars		
	Wholesale Trade	Manufacturing Product	Construction Value
1869	13.0	1.6	1.9
1870	15.1	1.9	2.1
1871	17.7	-	2.2
1872	22.5	-	3.0
1873	24.2	-	-
	. . . .	. . . .	
1878	32.6	-	-
1879	36.9	7.7	1.3
1880	-	10.5	2.9
1881	49.7	10.7	4.9
1882	64.0	14.5	8.3
1883	68.4	12.4	15.0
1884	70.3	18.4	8.6
1885	75.9	21.2	7.6
1886	76.6	18.9	11.5
1887	90.9	20.9	15.4
1888	94.4	20.3	17.5
1889	94.9	27.6	16.7
1890	105.1	40.2	-
1891	-	-	11.4
1892	-	-	4.1
1893	-	-	-
1894	-	-	1.6
1895	118.6	49.8	2.5
1896	-	-	2.1
1897	128.3	55.2	1.7
1898	-	-	2.2
1899	-	-	3.3

Sources: St. Paul Chamber of Commerce, Annual Reports.

Notes: Wholesale trade totals for 1881 - 1890 from Annual Report for 1890, p. 30. Manufacturing totals for 1885 - 1890 calculated by subtracting "Construction" totals from "Manufacturing" totals in the Annual Report for 1890, pp. 30,41. Manufacturing totals for 1881 calculated by subtracting the "Construction" value for that year (see Table 40, Chapter 2) from the "Manufacturing" total in the Annual Report for 1890, p. 30. For sources of price indexes see Table 51.

Table 50

Production Value Growth Rates (1879 = 100), Wholesale Trade, Manufacturing, and Construction in St. Paul, 1869 to 1899, Based on Constant 1879 Dollars

	Wholesale Trade	Manufacturing Product	Construction Value
1869	35	21	146
1870	41	25	162
1871	48	-	169
1872	61	-	231
1873	66	-	-
	. . . .	. . . .	
1878	88	-	-
1879	100	100	100
1880	-	136	223
1881	135	139	377
1882	173	188	638
1883	185	161	1154
1884	191	239	662
1885	206	275	585
1886	208	245	885
1887	246	271	1185
1888	256	264	1346
1889	257	358	1285
1890	285	522	-
1891	-	-	877
1892	-	-	315
1893	-	-	-
1894	-	-	123
1895	321	647	192
1896	-	-	162
1897	348	717	131
1898	-	-	170
1899	-	-	254

Source: Table 49.

Table 51

Price Indexes for Product Values in Wholesale Trade, Manufacturing, and Construction Sectors, St. Paul, 1869 to 1899

(1879 = 100)

	Wholesale Trade	Manufacturing Product	Construction Value
1869	147	151	133
1870	142	145	131
1871	137	139	129
1872	132	133	127
1873	127	127	125
1874	122	122	124
1875	117	117	119
1876	112	113	114
1877	107	109	109
1878	102	105	104
1879	100	100	100
1880	98	99	104
1881	97	98	108
1882	96	97	112
1883	95	96	116
1884	94	95	118
1885	93	92	118
1886	91	89	118
1887	90	86	119
1888	89	83	119
1889	87	80	119
1890	86	77	119
1891	85	74	118
1892	84	71	118
1893	83	68	117
1894	82	66	116
1895	81	69	118
1896	80	72	120
1897	79	75	122
1898	79	78	124
1899	78	80	126

Sources: Manufacturing and construction from: Robert E. Gallman, "Commodity Output, 1839-1899," in National Bureau of Economic Research, _Trends in the American Economy in the Nineteenth Century_ (Princeton, 1960), p. 40; "Construction Variant A" used. Wholesale trade index is an average for major products of wholesale trade in St. Paul, using specific product indexes from: Dorothy S. Brady, "Price Deflators for Final Product Estimates," in National Bureau of Economic Research, _Output, Employment, and Productivity in the United States after 1800_ (Princeton, 1966), 108-109, 111; the Brady index was converted to 1879 base by setting the 1879 index value at 100. Index values between decadal values given by sources were estimated by linear interpolation.

occurred in manufacturing between 1890 and 1894 but the Chamber of Commerce failed to report totals for those years.

Comparing Tables 49 and 50 to Table 48, it seems fair to conclude that cyclic fluctuations in economic production were much less important than long trends of development in St. Paul _except_ in the construction sector. The "shrinkage" of relative manufacturing _employment_ between 1884 and 1890, however was quite sharp (-9%) and apparently was _not_ the result of declining production. The alternative explanation is increased output per worker created by technological change. We shall examine this possibility below at greater length.

The odd fact that employment in the construction sector (Table 48) did not seem to fluctuate markedly with the pattern of the long swing in construction product (Tables 49 and 50), suggests still another factor: unemployment. The proportions in Table 48 are the "regular occupations" reported to census-takers and do not reflect actual current employment in that occupation. As we have seen in Chapter 1 (Table 19) unemployment rates among construction workers ran as high as 40% in some construction trades in 1890, before the onset of the depression of the 1890's (compared to an overall rate of 6% for all male workers). The rate for unskilled laborers in 1890 was 23% unemployed. Despite the rapid growth of the wholesale trade and manufacturing sectors in the late 1880's and the 1890's, a high proportion of workmen in construction and unskilled labor apparently were "trapped" in unemployment or under-employment, unable to move to other industrial sectors of the economy or to migrate out of the city. At the same time, craftsmen in the apparel trades seemed to fare better during the 1880's, despite the relative decline of manufacturing employment from 1884 to 1890. As Table 19 indicates, boot and shoe makers and tailors had unemployment rates of 4% and 5%, respectively, in 1890, less than the average of 6% for the male workforce.

The implication of this combination of short term factors - cyclic fluctuations in production, technological innovation in some manufacturing areas, and rigidities which prevented mobility out of shrinking sectors - seems to be that construction workers and unskilled laborers suffered from a double handicap during the downturn in construction from 1888 to 1894. The overall trend of St. Paul's economic development was decreasing the need for such workers, and they were unable to move out of the sector to other industries when construction activity turned downward at the end of the long swing. Under these circumstances, we should expect to find a strong tendency

Table 52

Median Capitalization of Major Manufacturing Firms, St. Paul, 1860 and 1880

1860		1880	
Lumber	$10,000	Flour	($20,500)*
Beverages	3,000	Leather	15,000
Flour	2,000	Lumber	10,000
Leather	1,500	Printing	5,000
Wagons	1,450	Beverages	4,000
Meats	1,200	Machinery	3,750
Sash & Door	1,000	Metal	2,500
Brooms	1,000	Wagons	2,000
Clothing	1,000	Harness	2,000
Furniture	800	Baking	1,350

Source: U. S. Census Bureau, manuscript schedules of the Manufacturing Census, 1860 and 1880.

*Mean, calculated from published census of manufacturing.

Note: For classification system see Appendix.

Table 53

Median Number of Employees Per Manufacturing Firm, St. Paul, 1860 and 1880

1860		1880	
Lumber	18	Lumber	15
Sash & Door	8	Leather	11
Wagons	6	Machinery	6.5
Brooms	4	Construction	6
Shoes	3	Flour	(5.7)*
Whiskey	3	Printing	5
Flour	3	Metal	5
Meat	2.5	Clothing	5
		Wagons	4.5
		Furniture	3
		Harness	3
		Beverages	3
		Cooperage	2.5

Source: U. S. Census Bureau, manuscript schedules of the Manufacturing Census, 1860 and 1880.

*Mean, calculated from published census of manufactures.

Note: For classification system, see Appendix.

Table 54

Proportions of Manufacturing Firms Using Steam or Water Power, St. Paul, 1860 and 1880

1860

	No.	%
Flour Milling	3	100
Lumber	3	67
Beverages & Vinegar	9	50
Furniture	10	10
Metal	12	8
Other Firms	57	0
All Firms	83	14

1880

	No.	%
Lumber	4	100
Machinery	12	50
Beverages	12	42
Printing	41	39
Metal	9	33
Baking	34	21
Household	60	13
Other Firms	449	5
All Firms	621	10

Source: U. S. Census Bureau, manuscript schedules of the Manufacturing Census, 1860 and 1880.

Notes: Data on flour milling in 1880 not available. For classification system see Appendix.

Table 55

Manufacturing Firms in Philadelphia and St. Paul in 1880

	Median Capitalization ($000)		Median No. of Employees		Proportion Using Steam or Water Power	
	St. Paul	Philadelphia	St. Paul	Philadelphia	St. Paul	Philadelphia
Flour	(20.5)[a]	-	(5.7)[b]	-	100	-
Leather	15.0	-	11	-	-	-
Lumber	10.0	-	15	-	100	-
Printing	5.0	5.2	5	9.8	39	39
Beverages	4.0	-	3	-	42	-
Machinery	3.8	5.3	6.5	6.9	50	67
Metal	2.5	1.3	5	2.5	33	9
Wagons	2.0	-	4.5	-	-	-
Harness	2.0	0.8	3	1.5	-	3
Baking	1.6	1.0	-	1.6	21	3

[a]Mean, taken from published U. S. Census of 1880.

[b]Mean, taken from published U. S. Census of 1880.

Sources: U. S. Census of Manufactures, manuscript schedules for St. Paul; Bruce Laurie, Theodore Hershberg and George Alter, "Immigrants and Industry: The Philadelphia Experience, 1850 - 1880," Journal of Social History, 9(Winter, 1975),

for new migrants to St. Paul in the late 1880's and 1890's, of whatever nationality, to avoid unskilled labor and construction employment, and seek work in trade, transportation, manufacturing and service instead.

Though we are unable to directly measure trends in technological innovation in the manufacturing sector during the years from 1884 to 1894 when they apparently had the greatest effect on employment, some trend data is available for the years 1860 to 1890. As Tables 52-54 indicate, a group of technologically advanced "export sector" industries had emerged in St. Paul by 1880, characterized by relatively high median capitalization per firm, median employees per firm and proportions using steam or water power. Flour, lumber, leather, metal, machinery, printing and beverages all ranked highest among manufacturing firms in St. Paul according to these indicators of technological innovation. As Table 55 suggests, the median levels of these indicators in 1880 were surprisingly close to the medians for Philadelphia in the same year in the printing, machinery and metal industries. As a glance at Table 56 indicates, however, the most technologically advanced of the "export sector" industries actually employed a rather small proportion of the total workforce in 1884. Though the median size of machinery manufacturing firms in 1880 was 6.5 employees,

Table 56

Employment Opportunities in St. Paul, Manufacturing, Construction, and Wholesale Trade Sectors, 1884

	No. of Firms	No. of Employees	Ave. No. Per Firm	Prop. of Workforce
Manufacturing				
Clothing	81	1500	19	
Printing & Publishing	33	1200	36	
R.R. Repair, Car Making	4	1050	263	
Cigars	49	962	20	
Boots & Shoes	28	635	23	
Machinery, Foundries, Boilers	20	472	24	
Wagons, Carrg.	19	311	16	
Crackers, Bakery Prod.	30	300	10	
Subtotals, Large Firms	264	6430	24	14
Totals, All Mfg. Firms	641	9972	15	22
Large Firms as % of All Mfg. Firms	41	64		
Construction				
Contractors & Builders	153	4111	27	
Marble & Stone Cutting	22	1000	45	
Bricks & Tile	16	320	20	
Sash, Door, Box, Planing Mills	11	322	29	
Totals	202	5753	28	12
Wholesale Trade				
Lumber	21	684	33	
Dry Goods	6	518	86	
Fuel & Pig Iron	17	484	28	
Groceries	10	404	40	
Provisions & Dressed Meats	12	340	28	
Bricks & Tile	16	275	17	
Machinery & Mill Supplies	14	263	19	

- continued -

	No. of Firms	No. of Employees	Ave. No. Per Firm	Prop. of Workforce
Wholesale Trade, continued				
Drugs, Paints	11	223	20	
Subtotals, Large Firms	107	3191	30	7
Totals, All Wholesale Firms	396	6010	15	13
Large Firms as % of All Whlsle. Firms	27	53		

Source: St. Paul Chamber of Commerce, Annual Reports, 1884, 16,20.

for example, such firms employed only 5% of the total manufacturing workforce in 1884. Firms with lower capitalization levels such as clothing, cigars and boots and shoes also were major employers in Table 56. The high "median employees per firm" levels for lumber, leather, machinery, and flour thus are misleading indicators of the importance of these firms for workmen seeking employment in St. Paul in 1880. The major source of the downward pressure of technological change on the proportion of workmen employed in manufacturing after 1884 (observed in Table 48) thus must be sought among those industries in the second rank of technological change in the early 1880's - most typically, the clothing, cigar and boot and shoe industries - which together made up 27% of all manufacturing employment in 1884 (see Table 56).

Though facts are hard to come by for the history of manufacturing in St. Paul in the late 1880's, several observations can be made about one of these industries - boot and shoe manufacturing - which employed large numbers of workers though their levels of capitalization in 1880 were quite low. Three large firms, C. Gotzian and Co., Foot, Schulze and Co., and Tarbox, Schlick and Co. emerged to dominate the boot and shoe business in the mid-1880's, in each case incorporating the assets of several smaller firms.[17] Since the "big three" boot and shoe companies engaged in wholesale trade as well as manufacturing their manufactured product was not included in the U. S. Census of Manufacturing for 1890 for St. Paul.[18] According to a history of St. Paul published in 1890, however, the boot and shoe factories of these three large firms dominated the local industry. In 1890, C. Gotzian and Company employed 480 operatives at its factory on the corner of Isabel and Fifth Streets, which produced 1,000 pairs of shoes per day and had sales exceeding $1,800,000 in 1888. Foot, Schulze and Company employed 300 hands at its five-story factory on the corner of Third and Wacouta streets. The Tarbox, Schlick and Company factory was located in South St. Paul, with sales offices in downtown St. Paul. All three firms marketed their manufactured products throughout the vast wholesale trade area of St. Paul in the 1880's, extending as far east as Michigan and west to the Pacific slope.[19]

In stark contrast, the 76 smaller boot and shoe firms of St. Paul in 1890 which were enumerated by the U. S. Census of Manufacturers in that year had a combined product of $133,375 (in current dollars) and a total of 80 adult male workmen employed. Comparing the 1880 Census of boot and shoe manufacturers to the 1890 Census (limited to the 76 small manufacturers only), the "value added per worker" increased from $900 to $936 (in constant 1879 dollars) among these smaller firms enumerated by the U. S. Census and the average number of workers employed decreased from 325 among 41 firms in 1880 to 80 among 76 firms in 1890 (see Table 57). Despite this shrinkage of employment among the smaller firms, the unemployment rate of boot and shoemakers in 1890 was only 4% (Table 19) and it seems safe to presume that the craftsmen who lost their positions became operatives in the large factories of Gotzian and Foot-Schulze or left the city. The conclusion seems to be that boot and shoe making employment <u>increased</u> from 635 in 1884 to 860+ in 1890 if we count the operatives employed in the factories of Gotzian and Foot-Schulze.

Among the other major manufacturing employers of 1884, clothing and tobacco products, Table 57 indicates dramatic <u>increases</u> in these industries as a result of the introduction of the factory system, though the increase may have occurred mostly because of the entry of large numbers of women into the clothing and boot and shoe factories established in the 1880's. The occupational tables of the U. S. Censuses of St. Paul for 1880 and 1890 show that the total numbers of gainfully occupied women aged 10 and older increased from 3,081 to 11,991 during the decade (from 17% to 21% of the total work-

Table 57

Value Added per Worker and Capitalization per Worker (1879 Dollars), Boots and Shoes, Clothing, and Tobacco Manufacturing Industries, St. Paul, 1880 and 1890

	No. of Firms	Average No. of Workers in Year	Prop. of Workers Women, Children	Prop. of Workers Piecework	Value Added per Worker	Capital per Worker
<u>Boots & Shoes, Custom</u>						
1880	41	325	12	NA	900	838
1890	76	80	0	33	936	1483
<u>Boots & Shoes, Factory</u>						
1890	(6)*	(780)*	NA	NA	NA	NA
<u>Men's Clothing, Custom</u>						
1880	22	642	76	NA	649	408
1890	79	496	2	74	928	1418
<u>Men's Clothing, Factory</u>						
1890	5	666	91	39	477	842
<u>Tobacco, Cigars</u>						
1880	27	150	23	NA	1591	523
1890	47	285	20	62	879	111

Sources: U. S. Census Bureau,

force). These increases in absolute numbers of manufacturing workers also apparently represented slight increases in the relative proportions of such workers in the total workforce from 1880 to 1890 as the ratios at the bottom of Table 57 indicate. Thus, technological innovation is not an explanation for the relative decline in the proportion of the total gainfully occupied workforce engaged in manufacturing in St. Paul between 1884 and 1890. Such innovations in the manufacturing industries where most workers were employed in 1884 (i.e. boots and shoes, clothing, tobacco) actually produced a doubling of absolute employment in those industries and a slight proportional increase in the overall manufacturing total as well. Since "value added per worker" actually decreased with the introduction of the factory system in the men's clothing industry ($928 for custom workers in 1890 compared to $477 for factory workers) we may presume that factory profits were gained by hiring more low paid women and children workers to cut production costs.

How then do we account for the relative shrinkage of total manufacturing employment from 22% in 1884 to 14% in 1890 (Table 48) while total manufacturing production increased by 283% in constant dollars (Table 50)? The answer seems to lie in a decline in the proportional size of employment among small handcraft industries other than those most affected by technological innovation such as clothing and boots and shoes. The new factories which emerged in St. Paul in the 1880's vastly increased the gross value of manufacturing product during the decade despite the relative shrinkage of total manufacturing employment.

In sum, we have discovered that over the long term from 1860 to 1900 the proportions of workers "gainfully occupied" in St. Paul decreased in construction and unskilled labor and increased in trade and manufacturing. Short term cyclic fluctuations in these trends were most pronounced in manufacturing from 1884 to 1890 when a -9% decrease in reported occupations occurred, and in services from 1890 to 1895 when a -12% decrease occurred. A small increase occurred in the construction sector between 1880 and 1884 (+4%), but for the most part the long trends in trade, construction and unskilled labor were unaffected by major cyclic fluctuations. In response to these long trends mobility among industrial sectors and among skill levels within such sectors varied substantially by industry. Workmen in construction and unskilled labor sectors were trapped in an unemployed status after the construction boom had passed following 1888. Workers in clothing and boots and shoes in the late 1880's, on the other hand, found factory employment and were able to avoid unemployment (though incomes probably declined if they were male craftsmen before the change).

As a result of these changes in the structure of employment opportunities, we should expect fewer workers in construction and labor and more workers in trade and manufacturing at the end of our period. In the short term, we should expect that workers had the widest range of voluntary choice among major employment sectors between 1880 and 1884. In the late 1880's, especially after 1888, workers in construction, unskilled labor and manufacturing faced diminished opportunities. Construction and labor opportunities remained grim thereafter and manufacturing opportunities did not reach mid-1880 levels until the late 1890's. The trade sector, especially wholesale trade enjoyed steady growth of employment opportunities with no major interruption by cyclic fluctuations, attracting a steadily increasing share of the workforce throughout the period. Transportation and local services maintained an essentially stable share of the workforce over the long term, though transportation gained ground between 1890 and 1895 (+4%).

Occupations of Ethnic Generations in St. Paul

With the above knowledge of the limits on occupational choices imposed by structural considerations in

St. Paul, we turn again to the question of distinctive occupational distributions among Irish and German immigrants and their children. We have proposed above that we would expect the sons of German immigrants to remain heavily concentrated in manufacturing occupations as a result of ethnic circumstance (high proportions of immigrants who were initially trained as craftsmen), ethnic preference (more authority-centered, formal, object-oriented family values), and ethnic resources (strong kinship and trade union networks of information and aid in the trades). The Irish second generation, we suggested, should be found concentrated much less strongly in unskilled labor than their fathers and more strongly concentrated in positions which gave opportunities for social interaction such as governmental service. We should expect such concentrations from the Irish second generation both because of ethnic preference (family values favoring social interaction) and because of ethnic resources (aid networks established by immigrant generations in government service and transportation, especially steam railroad companies). We also would expect the second generation Irish to exhibit high concentrations in construction occupations because of the existence of Irish ethnic resources in such occupations (established by the first generation).

Before discovering whether such ethnic and generational distributions of occupations actually occurred as expected in St. Paul, we must pause first to decide which of these expectations about ethnic concentrations coincided with structural changes in employment opportunities. Quite obviously, several of these expectations based on ethnicity in fact coincided with general trends in the occupational marketplace. Some movement of both first and second generation Irishmen out of labor and into trade and service occupations between 1860 and 1895 could be predicted on structural grounds alone (see Table 48), but an above average _pace_ of such change might suggest a role for ethnicity. The avoidance of manufacturing occupations by second generation Irish _men_ in 1895 might also be expected given the declining opportunities for men in this sector between 1884 and 1895 which we outlined in the previous section. On the other hand, we would _not_ expect second generation Germans to remain concentrated heavily in manufacturing trades in 1895 for the same structural reasons, and if we find such a concentration it is plausible to argue that ethnicity in part explains it. Likewise, we would not expect Germans to have low concentrations in the transportation sector in 1895, given the momentary surge in such occupations between 1890 and 1895 (see Table 48).

With this mix of expectations based on ethnicity and structural change, we turn to the actual occupational distributions of ethnic groups in St. Paul in 1860 and 1895 (Tables 58 and 59). In Table 58 it is clear, first of all, that Irish and German distributions coincided with our expectations for the first generation based on ethnic circumstance and the structure of employment in St. Paul in 1860, with the possible exception of high Irish concentration in transportation (16% compared to 10% for all workers). These group differences based on ethnic circumstance at the time of immigration are not the result of group differences in ages or family positions or chance variations because of sampling procedures as the data and statistics indicate.

In Table 59 the occupational distributions of both generations are compared for 1895, and here ethnic differences are much less pronounced. Though differences the percentage distributions of the ethnic groups as a whole are different to a statistically significant degree for both generations, the strength of association between ethnic background and occupational sector is weaker in 1895, particularly in the first generation (Cramer's V in 1860 was 0.31; for 1895, first generation value was 0.13, second generation value was 0.20).

To discover whether the overall ethnic occupational

Table 58

Percentage Distribution Among Occupational Sectors, Gainfully Occupied Males Aged 15 Years and Over, by Place of Birth, Age, and Relationship to Household Head, St. Paul, 1860

	Place of Birth				
	Ireland	Germany	Other Foreign	U. S.	All
Manufacturing					
15-20 years	0	33.3	33.3	21.1	26.1
21-34	7.7	30.0	33.3	13.9	20.1
35+	2.1	18.9	20.0	12.3	13.5
Heads	6.7	26.8	20.9	9.0	15.3
Kin	0	16.7	55.6	12.5	21.6
Lodgers	3.4	29.2	38.2	28.0	26.1
All	5.8	27.0	27.7	14.0	18.3
N's	9	48	36	28	121
Construction					
15-20 years	0	13.3	0	5.3	6.5
21-34	10.6	20.9	19.7	15.7	16.5
35+	14.6	15.1	23.6	11.0	15.7
Heads	12.5	22.0	27.9	12.7	17.9
Kin	0	0	0	12.5	5.4
Lodgers	10.3	12.5	2.9	14.0	10.6
All	11.6	18.5	20.0	13.0	15.5
N's	18	33	26	26	103

- continued -

Table 58, continued

	Ireland	Germany	Other Foreign	U. S.	All
Trade and Service					
15-20 years	0	20.0	22.2	47.4	30.4
21-34	10.6	26.4	25.8	49.1	28.4
35+	12.5	26.4	34.5	58.9	35.8
Heads	14.2	23.6	31.4	61.2	33.5
Kin	0	50.0	11.1	68.8	40.5
Lodgers	0	29.2	29.4	24.0	22.4
All	11.0	25.8	29.2	52.5	31.1
N's	17	46	38	105	206
Labor					
15-20 years	33.3	13.3	22.2	21.1	19.6
21-34	50.0	10.9	12.1	7.4	20.6
35+	54.2	20.8	10.9	6.8	21.0
Heads	52.5	12.2	9.3	6.7	20.5
Kin	83.3	16.7	11.1	0	18.9
Lodgers	37.9	16.7	20.6	16.0	21.1
All	51.0	14.0	12.3	8.5	20.7
N's	79	25	16	17	137

- continued -

Table 58, continued

	Ireland	Germany	Other Foreign	U. S.	All
Transportation					
15-20 years	66.7	20.0	11.1	5.3	15.2
21-34	19.2	10.0	7.6	6.5	11.1
35+	4.2	9.4	7.3	5.5	6.6
Heads	8.3	9.8	8.1	6.0	8.0
Kin	0	16.7	11.1	6.3	8.1
Lodgers	48.3	12.5	5.9	6.0	15.5
All	15.5	10.7	7.7	6.0	9.8
N's	24	19	10	12	65
Agriculture & Extractive					
15-20 years	0	0	11.1	0	2.2
21-34	1.9	1.8	1.5	7.4	3.4
35+	12.5	9.4	3.6	5.5	7.4
Heads	5.8	5.7	2.3	4.5	4.8
Kin	16.7	0	11.1	0	5.4
Lodgers	0	0	2.9	12.0	4.3
All	5.2	3.9	3.1	6.0	4.7
N's	8	7	4	12	31
Total N's	155	178	130	200	663

- continued -

Table 58, continued

Relationship between occupational sector and place of birth:

	Significance Level	Cramer's V	N's
15-20 years	NS	NS	46
21-34	***	.33	388
35+	***	.32	229
Heads	***	.34	463
Kin	***	.58	37
Lodgers	***	.35	161
All	***	.31	663

Note: Significance level of "***" $< .001$; "NS" means not significant, $p > .10$.

Source: Sample data.

Table 59

Percentage Distribution Among Occupational Sectors, Gainfully Occupied Males Aged 15 Years and Over, By Generation, Age and Relationship to Household Head, St. Paul, 1895

	Ethnic Origin				
	Irish	German	Other Foreign	U. S. and Other Foreign	All
Manufacturing					
First Generation					
15-20 years	0	42.9	37.5	-	38.7
21-34	5.9	27.8	14.1	-	16.9
35+	5.0	22.4	13.9	-	14.7
Heads	3.1	27.6	16.5	-	18.3
Kin	0	36.8	28.2	-	29.5
Lodgers	9.1	9.1	9.3	-	9.2
All	5.3	25.8	15.7	-	17.1
Second Gen.					
15-20	9.4	0	-	18.2	10.4
21-34	11.9	12.9	--	23.8	13.4
35+	20.3	15.8	-	7.7	18.7
Heads	21.3	12.5	-	31.6	21.2
Kin	11.5	8.0	-	13.3	10.9
Lodgers	6.1	33.3	-	0	7.1
All	15.2	12.7	-	17.8	15.2

- continued -

Table 59, continued

	Irish	German	Other Foreign	U. S. and Other Foreign	All
Construction					
First Gen.					
15-20 years	0	0	0	-	0
21-34	11.8	13.0	10.6	-	11.3
35+	20.0	14.9	18.1	-	17.5
Heads	28.1	17.2	19.3	-	19.7
Kin	33.3	10.5	2.6	-	6.6
Lodgers	0	0	6.2	-	4.3
All	17.5	13.3	13.1	-	13.7
Sec. Gen.					
15-20	6.3	0	-	0	4.2
21-34	5.2	16.1	-	4.8	7.0
35+	7.3	5.3	-	15.4	7.7
Heads	9.0	4.2	-	5.3	8.1
Kin	5.8	20.0	-	6.7	9.8
Lodgers	1.2	0	-	9.1	2.0
All	6.2	10.9	-	6.7	6.9

- continued -

Table 59, continued

	Irish	German	Other Foreign	U. S. and Other Foreign	All
Trade and Service					
First Gen.					
15-20 years	0	28.6	41.7	-	38.7
21-34	29.4	27.8	29.6	-	29.1
35+	25.0	31.3	36.8	-	33.5
Heads	15.6	29.9	34.1	-	30.8
Kin	0	10.5	28.2	-	21.3
Lodgers	45.5	45.5	37.1	-	39.7
All	26.3	29.7	34.3	-	32.2
Second Gen.					
15-20	78.1	20.0	-	72.7	70.8
21-34	41.8	41.9	-	66.7	44.6
35+	47.2	52.6	-	61.5	49.0
Heads	42.6	58.3	-	52.6	45.5
Kin	67.3	28.0	-	73.3	57.6
Lodgers	46.3	50.0	-	81.8	50.5
All	48.1	43.6	-	66.7	49.6

- continued -

Table 59, continued

	Irish	German	Other Foreign	U. S. and Other Foreign	All
Labor					
First Gen.					
15-20 years	0	0	12.5	-	9.7
21-34	29.4	20.4	26.8	-	25.4
35+	35.0	22.4	20.1	-	23.1
Heads	31.3	14.9	17.6	-	18.3
Kin	33.3	26.3	25.6	-	26.2
Lodgers	45.5	45.5	37.1	-	39.7
All	33.3	20.3	22.4	-	23.1
Second Gen.					
15-20	0	60.0	-	0	6.3
21-34	7.5	12.9	-	0	7.5
35+	8.9	10.5	-	0	8.4
Heads	5.8	4.2	-	0	5.1
Kin	1.9	32.0	-	0	9.8
Lodgers	13.4	0	-	0	11.1
All	7.3	16.4	-	0	7.7

- continued -

Table 59, continued

	Irish	German	Other Foreign	U. S. and Other Foreign	All
<u>Transportation</u>					
<u>First Gen.</u>					
15-20 years	0	0	8.3	-	6.5
21-34	23.5	11.1	17.6	-	16.4
35+	12.5	7.5	9.0	-	9.2
Heads	18.8	9.2	10.8	-	11.2
Kin	33.3	5.3	12.8	-	11.5
Lodgers	9.1	9.1	16.5	-	14.2
All	15.8	8.6	12.8	-	12.1
<u>Second Gen.</u>					
15-20	6.3	0	-	9.1	6.3
21-34	33.6	12.9	-	4.8	26.9
35+	16.3	15.8	-	15.4	16.1
Heads	21.3	20.8	-	10.5	20.2
Kin	13.5	4.0	-	6.7	9.8
Lodgers	32.9	16.7	-	9.1	29.3
All	23.2	12.7	-	8.9	20.1

- continued -

Table 59, continued

	Irish	German	Other Foreign	U. S. and Other Foreign	All
Agriculture & Extractive					
First Gen.					
15-20 years	0	28.6	0	-	1.8
21-34	0	0	1.4	-	0.9
35+	2.5	1.5	2.1	-	2.0
Heads	3.1	1.1	1.7	-	1.7
Kin	0	10.5	2.6	-	4.9
Lodgers	0	0	1.0	-	0.7
All	1.8	2.3	1.6	-	1.8
Second Gen.					
15-20	0	20.0	-	0	2.1
21-34	0	3.2	-	0	0.5
35+	0	0	-	0	0
Heads	0	0	-	0	0
Kin	0	8.0	-	0	2.2
Lodgers	0	0	-	0	0
All	0	3.6	-	0	0.5

- continued -

Table 59, continued

	Irish	German	Other Foreign	U. S. and Other Foreign	All
Total N's					
First Gen.	57	128	312	-	497
Second Gen.	289	55	-	45	389

Relationship between occupational sector and ethnic origin:

*** p < .001
** p < .05 > .001
* p < .10 > .05
NS p > .10

	Significance Level	Cramer's V	N's
First Generation			
15-20 years	*	.53	31
21-34	NS	NS	213
35+	NS	NS	251
Heads	**	.18	295
Kin	NS	NS	61
Lodgers	NS	NS	141
All	*	.13	497
Second Generation			
15-20	***	.64	48
21-34	**	.26	186
35+	NS	NS	155
Heads	NS	NS	198
Kin	***	.43	92
Lodgers	**	.29	99
All	***	.20	389

distributions in 1895 were the results of ethnicity or structural considerations, we turn to Tables 60 and 61. In Table 60 the percentage distributions of Tables 58 and 59 have been converted to "relative concentrations" of each group and generation within broad occupational sectors, allowing us to compare changes from 1860 to 1895 while "controlling" for changes in the occupational structures in both years. Some of our expectations are confirmed by Table 60 but some of the findings are completely unexpected:

a) for the first generation Irish, the gains from 1860 to 1895 in transportation and construction were expected because of Irish resources in those sectors; low proportions in manufacturing and high proportions in labor are also expected because of ethnic curcumstance;

b) for first generation Germans, however, only the gains in manufacturing were predicted by ethnicity;

c) for second generation Irish, the dramatic gain in trade and services and the sharp decline in labor were expected by ethnic preference and the gain in construction by ethnic resources;

d) the results for second generation Germans runs almost entirely <u>contrary</u> to expectations based on ethnicity, including substantial losses in manufacturing and gains in unskilled labor.

Table 60

Relative Concentrations of Gainfully Occupied Males Aged 15 Years and Over in Occupational Sectors, By Ethnic Origin and Generation, St. Paul, 1860 and 1895, Irish and Germans

	Irish			Germans		
	First Gen.		Second Gen.	First Gen.		Second Gen.
	'60	'95	'95	'60	'95	'95
Manufacturing	32	33	94	148	160	79
Transportation	158	164	58	109	124	102
Labor	246	223	49	68	136	110
Trade, Service	35	64	116	83	72	106
Construction	75	148	217	119	80	119

Source: Tables 58 and 59.

Overall it seems reasonable to say that ethnic preferences and resources were more influential in predicting the concentrations of Irish than Germans. Among the Irish, ethnic resources in construction were strong in both first and second generations despite the depressed state of the construction market in St. Paul. Steady gains by the Irish in trade and service occupations between 1860 and 1895 also suggest both ethnic preference and ethnic resources in that sector.

Another way of examining the effects of ethnic resources within occupational sectors is to compare the occupational distributions of recent migrants with longer-term migrants to St. Paul. Presumably, the longer-term migrants had more opportunity to take advantage of ethnic resource networks within an occupation and their occupational patterns should conform more closely to distinctive ethnic distributions in the city. Table 61 compares the occupational distributions of recently-arrived with longer-term migrants among first generation men only. It is very clear here that longer-term migrants took more effective advantage of ethnic resources than did those more recently arrived. German immigrants, for example, increased their proportions in manufacturing from 15% to 30% after residence in St. Paul of 8 years or more,

Table 61

Percentage Distributions Among Occupational Sectors, Gainfully Occupied Males Aged 21 Years and Over Who Were Residents of Minnesota for 22 Years or Less, By Place of Birth and Length of Residence in Minnesota, St. Paul, 1895

Length of Residence (Years)	Ireland	Germany	Other Foreign	U. S.	All	N's
Trade, Services						
1 year	50.0	66.7	42.9	39.1	42.9	18
2-7 yrs.	22.2	17.6	33.3	58.3	40.9	95
8-17 yrs.	26.1	24.6	31.3	44.3	33.2	105
18-22 yrs.	60.0	0	40.0	50.0	46.2	24
All	26.3	29.7	34.3	49.6	39.8	353
Manufacturing						
1 year	0	33.3	7.1	0	4.8	2
2-7 yrs.	11.1	14.7	10.8	7.3	9.9	23
8-17 yrs.	4.3	29.5	16.7	18.2	18.7	59
18-22 yrs.	0	33.3	10.0	29.4	23.1	12
All	5.3	25.8	15.7	15.2	16.3	144
Labor						
1 year	0	0	7.1	8.7	7.1	3
2-7 yrs.	55.6	47.1	35.5	6.3	25.9	60
8-17 yrs.	26.1	14.8	20.8	9.1	16.8	53
18-22 yrs.	20.0	33.3	30.0	8.8	15.4	8
All	33.3	70.3	22.4	7.7	16.4	145

- continued -

Table 61, continued

Length of Residence (Years)	Ireland	Germany	Other Foreign	U. S.	All	N's
<u>Transportation</u>						
1 year	0	0	28.6	47.8	35.7	15
2-7 yrs.	11.1	8.8	16.1	28.	19.8	46
8-17 yrs.	26.1	11.5	9.7	15.9	13.0	41
18-22 yrs.	20.0	33.3	10.0	8.8	11.5	36
All	15.8	8.6	12.8	20.1	15.6	138
<u>Construction</u>						
1 year	50.0	0	14.3	4.3	9.5	4
2-7 yrs.	0	8.8	4.3	0	3.0	7
8-17 yrs.	13.0	19.7	18.8	11.4	16.5	52
18-22	0	0	10.0	2.9	3.8	2
All	17.5	13.3	13.1	6.9	10.7	95
<u>Agriculture & Extractive</u>						
1 year	0	0	0	0	0	0
2-7 yrs.	0	2.9	0	0	0.4	1
8-17 yrs.	4.3	0	2.8	1.1	1.9	6
18-22 yrs.	0	0	0	0	0	0
All	1.8	2.3	1.6	0.5	1.2	11
N's	57	128	312	389	886	

- continued -

Table 61, continued

Relationship between occupational sector and place of birth:

Length of Residence	Level of Significance	Cramer's V	N's
1 year	NS	NS	42
2-7 years	***	.30	232
8-17 years	**	.17	316
18&22 years	NS	NS	52
All	***	.18	886

Significance levels:

*** $p < .001$
** $p < .05 > .001$
* $p < .10$ - $.05$
NS $p > .10$

compared to an overall increase among all migrants from 10% to 19% for the same length of stay. The same effect occurred among the Irish in transportation and construction occupations.

On balance, it seems that Irish generations were more influenced by ethnicity than were German generations in St. Paul in 1895 and that ethnic resources were more influential than ethnic preferences as factors affecting voluntary occupational decisions. Over the long term from 1860 to 1895, the effect of ethnic origin on occupational placement gradually shifted from simply ethnic circumstance at the time of international migration at the beginning of the period to a greater role for ethnic resources by 1895. Of course, in some cases ethnic resources in an occupation coincided with ethnic preference for the occupation (such we believe as the Irish in politics). The failure of second generation Germans to reflect either the preferences or resources of the immigrant Germans, however, argues against a strong role for ethnic preference when economic factors militated against movement into a particular sector, at least in some cases. As we have described above, the handcraft skills which the immigrant Germans brought with them and their dominance of those trades in St. Paul were of less value after the rise of the boot and shoe and clothing factories in St. Paul in the late 1880's, and the lower than average concentrations of the second generation in manufacturing reflected that fact in 1895.

The year 1895 was near the trough of the great depression of the 1890's and economic pressures thus had their greatest effect on occupational decisions in such a year, particularly in sectors most affected by the business climate. It is also wise to examine the role of ethnicity in more prosperous times when greater freedom existed for expressing preferences in the job market. To include such times of choice, we turn next to a study of intergenerational "inheritance" of occupations among Irish and Germans in St. Paul from 1880 to 1885 and 1895 to 1900.

Ethnic Fathers and Sons in St. Paul

In Tables 58 and 59 we compared the occupational distributions of generations within ethnic groups and of "heads of household" and "kin" within ethno-generational groups. Such comparisons are suggestive of the cumulative influence of ethnic preferences and ethnic resources among all members of generations or persons of specific family positions. To specify more precisely the effects of ethnic preference as learned in the ethnic family, we turn in Tables 62-65 to a consideration of fathers and their co-resident sons aged 15 years or older in St. Paul. To investigate the strength of the family influence of fathers on sons we will examine father-son occupational similarities in a time of greatest freedom for voluntary choice of occupation (1880 - 1885) and a time of somewhat less freedom of choice (1895 - 1900) when St. Paul's economy was recovering from the severe depression of the mid-1890's. The relatively small sample size necessarily limits conclusions to suggestions of apparent patterns only.

In Tables 62 and 63 we examine first the changes in the occupational distributions of co-resident sons, by major occupational sectors. Table 62 for the period 1880 - 1885 demonstrates that ethnicity influenced choices among Irish and German sons during these prosperous times. In contrast to changes in average distributions, the Irish sons followed ethnic resources by moving more strongly than average into construction and transportation sectors and demonstrated ethnic preferences by moving more strongly than average out of labor and into trade. German sons moved more strongly than average into manufacturing (which we would expect from both ethnic preferences and resources), though their other occupational movements conformed closely to the average for all sons.

During the period 1895 - 1900, however, Irish sons

Table 62

Percentage Distributions Among Occupational Sectors, Sons Who Were Aged 15 Years Or Over and Co-resident with Fathers in St. Paul in 1880, By Father's Place of Birth, St. Paul, 1880 and 1885

Fathers' Birthplace	Agric. & Extract.	Mfg.	Construct.	Labor	Trade	Transp.	Student	Serv.	N
Ireland									
Fathers	4	0	12	53	22	8	0	0	49
Sons, 1880	0	16	14	22	20	12	10	4	49
Sons, 1885	0	12	24	12	30	21	0	0	33
5 yr. diff.	0	-4	+10	-10	+10	+9	-10	-4	
Germany									
Fathers	3	43	26	11	17	0	0	0	35
Sons, 1880	0	40	11	6	14	3	17	9	35
Sons, 1885	0	52	13	0	26	9	0	0	23
5 yr. diff.	0	+12	+3	-6	+12	+6	-17	-9	
Other Foreign									
Fathers	0	17	30	13	22	17	0	0	23
Sons, 1880	0	30	13	4	17	0	9	26	23
Sons, 1885	0	33	11	6	39	6	0	6	18
5 yr. diff.	0	+3	-2	+2	+12	+6	-9	-20	
U. S.									
Fathers	0	21	11	3	66	0	0	0	38
Sons, 1880	0	18	5	3	39	0	26	8	38
Sons, 1885	0	21	7	0	48	7	10	7	29
5 yr. diff.	0	+3	+2	-3	+9	+7	-16	-1	
Total									
Fathers	2	19	18	23	32	6	0	0	145
Sons, 1880	0	25	11	10	23	5	16	10	145
Sons, 1885	0	27	15	5	36	12	3	3	103
5 yr. diff.	0	+2	+4	-5	+13	+7	-13	-7	

Table 63

Percentage Distributions Among Occupational Sectors, Sons Who Were Aged 15 Years Or Over and Co-resident with Fathers in St. Paul in 1895, By Father's Place of Birth, St. Paul, 1895 and 1900

Fathers' Birthplace	Agric. & Extract.	Mfg.	Construct.	Labor	Trade	Transp.	Student	Serv.	N
Ireland									
Fathers	0	0	46	29	21	4	0	0	24
Sons, 1895	0	0	29	29	13	0	0	29	24
Sons, 1900	0	9	27	14	23	14	0	14	22
5 yr. diff.	0	+9	-2	-15	+10	+14	0	-15	
Germany									
Fathers	0	23	13	29	35	0	0	0	31
Sons, 1895	3	19	6	6	23	0	0	42	31
Sons, 1900	0	33	6	6	39	0	0	17	18
5 yr. diff.	-3	+14	0	0	+16	0	0	-25	
Other Foreign									
Fathers	1	22	12	10	50	5	0	0	60
Sons, 1895	1	23	0	7	22	6	1	40	60
Sons, 1900	0	10	15	2	56	10	2	5	41
5 yr. diff.	-1	-13	+15	-5	+34	+4	+1	-35	
U. S.									
Fathers	0	18	9	2	66	5	0	0	44
Sons, 1895	0	5	2	2	39	2	5	45	44
Sons, 1900	0	17	7	3	48	7	10	7	29
5 yr. diff.	0	+12	+5	+1	+9	+5	+5	-38	
Total									
Fathers	1	18	16	14	47	4	0	0	159
Sons, 1895	1	14	6	9	25	3	2	40	159
Sons, 1900	0	5	14	5	45	8	4	9	110
5 yr. diff.	-1	+1	+8	-4	+20	+5	+2	-31	

apparently departed from the expected effects of ethnicity. As Table 63 indicates, Irish sons continued to move into transportation in the latter period, but they also moved out of construction and into manufacturing, seemingly in response to purely structural considerations. In other words, Irish sons turned away from the strong Irish resource network in construction because of the depressed state of construction activity and turned toward the manufacturing sector where new semi-skilled manual jobs were to be had despite their putative lack of taste for routine mechanical work. German sons in the latter period, continued to follow ethnic preference and resources in manufacturing, but then, structural considerations favored such a movement in any case.

In Tables 62 and 63 we have compared the changes in occupational distributions of ethnic sons. In Tables 64 and 65 we now consider ethnic fathers. How effectively did the fathers' occupational statuses influence the occupational positions of their sons during the two time periods? As Tables 64 and 65 indicate, the proportions of Irish and German father and son pairs whose occupational sectors were identical in each year tends to confirm the patterns noted in Tables 62 and 63; i.e. Irish father-son "pair identity" was strong among sectors where ethnicity favored such concentrations during the

Table 64

Proportions of Father-Son Pairs Who Were in Identical Occupational Sectors, Fathers With Co-resident Sons Aged 15 Years and Over in 1880, By Father's Place of Birth and Father's Occupational Sector in 1880, St. Paul, 1880 and 1885

Father's Occupation in 1880	Father's Place of Birth: Ireland		Germany		Other Foreign		U. S.		All	
	1880	1885	1880	1885	1880	1885	1880	1885	1880	1885
Agric. & Extract.	0	0	0	0	-	-	-	-	0	0
Manufacturing	-	-	40	30	50	67	38	60	41	48
Construction	67	100	22	17	29	0	0	0	31	32
Labor	31	19	0	0	33	0	0	0	29	14
Trade & Service	55	88	17	25	60	25	52	60	49	58
Transport.	50	100	-	-	0	0	-	-	25	43
N's	49	33	35	23	23	18	38	29	145	103

Table 65

Proportions of Father-Son Pairs Who Were in Identical Occupational Sectors, Fathers With Co-resident Sons Aged 15 Years and Over in 1895, By Father's Place of Birth and Father's Occupational Sector in 1895, St. Paul, 1895 and 1900

Father's Occupation in 1895	Father's Place of Birth: Ireland		Germany		Other Foreign		U. S.		All	
	1895	1900	1895	1900	1895	1900	1895	1900	1895	1900
Agric. & Extract.	-	-	-	-	100	0	-	-	100	-
Manufacturing	-	-	0	40	46	17	13	67	25	36
Construction	45	36	25	0	0	60	0	50	23	35
Labor	71	50	11	0	17	25	100	0	35	27
Trade & Serv.	20	60	36	60	33	65	48	57	39	64
Transportation	0	-	-	-	0	68	50	-	17	0
N's	24	22	31	18	60	41	44	29	159	110

early 1880's, but movement away from expected ethnic patterns occurred among Irish sons in the late 1890's, especially in the construction sector. German father-son identity remained strong in both periods.

Another reason for the departure of Irish sons from expected ethnic occupational concentrations in the late 1890's is revealed by Table 66, which compares the persistence rates of co-resident sons for the two time periods. Despite the generally higher rate of mortality for Irish compared to German adolescent and young adult men, the Irish persistence rate was substantially higher than the German rate in the late 1890's. Irish sons remained in St. Paul at a far higher rate than German sons, and it is likely, therefore, that a higher proportion of Irish sons were forced to enter occupations (such as manufacturing) which they did not prefer for ethnic reasons simply to find a subsistence in St. Paul. German sons apparently were more free to move out of the city if jobs to their liking were not available in St. Paul.

Taking our findings about the occupational similarities of ethnic fathers and sons as a whole, they seem to conflict with previously stated findings about ethnic generations. We found above, for example, that second generation Irish men in St. Paul in 1895 were more likely

Table 66

Persistence Rates of Sons Aged 15 Years and Over Who Were Co-resident with Fathers in 1880 or in 1895, By Father's Place of Birth, St. Paul, 1880 - 1885 and 1895 - 1900

	Father's Place of Birth				
	Ireland	Germany	Other Foreign	U. S.	All
1880 - 1885					
No. in 1880	49	35	23	38	145
No. in 1885	33	23	18	29	103
Prop. persistent	67	66	78	76	71
1895 - 1900					
No. in 1895	24	31	60	44	159
No. in 1900	22	18	41	29	110
Prop. persistent	92	58	68	66	69

to reflect ethnic preferences and resources than second generation German men (measured for example by the lower than average concentrations of Germans in manufacturing and higher than average concentrations of Irish in construction noted in Table 60). Among co-resident sons, however, German sons strongly reflected ethnic preferences for manufacturing in the late 1890's, while Irish sons moved out of the traditional Irish concentration in construction. The explanation of this apparent contradiction is that comparing generations is not the same as comparing a group of fathers to their own sons. Each of the ethnic generations in St. Paul in 1895 were composed of both fathers and of sons, and of men who were recently arrived as well as those who were long time residents. The father-son pairs of Tables 62-65 allow us to examine directly the socializing effects of the ethnic family upon occupational decisions and we have found that this effect remained strong for co-resident German sons in the late 1890's, despite the lower than average concentrations of all second generation German men in manufacturing in 1895 (Table 60). Though Irish sons began to move away from ethnic resources in construction and to forego ethnic preferences by entering manufacturing jobs in the late 1890's, the overall second generation Irish pattern in 1895 was still distinctively similar to our expectations based on ethnicity.

The overall conclusion which we can draw from our study of generational patterns over the long term (1860 - 1895) and of father-son similarities in two shorter periods (1880-1885 and 1895 - 1900) is that a three-stage process of ethnic influence on occupational position was at work. Initially, during the period of new settlement in St. Paul in 1860, Irish and German occupational distributions simply reflected ethnic circumstances at the time of immigration, with most Irish men in unskilled labor and most German men in the crafts. By the time of the economic boom of the early 1880's, the sons of Irish and German immigrants (and the recently-arrived immigrants) were able to enter certain sectors (transportation and construction for the Irish, manufacturing for the Germans) more easily because of ethnic resources, and were better able to escape certain sectors (such as unskilled labor for the Irish) where ethnic preferences dictated a change. By the end of the century, with the local economy coming out of the depression of the 1890's, Irish sons began to move away from ethnic resource networks in construction (despite the recovery in that sector), and into white collar positions in the trade and service sectors which attracted them because of ethnic preference. Despite a setback for the German second generation men in the manufacturing sector in the late 1880's and early 1890's as a result of technological and organizational change, German <u>sons</u> continued to move into manufacturing in the late 1890's as a result of family preferences and resources.

In sum, the effect of ethnic background upon the occupational position of Irish and German workmen in St. Paul in the nineteenth century shifted from the primary influence of ethnic circumstance in 1860 for the immigrant generation to a stronger effect of ethnic resources in the 1880's, and, finally, to a movement away from ethnic resources toward ethnic preferences by Irish sons at the end of the century, where ethnic resources in a sector did not allow maximum opportunities for expression of ethnic preference (as in the construction sector).

This three-stage historical process of ethnic influence on occupational position, of course, was constrained by structural shifts in occupational opportunities, both because of cyclic fluctuation (as in construction between 1888 and 1898) and because of technological reorganization of an industry (as in the manufacture of clothing and boots and shoes in the late 1880's). Of the three sorts of ethnic influence, ethnic resources in a sector were perhaps most influential and least affected by structural shifts in the local economy. The solid roots in transportation and construction built by the Irish and the roots in manufacturing built by the Germans remained influential and were spurned voluntarily (all else being equal), only when second generation Irish sons began to forsake construction for white collar work at the end of the century.

Verbal Statements of Ethnic Occupational Values

In our overall strategy for the historical study of voluntary occupational decisions which we outlined at the beginning of the chapter, we "predicted" that actual verbal statements of ethnic occupational values would appear in some form among the surviving ethnic documents of the nineteenth century. Our review of occupational distributions and concentrations in St. Paul confirmed our expectations about Irish and German occupational preferences, under limitations dictated by structural changes in the occupational marketplace, especially among young co-resident sons entering the workforce in the late 1890's. Though ethnic resources in major occupational sectors were apparently more influential than ethnic preferences when the two were in tension (such as the Irish in construction work), we concluded that second generation Irish sons demonstrated ethnic preferences for work allowing social interaction by their movement out of construction and into low white collar work by 1900. German sons also demonstrated ethnic preferences by remaining in manufacturing in the late 1890's, though their choices were aided by expanding opportunities in this sector. If behavior thus conformed to expectations about values, what evidence is there that the Irish and Germans verbalized these values in writing?

Several explicit statements of such values appeared in the Irish press in St. Paul and Minneapolis during our period. A publication of the Minnesota Irish Emigration Convention, an organization of Irish residents in St. Paul led by Father John Ireland (later Archbishop Ireland), argued in 1860, for example, that the "traits" of Irish character were dangerous in large cities. The Irish were "sociable by nature," "warm-hearted," and "generous to a fault," the pamphlet argued, and thus should seek agricultural land in Minnesota where such traits would not be taken advantage of by the unscrupulous.[20] Ireland's views in this pamphlet proved to be ill-conceived; the Irish avoided farming in Minnesota for the most part and their sociable "traits" proved to be an advantage for many in St. Paul. Still, Ireland's perception of his countrymen's character coincided closely with Greeley's survey data 100 years later.

Perhaps the most detailed local discussion of Irish occupational values in the nineteenth century appeared in the *Irish Standard* (published in Minneapolis) in 1905. In an article titled "Why so Few Irish in Business.", the editors asked why "in the great cities of the country the Irish are the leaders in the professions and in politics, but in business they have made a sorry record." The answer seemed to lie in the Irish character:

> The cold mathematics of business do not appeal to the Celtic nature. The Celtic ideal is ambition in the extreme...The Irishman is, ordinarily, desirous of following a life where there is opportunity to display personality. The professions and politics give these opportunities where there is ability sufficient to give success. . . . Too many young men of immigrants think that the acme of success is to be as different as possible from their parents. They refer to what is called "society" and are much too likely to judge others and to expect to be judged by the cut of their coats rather than by what they accomplish in life. In preference to that class of young Irish-Americans give us the Irish immigrant who worked upon the street and in the sewer; the man who built the railroads in this country and all its great public works. . .[21]

Though there is implied criticism in this statement of the "Celtic nature" which gave rise to "ambition" in the second generation, the editors clearly are generalizing from their own observation of their countrymen's attitudes and behavior. The shift among young members of the Irish second generation away from the resources of their fathers toward occupations which gave more opportunity for preference (which we observed in the late 1890's) evidently occurred amidst some soul-searching by the older generation represented by the editors. Other reports in the *Irish Standard* made similar points.[22]

Though such explicit statements of occupational values seem to be rare in the German press in the Midwest, the more frequent discussions of the importance of discipline of children and the dangers of too much independence for children seem to coincide with the Greeley data on Germans in the twentieth century. The editors of the *Illinois Staats Zeitung*, a liberal "Forty-Eighter" paper published in Chicago, for example, denounced the growing lack of discipline and respect among young German-Americans in 1874:

> The cause of all this can easily be traced. The parents make their childrn earn money as soon as possible. Although they came from a country where school attendance for children is obligatory, here they do not consider it necessary to have their children learn anything. Many go thus to the universities for loafers, the factories. The first thing they learn is that their parents have no authority over them. Often they run away . . . . To do away with such evils, it is necessary to reestablish the right relations between parents and children.[23]

As this statement suggests, the transition from work for the young family craft shops under familial supervision to employment in the new factories of the era was not easy for the German family. Traditions of family discipline were interrupted in the process. Nevertheless, the statement reflects middle class, immigrant generation values about the dangers of autonomy and lack of respect for convention which coincide with Greeley's survey data about German ethnic attitudes ninety years later.

Conclusions

At the beginning of this chapter we proposed that ethnicity, as well as the circumstances of immigration and of economic opportunity, helped to account for the distinctive occupational concentrations of Irish and Germans in the American workforce in the nineteenth century. We anticipated that ethnicity - which we defined as either ethnic resources or ethnic preferences - would have greater effect on the occupational positions of the second than on the first generation in America. We cited a national survey of ethnic group values in the twentieth century to suggest that Irish workers preferred jobs which allowed higher degrees of autonomy and social interaction than jobs preferred by Germans (all else being equal). By considering the economic and demographic factors affecting occupational positions in St. Paul, we argued that the limits on voluntary occupational choices by the Irish and Germans could be set, and the influence of ethnicity examined directly both with census and verbal data.

The results of the study of the Irish in St. Paul indicate that ethnic resources in the construction, transportation and governmental service sectors were more important than ethnic preferences where conflicts existed between resources and preferences. Resources were more influential than preferences for autonomous and socially interactive work in the construction sector for both the first and second generation Irish until the end of the century, when a study of Irish sons found a movement away from construction. Though the Irish in St. Paul verbally expressed values which coincided with our expectations, and their strong concentrations in governmental service were an example of applying preferences to occupational decisions, it is clear from the evidence that ethnic communal resource networks channelled most voluntary occupational decisions among the Irish after the initial period of immigration and settlement.

The results for the Germans show steady concentration in manufacturing occupations in St. Paul for both first and second generations from 1860 to 1900, with one important exception: the second generation shift in the early 1890's. After a period of technological change and reorganization of the tobacco, boot and shoe, and clothing industries in St. Paul in the late 1880's which undercut the business of German craftsmen, the German second generation moved out of manufacturing occupations by 1895. After the long trend toward increased proportions of manufacturing jobs resumed in the late 1890's, however, German second generation youth resumed their concentrations in the manufacturing sector, presumably as semi-skilled workers in the new factories of the city.

Though the long trend changes in St. Paul's occupational structure (gains for trade and manufacturing, loss for unskilled labor and construction) accounted for some of the Irish and German occupational concentrations, the importance of ethnic resources despite such structural changes was nowhere more obvious than among Irish construction workers in the late 1880's and early 1890's. Despite dramatic decreases in construction work in St. Paul after 1888, high concentrations of Irish of both generations reported construction occupations in 1895. The high unemployment rates in some construction trades in 1890 reflected the grim realities of Irish concentration in this sector.

The prevailing view that ethnic occupational distributions in the nineteenth century - particularly those of the Irish - simply reflected circumstances in the Old Country at the time of immigration thus needs to be modified to include ethnic resources as well. When the structure of economic opportunity allowed a range of options to ethnic workmen (most notably in the early 1880's in the case of St. Paul), a three-stage historical process of ethnic influence was at work in the new cities which sprang up in the Midwest after 1850. Though circumstances seemed to dictate the occupational concentrations of Irish and German immigrants who arrived in 1860 when the city was young, strong ethnic resource networks emerged over the years in several occupational sectors, attracting increasing concentrations of both first and second generation immigrants. Where such ethnic resources failed to allow sufficient opportunities for the expression of ethnic preferences (as for the Irish in construction in the 1890's and the second generation Germans in the early 1890's), movements out of the sphere of ethnic resources began. This third stage of occupational movement, however, thus reflected ethnic preferences to some degree, particularly the second generation Irish movement into white collar positions at higher than average rates at the national level by 1900 and among second generation Irish sons in St. Paul, 1895 to 1900.

Finally, comparisons of immigrant occupational concentrations in St. Paul and at the national level, 1880 and 1890, suggest that a regional factor must be considered as well. The Irish in St. Paul were more highly concentrated in governmental service, unskilled labor, and local transportation jobs than was the case nationally. The Germans were less highly concentrated in manufacturing jobs in St. Paul than was the case nationally for Germans. The explanation of both ethnic patterns seems to be that the "urban fringe" location of St. Paul and the necessities of building a new economy on the frontier demanded more workers in the "frontier building" sectors - construction, labor, local transportation- and less in manufacturing work. The Midwestern location of St. Paul thus encouraged the development of Irish resource networks in their "typical" occupations more so than the Germans in their "typical" sector. In the next chapter we will explore the regional factor at greater length, and consider the broader implications of ethnic resources in construction, transportation and manufacturing for urban growth in the Midwest in the nineteenth century.

Footnotes

[1]Comparative studies of Irish and Germans in American and Canadian cities for census years between 1860 and 1900 include: Stephan Thernstrom, The Other Bostonians: Poverty and Progress in the American Metropolis, 1880 - 1970 (Cambridge, Mass., 1973), and Theodore Hershberg, et al., "Occupation and Ethnicity in Five Nineteenth-Century Cities: A Collaborative Inquiry," Historical Methods Newsletter, 7 (June, 1974), 174-216. Important comparisons of Irish and German occupational patterns in single localities are: Clyde Griffen, "Workers Divided: The Effect of Craft and Ethnic Differences in Poughkeepsie, New York, 1850 - 1880," in Stephan Thernstrom and Richard Sennett, eds., Essays in the New Urban History (New Haven, 1969), 124-164; Bruce Laurie, Theodore Hershberg and George Alter, "Immigrants and Industry: The Philadelphia Experience, 1850 - 1880," Journal of Social History, 9 (Winter, 1975), 219-248; and Michael B. Katz, The People of Hamilton, Canada West: Family and Class in a Mid-Nineteenth-Century City (Cambridge, Mass., 1975).

[2]See for example: Laurie, Hershberg and Alter, Immigrants and Industry," 234, 240.

[3]One of the few studies of the ethnic role in occupational placement based on factory records from the nineteenth century is: Gerd Korman, Industrialization, Immigrants and Americanizers: The View from Milwaukee, 1866 - 1921 (Madison, 1967), Chapter 3.

[4]John Bodnar, "Immigration and Modernization: The Case of the Slavic Peasants in Industrial America," Journal of Social History 10 (Fall, 1976), 44-71; suggests the importance of this factor.

[5]Richard A. Easterlin, Population, Labor Force, and Long Swings in Economic Growth: The American Experience (New York, 1968), Chapter 2; David Ward, Cities and Immigrants (New York, 1971), 39-49, 85-93; Stanley Lebergott, "Labor Force and Employment, 1800 - 1960," in National Bureau of Economic Research, Output, Employment, and Productivity in the United States after 1800 (New York, 1966), 117-204; and H. Dewey Anderson and Percy E. Davidson, Occupational Trends in the United States (Stanford University, 1940), Chapter 1.

[6]See Table 4 in Chapter 1 for an indication of the range of variation in the proportion of the workforce engaged in manufacturing in cities of various sizes and regional locations. On regional urban development patterns in the United States generally, see Ward, Cities and Immigrants, Chapters 1 and 2 and Eric E. Lampard, "The Evolving System of Cities in the United States: Urbanization and Economic Development," in Harvey S. Perloff and Lowdon Wingo, Jr., eds., Issues in Urban Economics (New York, 1968), 81-140.

[7]Stanley Elkins and Eric McKitrick, "A Meaning for Turner's Frontier: Part I: Democracy in the Old Northwest," Political Science Quarterly, LXIX (September, 1954), 321-353.

[8]Cf. John Archer Jackson, The Irish in Britain (London, 1963), 72-95.

[9]Andrew M. Greely, That Most Distressful Nation: The Taming of the American Irish (Chicago, 1972), 147, 158-165; Greeley, Why Can't They Be Like Us? America's White Ethnic Groups (New York, 1971), 213.

[10]See, e.g., Charles E. Werts, "Social Class and Initial Career Choices of College Freshmen", Sociology of Education, 39 (Winter, 1966), 74-85.

[11]Jeylan T. Mortimer, "Patterns of Intergenerational Occupational Movements: A Smallest - Space Analysis," American Journal of Sociology, 79 (March, 1974), 1278-1299.

[12]Kohn, Class and Conformity: Kohn and Carmi Schooler, "Class, Occupation, and Orientation," American Sociological Review 34 (October, 1969), 659-678; David R. Miller and Guy Swanson, The Changing American Parent (New York, 1958).

[13]A study of "as many members of Minnesota trade unions as possible" conducted by the Minnesota Bureau of Labor in the summer of 1893 found 970 union members in St. Paul and a total of 3344 in all of Minnesota; among all Minnesota union members, the German-born were most heavily concentrated in German printing (71%), cigarmaking (35%), brick making (26%), and tailoring (20%): Minnesota Bureau of Labor, Fourth Biennial Report, 1893-1894 (St. Paul, 1895), 177-187.

[14]Ibid., 210, 215, 236-237, and 301 describe the general pattern of ignoring apprenticeship rules among trade unions in St. Paul; in boot and shoe making, for example, the report states that "local unions at St. Paul and Minneapolis have no rules governing apprentices. No limitations are placed upon persons desiring to enter the trade." (Ibid., 301).

[15]Edward M. Levine, The Irish and Irish Politicians: A Study of Cultural and Social Alienation (Notre Dame, Ind., 1966), Chapter 6.

[16] "The Irish Ethic and the Spirit of Patronage," Ethnicity 2 (1975), 305-359.

[17]C. C. Andrews, History of St. Paul, Minn.(Syracuse, N. Y., 1890), 439-440.

[18]U. S. Census Bureau, Census of 1890, Manufacturing, 518-519; see also: R. L. Polk and Company, St. Paul City Directory, 1890-91, 1457-1458. The Directory listed the large boot and shoe companies separately as "Manufacturers and Wholesale Dealers," along with: Kellogg, Johnson and Company; Minnesota Shoe Company; and Schnittger, Stickney and Company. The Minnesota Bureau of Labor's Seventh Biennial Report, 1899-1900 reported three boot and shoe factories; Foot, Schulze and Company, Minnesota Shoe Company, and Sharood and Crooks, with a total of 1081 employees in 1899 (p.19).

[19]Andrews, History of St. Paul, Minn., 439-440

[20]Address of the Minnesota Irish Emigration Convention, Held in the City of Saint Paul, Minnesota, January 20th, 1869, to the People of Ireland (St. Paul, 1869), 2.

[21]Irish Standard (Minneapolis), February 25, 1905

[22]See: "Masters or Servants," (May 30, 1903); "Our Newsboys" (March 23, 1894); and "The Achievement of an Irish Emigrant" (June 6, 1903); all in the Irish Standard (Minneapolis).

[23]Illinois Staats Zeitung (Chicago), May 18, 1874, translated by the Chicago Foreign Language Press Survey.

Chapter 5

Households, Homes and Jobs: Ethnic Patterns and Urban Development in Regional and National Perspective

A common deficiency of many of the new studies of ninteenth century American cities is their lack of comparative perspective. However insightful a local urban study may be, those readers who are primarily concerned with broad processes of social change are often left to wonder whether local patterns are representative of larger ones. While a perceptive local study may break new ground by posing new questions about broader processes of change, the significance of such studies must eventually be enhanced by examining local and regional variation as it interacts with lower-level processes discussed in the case study. In this chapter we turn to a comparison of demographic and economic trends in St. Paul in the late nineteenth century with those of other large cities of the country.

In the first two chapters we linked trends in household formation and household residence in single family dwellings among immigrants and native-born migrants in late nineteenth century St. Paul to local patterns of secular and cyclic economic change. We also argued that, at least marginally in St. Paul, all else being equal, the national differences in the behavior of the Irish, German and native-born indicated the probable persistence in the American setting of distinctive ethnic norms. Though the possibility remains that observed differences in group behavior among these nationality groups could be explained by demographic or economic factors which we were unable to identify, a search of the available "normative" documents among Germans and Irish in the Midwest suggested that similar group differences in verbally expressed value statements appeared with some regularity at least among those mostly middle class persons from both ethnic groups whose verbal documents have survived to the present. In Chapter Four we considered the probable causes of higher-than-average concentrations of ethnic workers in major occupational sectors of St. Paul's economy. Though the changing opportunities provided by St. Paul's development and the prior circumstances of immigrants both established constraints on occupational career decisions, we concluded that local patterns of ethnic job recruitment (or occupational "resource networks") also contributed significantly to ethnically specific concentrations, especially among first generation workers.

The dates of our local study, 1860 to 1900, enclosed most of the major period of frontier settlement in

St. Paul. In 1860 St. Paul's population barely exceeded 10,000 but was growing rapidly. By 1900 growth rates had leveled off and the era of metropolitan combination with nearby Minneapolis had begun. During this era of "filling up" the household formation rates of St. Paul's population declined by a remarkable 31% among all men aged 25-34 as indicated by Table 72. Though a shift in the tenure composition of demand for housing in St. Paul toward increased rental of dwellings occurred during this period, the homeownership level in 1890 remained among the highest recorded levels in the country at 40% of all households. The structure of employment opportunities in St. Paul likewise reflected the developmental trend; the proportions of workers in construction and labor declined and the proportions in commerce and manufacturing increased from 1860 to 1900 as the "frontier building" era passed.

In addition to these secular trends we also found some evidence that downturns in both "long swing" investment cycles and short term business cycles affected patterns of household formation, occupational distribution and perhaps also homeownership - either directly through lowered income expectations or indirectly by encouraging out-migration. Construction activity in St. Paul conformed roughly to the 20 year "long swing" cycles of urban development documented by Richard Easterlin and others at the national level, with peaks in 1872 and 1888 and troughs in the mid 1870's and mid 1890's. The sharp downswing in construction activity which began in 1889 combined with the effects of the financial panic of 1893 produced high rates of unemployment at least as early as 1890 in St. Paul, especially among blue collar workers. The depression of the nineties seemingly contributed in some measure to lowered household headship rates, the shift from sales to rental housing, and the relative decline of construction and labor employment in the city until an upswing began in the late 1890's.

How far were these local patterns representative of other urban places, both among Midwestern cities and the cities of the nation generally? How far did the observed ethnic differences affect city-to-city variation in household formation and homeownership in the late nineteenth century, all else being equal, and how much impact did these have on ethnic differentiation and local ethnic composition on urban development? The purpose of this chapter is to test these questions as far as available published census data will allow. In some ways St. Paul in the late nineteenth century was an ideal site for measurement of local ethnic patterns of headship and homeownership; if such differences existed for normative reasons the relatively open structure and rapid growth of a frontier city should reveal them most clearly. On the other hand, St. Paul was not "typical"; it remained largely a regional wholesale distribution center, ranked 22nd among the nation's cities in 1890 in population and geographically distant from major markets in the East. The independent effects of city age, city size, and level of industrialization upon local urban populations needs to be examined directly along the range of variation in the national urban system if we are to speak confidently about the generality of St. Paul's patterns.

Fortunately for our purposes, the U. S. census provides comparable information for the 27 largest American cities for the first time in 1890.[1] Though the data is cross-sectional, our analysis will show that city age was a predominant factor affecting all of our concerns; thus, we will be able to infer local patterns of change through time as cities such as St. Paul passed from the frontier phase to later stages of development. The published data on population, housing and manufacturing for the 1890 census provide measures of several important factors potentially related to nuptiality,[2] homeownership and occupational concentrations. Our general approach will be essentially empirical, testing the statistical association of all likely independent variables with one another and with our primary concerns.

As a guide to our investigation, research on the determinants of nuptiality in the twentieth century and recent studies of historical trends in nuptiality, headship and the supply and demand for new housing all yield useful insights. The most striking fact about the timing of marriage in the late nineteenth century is the lack of significant change between 1867 and 1890 in the median age at first marriage, for males and females measured both at the national level beginning about 1885 and in the state of Massachusetts from 1867.[3] Though one study found that the total yearly marriage rate per 1000 population (including both first and other marriages among adults of all ages) fluctuated in Massachusetts with the rise and fall of the business cycle from 1870 to 1900, the proportions of young adults ever married apparently was little affected at the national level by cyclic economic trends.[4] Urban/rural and east/west differences in nuptiality in Michigan and New York in 1885 and 1875 were discovered but no change over time was observed.[5] Among married farm women in several states in 1860, age at birth of first child (a proxy for age at marriage) was found to decrease regularly from eastern to western rural areas, suggesting a developmental trend from higher to lower nuptiality levels among farm women in frontier area. This frontier phenomenon, however, apparently had little effect at the national level.[6]

Twentieth century nuptiality trends will not concern us here, but studies of the determinants of nuptiality at the censuses of 1890, 1920, 1950, 1960 and 1970 and a National Fertility Study of a cohort of women marrying in the mid-1940's all provide a useful list of independent variables for testing with our 1890 set of cities. High sex ratios (males age 25-29 per 100 females age 20-24) have regularly decreased male nuptiality and increased female nuptiality though the strength of this influence has declined since 1890.[7] The following factors at various times have tended to increase female nuptiality: high rates of in-migration of females, high ratio of males to females, average earnings, rural residence and Southern regional location.[8] On the other hand, the following factors have tended to decrease female nuptiality: a favorable female job opportunity structure, large proportions of population who were Catholic, large size of city, high cost of housing, high social class status, and the previous experience by an age cohort of a major national economic depression.[9] Among women from predominantly Catholic countries of origin of both immigrant or second generations in 1950, those of Irish background had the lowest level of nuptiality, with controls for socioeconomic status.[10]

The literature on urban homeownership rates is sparse but some understanding of historical trends and determinants can be achieved by looking at the literature on the national market for new housing, including demand (total and "tenure composition"[11] of demand for additional housing, rental or purchase); supply (percentage change in gross annual construction); and price. Looking first at trends in demand, one study at the national level found that the total demand for new dwelling units increased from the 1870's to the 1890's, though the rate of growth declined by nearly 50% during the 1890's.[12] The tenure composition of demand for new units shifted from an excess of rental to sales units of 235,000 in the 1870's to a lesser excess of 207,000 in the 1890's.[13] Assuming that preferences for sales housing and age-specific household headship rates for immigrants were the same as for native born migrants during this period (doubtful assumptions as we have seen in St. Paul) the same study estimated that immigration contributed 40% to 60% of demand for new rental housing though never more than 35% of demand for additional sales housing during the same period. The contribution of immigration to total new housing demand, as well as to each of the sales and rental sectors, also fluctuated cyclically, with high levels during the decades

1880-1890 and 1900-1910 and lower levels during the 1870's and 1890's.[14]

On the supply side, more precise trend data is available on the percentage annual change in gross construction, allowing us to delineate the "long swing"; during our period, the high points of the swing occurred in 1868, 1889 and 1901 with low points in 1860, 1874 and 1893.[15] As we noted in Chapter Two, the annual level of residential dwelling starts followed this cyclic pattern closely at the national level from 1885-1899 with a secular decline of 10% during the same period.[16] Price trends for construction from 1869 to 1899 were discussed in Chapter Four. As Table 51 indicates, the national construction price index declined to 1879 then moved upward to the end of the century with mild fluctuations corresponding to the long swing in construction output.

These national trends in the market for new housing represent a convenient frame of reference, but the crucial question for our purposes is whether trends existed in the price for residential dwellings and land among cities at different stages of their development. It would be useful to know what differences in housing price trends might have existed as cities passed from frontier to more mature stages in the nineteenth century. Richard Easterlin has argued that the expectation of return from investment in agricultural land among farm families in frontier areas at first increased and then declined as land prices rose during the latter stages of the development process, until a price plateau was reached at the point where most of the available tillable acreage was taken up. The trend in land prices, Easterlin argues, was responsible for changes in fertility and nuptiality. The first generation of rural settlers had somewhat higher levels of nuptiality and fertility than the population of their older rural areas of origin. The second generation (those reared from childhood in the frontier area) had highest levels of nuptiality and fertility, but as land prices climbed, the third generation again reduced fertility and nuptiality levels and began to migrate elsewhere at higher rates.[17]

Though land now represents about 5% of urban housing costs, the share of cost may have been higher in frontier cities and thus price trends of residential land may have prompted a similar response among urban residents as the settlement process gradually diminished economic expectations.[18] If this assumption is correct we should expect to find that nuptiality, headship and homeownership levels at first increased and then declined as residential land values increased in maturing frontier cities. Across the spectrum of cities at various stages of development in the late nineteenth century, then, we would expect a curvilinear pattern in homeownership levels. At one extreme, homeownership in older cities in the East should be low but moving upward over the long term. At the other extreme, homeownership in the youngest frontier cities should also be low but increasing to a maximum at about 60 years after settlement, then declining again as the cities reached a plateau of stable population growth. Since the total populations of new cities was small relative to the national population, the temporary frontier trend toward lower homeownership demand would have muted but not reversed the long trend at the national level. Movements in homewonership levels in the short term, of course, would also respond to the cyclic pattern of the housing market, with slower rates of increase during temporary downswings.

In addition to the stage of development as a factor, economic theory would predict that high average income levels would be associated with high levels of homeownership while high housing costs (including land) would be associated with low levels of ownership.[19] Since the average age at which demand for rental housing reaches maximum occurs at an earlier life cycle stage than the demand for owner-occupied housing[20] the immediate effect of a large in-migration to a city would be to increase demand for rental housing, given the fact that most migrants are young adults. The in-migration would increase demand for sales housing about 20 years later as the migrant population aged.[21] Two other factors, the increasing rate of mortality typical of growing cities before the introduction of effective public health measures in the 1890's, and the introduction of electric street railways in the 1890's, probably also affected homeownership: in the negative direction for mortality, in the positive direction for improved transportation.[22]

Still another factor affecting homeownership rates, of major concern in this study, are differentials in average wealth by ethnic group. A study of wealthholding (both real and personal estate) in Milwaukee in 1860 found that the average age-specific holdings of all native-born men was six times that of the foreign-born, though the average wealth of second generation immigrants apparently equalled the native born of native parentage.[23] Our analysis in Chapter One of real estate holdings among household heads in St. Paul (Table 22) indicated that the proportion of foreign-born heads who did not own real estate was nearly three times as great as for native born migrant heads (with controls for occupational category). These substantial differences strongly indicate that the effects of immigration cannot be estimated accurately by assuming that the immigrant contribution to rental demand was equal to that of native-born migrants in the nineteenth century. We would rather expect that large proportions of immigrants in a city population would increase demand for rental housing at a higher rate than native-born migrants.

As noted in an earlier chapter, the transition from marriage to the establishment of a separate household was not necessarily coincident in the nineteenth century. Since the acquisition of separate living quarters signified by household formation is more closely related to housing demand than is marriage, we turn next to a summary of the available literature on household headship. Like the average age at first marriage, household headship rates in young adult age groups has declined from 1890 to 1950 though not as rapidly as age at first marriage among males.[24] The proportion of young married men who had not formed separate households has also declined though there was little change, apparently, from 1880 to 1940.[25] The effects of labor force participation and income level on the headship rates of young men also apparently has shifted from lesser to greater influence, 1880 to 1970.[26] Economic theory would also predict that high rental costs would be associated with low headship and high rental vacancy rates with high headship among young adults.[27] Since interest rates on home mortgages represent an important cost factor primarily for home-ownership, rather than for separate household formation, the effect of changes in this variable have been considered "largely independent" of headship rates from 1890 to the present according to one recent study.[28] Finally, comparative age-specific household headship rates for immigrant populations have been reported for Buffalo, New York, at the middle of the nineteenth century (see Chapter One) suggesting that German headship rates were higher than average, though trends over time had not been reported separately for immigrants as a group or for specific nationalities.[29]

Data and Method

The 1890 census reports provide age-specific data for sex ratios and male and female nuptiality; hence, we shall examine for each city of 100,000 or more the proportion of males age 25 to 34 who were ever married, (i.e., who were no longer single) the proportion of females age 20 to 29 who were ever married, and the relationship of each to the number of males age 25 to 29 per 100 females age 20 to 24. The broader age groupings for nuptiality were chosen to coincide with the age groupings for headship in our local study of St. Paul, while the narrower sex ratio more precisely measures the role of this factor in the marriage market. Household headship can be represented crudely by the ratio of households (both "public" and "private") to adults aged 25 and over. The proportion of households who owned their own dwelling is given directly. Because most occupational categories except "carpenters" and "laborers" were small relative to the total workforce, we shall confine our study of city-to-city variations in ethnic occupational distribution to the proportions of gainfully occupied Irish and German males who were either carpenters or laborers. Other independent variables besides sex ratio are defined in Table 68. Because gains in manufacturing employment were an important indicator of expanding occupational opportunity in large cities in 1890, we include two measures of industrialization to represent city income levels. German and Irish subpopulations are represented here by the proportion of gainfully occupied males who were born in Germany or Ireland because of the limitations of the census reports. No age and sex breakdowns were provided for either first or second generation Irish or German populations of cities in 1890. Given the low rate of labor force participation by women in the nineteenth century, the best estimate of the proportion of adult population of a city who were German or Irish is provided by the proportions of male workers from each of

Table 67

GRAPH A

SCATTERGRAM OF (DOWN) PROPORTION OF MALES AGE 25 - 34 EVER MARRIED (ACROSS) CITY AGE (YEARS)

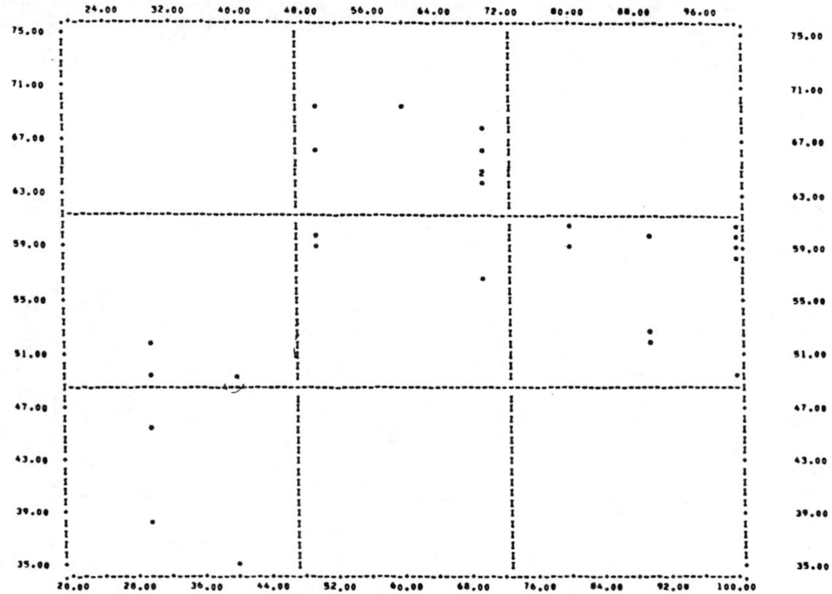

SCATTERGRAMS, 90
AGE AT MARRIAGE.90 — 77/05/23. PAGE 8

STATISTICS..

CORRELATION (R)-	.34404	R SQUARED -	.11837	SIGNIFICANCE R -	.07888
STD ERR OF EST -	8.51332	INTERCEPT (A) -	49.28703	STD ERROR OF A -	4.85929
SIGNIFICANCE A -	.00001	SLOPE (B) -	.12502	STD ERROR OF B -	.06824
SIGNIFICANCE B -	.07888				
PLOTTED VALUES -	27	EXCLUDED VALUES-	0	MISSING VALUES -	30

GRAPH B

SCATTERGRAM OF (DOWN) PROPORTION OF FEMALES AGE 20 - 29 EVER MARRIED (ACROSS) CITY AGE (YEARS)

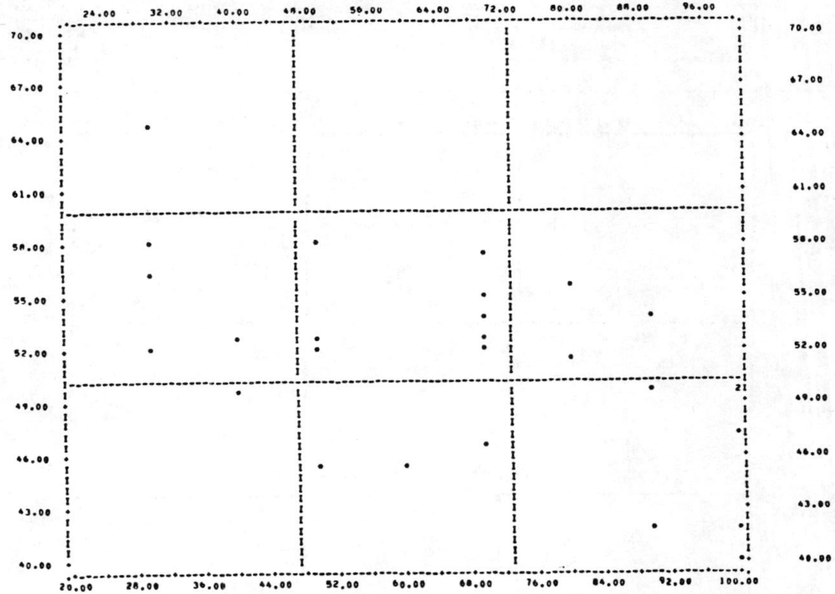

SCATTERGRAMS, 90 77/05/23. PAGE 58

AGE AT MARRIAGE,90

STATISTICS..

CORRELATION (R)-	-.55668	R SQUARED -	.30989	SIGNIFICANCE R -	.00256
STD ERR OF EST -	4.75373	INTERCEPT (A) -	60.06592	STD ERROR OF A -	2.71336
SIGNIFICANCE A -	.00001	SLOPE (B) -	-.12767	STD ERROR OF B -	.03811
SIGNIFICANCE B -	.00256				
PLOTTED VALUES -	27	EXCLUDED VALUES-	0	MISSING VALUES -	30

GRAPH C

SCATTERGRAM OF NUMBER OF HOUSEHOLDS PER 100 ADULTS AGE 25 AND OVER (ACROSS) CITY AGE (YEARS)

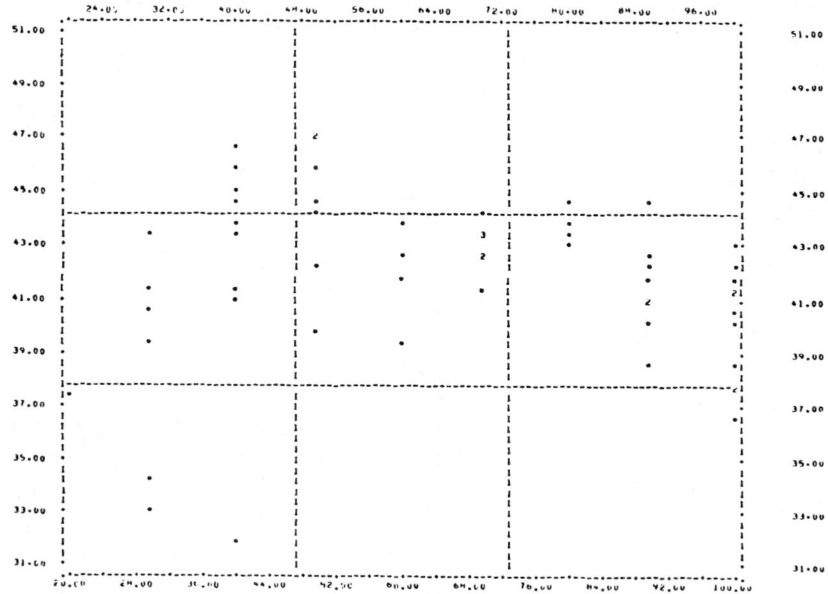

SCATTERGRAMS, SE
HOS/ADULTS, 90
STATISTICS..

11/05/23. PAGE 8

CORRELATION (R)-	-.02980	R SQUARED -	.00089	SIGNIFICANCE R -	.82583
STD ERR OF EST -	4.17631	INTERCEPT (A) -	42.22688	STD ERROR OF A -	1.16614
SIGNIFICANCE A -	.00001	SLOPE (B) -	-.00370	STD ERROR OF B -	.01672
SIGNIFICANCE B -	.82583				
PLOTTED VALUES -	57	EXCLUDED VALUES-	0	MISSING VALUES -	0

GRAPH D

SCATTERGRAM OF (DOWN) PROPORTION OF HOUSEHOLDS OWNING THEIR DWELLING (ACROSS) CITY AGE (YEARS)

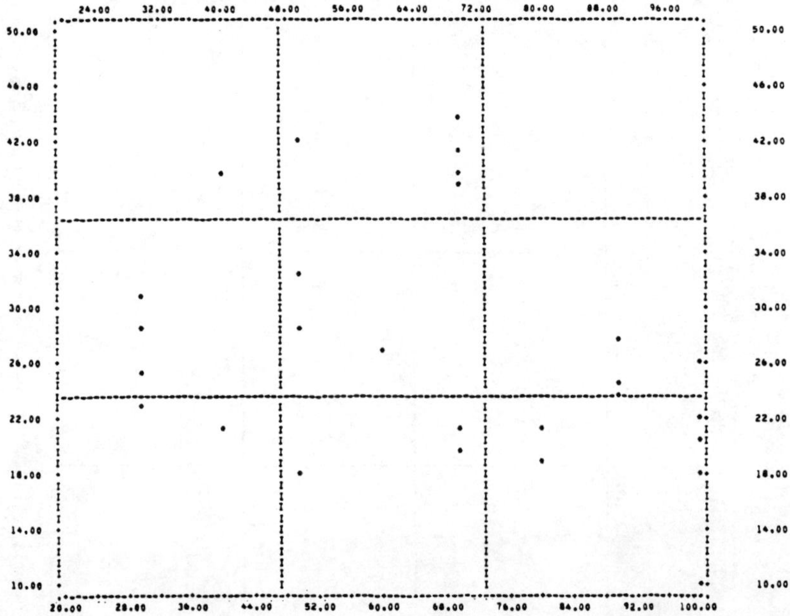

SCATTERGRAMS, 90
OWNERSHIP, 90

77/05/23. PAGE 8

STATISTICS..

CORRELATION (R)-	-.33004	R SQUARED -	.10892	SIGNIFICANCE R -	.09271
STD ERR OF EST -	8.36093	INTERCEPT (A) -	35.42449	STD ERROR OF A -	4.77231
SIGNIFICANCE A -	.00001	SLOPE (B) -	-.11716	STD ERROR OF B -	.06702
SIGNIFICANCE B -	.09271				
PLOTTED VALUES -	27	EXCLUDED VALUES-	0	MISSING VALUES -	30

******** IS PRINTED IF A COEFFICIENT CANNOT BE COMPUTED.

Table 68

Pearsonian Correlation Coefficients[a], Association Between Independents and Dependents, Large Cities, 1890

Independents	Dependents: Male Nuptiality[b]	Female Nuptiality[b]	Homeowner Proportion[b]	Headship Ratio[c]
V_1 Sex Ratio	-.690	+.453	---	-.723
V_2 Age of City	+.344*	-.557	-.330*	NS
V_3 Total Population	NS	NS	-.428	NS
V_4 % Heads Owners	+.323	NS	---	NS
V_5 Ave. Annual Interest, Home Mortgages	-.453	+.563	NS	NS
V_6 Rate of Pop. Growth, 1880-1890	-.452	+.447	+.284	NS
V_7 % of Workforce in Manufacturing	+.463	-.314	+.502	NS
V_8 Capitalization per Ave. Mfg. Employee	-.379	NS	NS	NS
V_9 % Male Workers Irish	NS	-.353	-.551	-.252
V_{10} % Male Workers German	+.480	NS	+.364	+.273
V_{11} Households per Dwelling	NS	NS	-.556	NS
V_{12} % Females Age 10-24 who were employed	NS	-.449	NS	NS
V_{13} % Male Workers Unemp. 4 mos. or more	NS	NS	+.502	NS
V_{14} % Change, Capitaliz. per Ave. Mfg. Employee, 1880-1890	-.423	+.342	NS	NS

[a]Significant at .10 level.

[b]Includes 27 cities of 100,000 population or more (combining Brooklyn with New York City). Due to an error, values of V_7, V_9, V_{10}, V_{12} and V_{13} for Washington, D. C. were not included in the data, reducing the total cases to 26 cities for these variables.

[c]57 cities of 50,000 population or more (except for varables V_7, V_9, V_{10}, V_{12} and V_{13} where 56 cities were reported, excluding Washington, D. C.).

*Indicates the form of the association is curvilinear.

Definitions

V_1	Ratio: Males age 25-29 per 100 females age 20-24.
V_2	Years in 1890 since first federal census of the city.
V_3	Total population of the city.
V_4	Proportion of households (both "public" and "private") who occupied a dwelling which they owned
V_5	Average annual interest rate on home mortgages
V_6	Percentage change in total population, 1880 to 1890
V_7	Ratio: Average Number of Manufacturing Workers Employed during the previous year per 100 gainfully occupied workers at the time of the census.
V_8	Ratio: Manufacturing capital (millions) per average number of manufacturing workers employed in the previous year.
V_9	Proportion of gainfully occupied males who were born in Ireland.
V_{10}	Proportion of gainfully occupied males who were born in Germany.
V_{11}	Ratio: Number of households per dwelling unit.
V_{12}	Proportion of females age 10 to 24 who were gainfully occupied.
V_{13}	Proportion of gainfully occupied males who were unemployed 4 months or more during the previous year.
V_{14}	Percentage Change, Manufacturing capital per average number of manufacturing workers employed in previous year.

these groups.

As a beginning point for analysis, the association between each of our dependent variables (i.e. male nuptiality, female nuptiality, household headship, homeownership level, and the proportions of ethnic workmen in major occupations) and those independent variables which we expected to have considerable impact was analyzed for each independent separately.[30] Two of our dependent variables (nuptiality and homeownership) were reported only for the 27 cities of 100,000 population or more in 1890, though a headship ratio and occupational proportions could be calculated for the 57 cities of 50,000 population or more. Because many of the independent variables were mutually associated with one another (see Table 69) a factor analysis was performed to identify the underlying structural dimensions or "factors" among those clusters of independent variables which were most strongly interrelated.[31] An index was then calculated for each of the underlying dimensions or factors and the indexes were incorporated into a linear regression equation as independents.[32] This technique thus allows us to assess the relative strength of influence of each cluster of independent variables upon our dependent variables while controlling for "interaction" or mutual association of independents with one another.

Table 69

Pearsonian Correlation Coefficients Among Significant Independent Variables[a], 26 Cities of 100,000 Population or More in 1890 (Excluding Washington, D. C.)

		V_1	V_2	V_4	V_6	V_7	V_9	V_{10}	V_{11}	V_{12}	V_{13}	V_{14}
V_1	Sex Ratio											
V_2	City Age	-.700										
V_4	% Homeowners	+.047	-.326									
V_6	Pop. Growth, 1880-90	+.728	-.703	+.280								
V_7	Mfg. Employ. Level	-.577	+.603	+.099	-.520							
V_9	% M. Workers, Irish	-.129	+.450	-.550	-.393	+.143						
V_{10}	% M. Workers, German	-.304	+.054	+.364	-.260	+.463	-.214					
V_{11}	Households/ Dwelling	-.261	+.361	-.569	-.265	+.243	+.523	-.014				
V_{12}	% Yng. Women, Employed	+.130	+.311	-.031	+.054	+.436	+.300	-.014	+.391			
V_{13}	Male Unemp.		-.036	+.502	+.070	+.157						
V_{14}	% Change, Cap./Mfg. Employee, 1880-90	+.542	-.371	+.191	+.505	-.303	-.104	-.082	-.225	+.108	-.247	

[a]"Significant" in the sense that each of the variables are significantly associated with one or more of the dependent variables in the previous Table. Some of the coefficients of association among independents above are not statistically significant but are reported here for reference because portions of this matrix are used in each of the factor analyses of independents reported in the following Table.

The linear regression equations and related statistics reported in Table 70 thus yield the following types of information which we will explore in detail below:

a) they allow us to examine simultaneously the direction and strength of influence of each of the independent factors or variables upon our dependent variables with control for interaction of independents;

b) they allow us to measure the predictive value of our set of independents, so that we may assess the relative importance of unknown variables which we have not identified (and the error introduced by assuming that all associations have a linear form);

c) in the case of an individual city such as St. Paul, they allow us to estimate those factors which most contributed to the particular level of nuptiality, homeownership, etc. which occurred in such cities in 1890.

In other words, these equations and statistics will allow us to give rough numerical estimates as answers to the general questions posed earlier in the chapter.

Table 70

Regression Equations for Nuptiality, Household Headship, Homeownership, and Ethnic Occupational Distributions, U. S. Cities of 100,000 Population or More, 1890 (Standard Errors and Beta Weights in Parentheses)

Nuptiality

$$Y_M = -.2924X_1* + .8031X_2 + 2.4776X_3 - 2.4175X_4 + 85.8891$$

(.0802) (1.6293) (1.7163) (2.1174) (Standard Errors)
(.7809) (.0859) (.0030) (.0010) (Beta Weights)

$R = .763$ $R^2 = .583$ $\bar{R}^2 = .507$

$$Y_F = -2.8887X_4* - 2.5591X_2* + 1.9572X_3 + .0661X_1 + 45.0141$$

(1.6344) (1.258) (1.325) (.0619)
(.4799) (.4338) (.0027) (.2796)

$R = .613$ $R^2 = .376$ $\bar{R}^2 = .262$

Household Headship

$$Y_H = .4155X_5 + .8635X_6 - .0897X_1* + 49.8022$$

(1.0065) (.5928) (.0351)
(.0965) (.2345) (.5811)

$R = .684$ $R^2 = .467$ $\bar{R}^2 = .398$

Homeownership

$$Y_O = -5.6016X_7* - 2.2213X_8* + 5.6922X_9* + 27.4507$$

(2.0635) (1.2117) (2.2870)
(.5555) (.3662) (.5632)

$R = .541$ $R^2 = .293$ $\bar{R}^2 = .210$

German Occupational Proportions

$$Y_{GL} = .6230X_{10} + 1.3451X_{11}* + 4.4455X_{12}* - 4.3151$$

(1.1612) (.1763) (.9121)
(.0474) (.6790) (.4498)

$R = .921$ $R^2 = .847$ $\bar{R}^2 = .827$

$$Y_{GC} = -.1315X_{10} + .729X_{12}* + .7302X_{13}* + 1.8958$$

(.6363) (.4073) (.4189)
(.0460) (.3389) (.4882)

$R = .786 \quad R^2 = .618 \quad \bar{R}^2 = .566$

Irish Occupational Proportions

$$Y_{IL} = .8938X_{10} + .6483X_{11}{}^{*} - 1.2700X_{12} + 22.3351$$

(1.3981) (.2123) (1.0982)
(.1207) (.3805) (.2279)

$R = .551 \quad R^2 = .304 \quad \bar{R}^2 = .209$

$$Y_{IC} = .1912X_{10} + .3234X_{13}{}^{*} - .1106X_{12} + 1.1342$$

(.2481) (.1633) (.1588)
(.2406) (.7777) (.1849)

$R = .499 \quad R^2 = .249 \quad \bar{R}^2 = .146$

Definitions of Independents[a]

X_1 = Sex Ratio (males age 25-29 per 100 females age 20-24)

X_2 = Female Employment Activity Factor

X_3 = Factor: Level of Manufacturing Employment plus Level of German Immigration

X_4 = Factor: Age of City less Rate of Population Growth, 1880-90

X_5 = Factor: Level of Manufacturing Employment plus Age of City less Rate of Population Growth, 1880-90

X_6 = Factor: Homeownership Level less Level of Irish Immigration

X_7 = Factor: Age of City less Rate of Population Growth, 1880-90

X_8 = Factor: Female Employment Activity plus Irish Immigration Level

X_9 = Factor: Level of Manufacturing Employment plus Level of German Immigration

X_{10} = Factor: City Age less Rate of Population Growth, 1880-90

X_{11} = Proportion of Male Workers who were Laborers

X_{12} = Homewownership Level Factor

X_{13} = Proportion of Male Workers who were Carpenters

---

[a]Factors refer to indexes created by factor analyses using the following general formula: Factor Index = Factor Score Coefficient X (Variable Score - Variable Mean) / Variable Standard Deviation.

*Starred coefficients significant at the .10 level.

Table 70, continued

Correlation Coefficients Among
Factors and Variables

Nuptiality:

	X_2	X_3	X_4	Y_M	Y_F
X_1	.11754	-.39553	-.75669	-.68978	.45311
X_2		.48287	-.10817	.15675	-.17975
X_3			.44251	.51821	-.1819
X_4				.45206	-.48944

Household Headship:

	X_5	X_6	Y_H
X_1	-.72566	.01949	-.64663
X_5		-.23802	.46244
X_6			.20018

Homeownership:

	X_8	X_9	Y_O
X_7	.00886	.47002	-.29396
X_8		.42717	-.13051
X_9			.14574

Occupational Proportions:

	X_{11}	X_{12}	X_{13}	Y_{GL}	Y_{GC}
X_{10}	-.19482	-.32376	-.76864	-.23044	-.53097
X_{11}		.34097		.82305	
X_{12}			.65874	.66588	.67536
X_{13}					.74679

	X_{11}	X_{12}	X_{13}	Y_{IL}	Y_{IC}
X_{10}	-.19482	-.32376	-.76864	.08143	-.29724
X_{11}		.34097		.47925	
X_{12}				-.06906	.24947
X_{13}					.47090

Results for 26 Large Cities

The regression equations reported in Table 70 generally confirm our expectations about the importance of the economic and demographic environment for predicting city-to-city variation in nuptiality, headship and homeownership. In the case of male nuptiality (Y_M) the most influential regression coefficient[34] in our equation is sex ratio (X_1), though the factor associated with industrial employment levels (X_3) tended to increase male nuptiality, and female employment levels (X_2) tended to decrease male nuptiality (i.e. nuptiality was higher in younger cities) as we expected, though the strength of this association is understated by the linear regression coefficient. The ages of cities in 1890 were associated in a curvilinear fashion with male nuptiality (Graph A) as we expected, with a peak at about a city age of 60 years. Male nuptiality levels in newer cities on the frontier such as St. Paul thus followed closely the "rising-then-falling" pattern observed by Easterlin among rural populations on the agricultural frontier during the same period, in response, apparently, to the same trend in frontier economic expectations.

The regression equation for female nuptiality (Y_F), on the other hand, suggests surprisingly little influence for sex ratio (X_1), though the reason that this is so in our equation doubtless is because the association was curvilinear in form and thus its strength was understated by our linear regression coefficient.[35] Female employment levels (X_2) as expected reduced female nuptiality, as did increasing city age (X_4). Female nuptiality steadily declined as city age increased (Graph B), suggesting that female marriage decisions on the frontier were less affected than those of males by the boom period of high economic expectations during the first 60 years in frontier towns.

The equations for both male and female nuptiality indicate that the "Irishness" or "Germanness" of city populations in 1890 had only a marginal influence upon city-to-city variation in nuptiality. Irish population proportions did not "load" importantly on the underlying dimensions identified by the factor analysis, and German population proportions apparently were important partly because Germans tended to settle in cities with high levels of manufacturing employment and thus of higher than average economic growth potential. A direct way of assessing the importance of the ethnic character of city populations for predicting nuptiality is given in Table 71. By setting all independents in the equation at their respective means except for the German population proportion, the range of direct influence of the "Germanness" of population on nuptiality levels can be estimated by substituting in the equation the extremes of the empirical range of the German population variable (from 1.9% to 32.4% of the male workforce). As Table 71 indicates, the full empirical range of the German population variable shifted male nuptiality by 3% and female nuptiality by 2.3%, or about 9% of the empirical range of the dependent in each case. In other words, if the ethnic composition of the population of one of our cities with a low proportion of Germans (e.g. Providence, Rhode Island with 2%) were to change to that of the highest proportion of Germans in a city in our set of cities (Milwaukee, with 32%), the level of nuptiality in the city would increase by only 3% among young men and 2.3% among young women, all else being equal.

The published literature on nuptiality during the twentieth century has found that the proportion Catholic is associated with low female nuptiality levels, as we reported above. Though we were unable to test this variable because data on religious affiliation was not available, we do know that a large proportion of U. S. Catholics in 1890 were Irish immigrants; thus, it is especially surprising that the "Irishness" of the populations of large cities in 1890 did not appear as significant in the factor analysis of nuptiality. In the case of household headship, however, the Irish population percentage (but not the German percentage) appears in the headship equation (Y_H) in Table 70 in the same factor with the level of homeownership (X_6). The close but negative association of homeownership levels with Irish proportions in the factor X_6 apparently means that the Irish tended to settle heavily in cities with low levels of homeownership (and, by inference, high rental costs). The independent effect of "Irishness", moreover, accounted for only 1% of the empirical range of the headship ratio (see Table 71).

Turning to the regression equation for homeownership (Y_O) in Table 70, we note by comparing the standardized regression coefficients ("beta weights") that the level of manufacturing employment (X_9) was associated with high levels of homeownership, city age (X_7) with low levels, and female employment activity (X_8) with low levels. Interestingly, Irish population proportions were clustered with female employment activity (X_8) and German proportions with manufacturing employment (X_9) in this equation, with the Irish proportion contributing more to the rental sector and the German proportion to the homeownership sector. These associations seem to mean that the

Table 71

Influence of Specific National Background Upon City-to-City Variation in Nuptiality, Household Headship, And Homeownership Levels, Cities of 100,000 Population or More, 1890

			Independents	
Dependent Variable	Factor		German Component	Irish Component
Male Nuptiality (Y_M)	(X_3)			
Minimum: 35.0%	53.7%		56.7%	
Maximum: 70.0%	62.7%		59.6%	
Range: 35.0%	9.0%		3.1%	
Proportion of Total Range Explained:	25.7%		8.9%	
Female Nuptiality (Y_F)	(X_3)			
Minimum: 40.0%	47.8%		50.3%	
Maximum: 64.7%	54.9%		52.5%	
Range: 24.7%	7.1%		2.3%	
Proportion of Total Range Explained:	28.7%		9.3%	
Household Headship (Y_H)	(X_6)			
Minimum: 31.9%	39.5%			40.5%
Maximum: 47.2%	42.7%			41.6%
Range: 15.3%	3.2%			1.1%
Proportion of Total Range Explained:	20.9%			7.2%
Homeownership (Y_O)	(X_9)	(X_8)		
Minimum: 10.6%	18.5%	23.3%	26.2%	25.3%
Maximum: 44.0%	36.7%	30.3%	28.7%	29.6%
Range: 33.4%	18.1%	7.1%	2.5%	4.3%
Proportion of Range Explained:	54.2%	21.3%	7.5%	12.9%

Note: Calculations based on regression equations reported in Table 70.

Irish contributed more to the rental sector partly because they settled in cities with high levels of female employment and that Germans contributed to higher levels of homeownership partly because they settled in cities with high manufacturing employment. Aside from this, the independent effects of Irish and German proportions upon homeownership levels given in Table 71 indicate that the Irish percentages accounted for 4.3% and the German 2.5% of the total empirical variation in homeownership levels among the 26 cities.

Though we cannot impute characteristics of cities to their German and Irish subpopulations directly, it is interesting to note that the direction of influence for each immigrant group upon city levels of nuptiality, headship and homeownership is the same as the ethnic differences in these patterns noted at the individual level of analysis for the German and Irish populations of St. Paul. Whatever the role of ethnic values, prior demographic circumstances, or distinctive settlement patterns in producing the observed effect, the role of specific national origin city-to-city variation in nuptiality, headship and homeownership clearly was marginal compared to the more central influence of economic and demographic circumstances. The curvilinear form of the associations between city age and male nuptiality, household headship, and homeownership (see Graphs A, C and D) further indicate that young cities went through a developmental pattern, with headship rising to a peak at about 50 years, male nuptiality at 60 years, and homeownership at 70 years after the first federal census in the young cities. German and Irish immigrants contributed to this developmental pattern by settling in large numbers in younger cities, but the specific influence of their particular places of origin upon the family and household formation and homeownership patterns was relatively a minor one.

Turning finally to the regression equations for ethnic occupational distributions in Table 70, the first point to be noted is that the occupational structure of cities in 1890, while clearly important, was not the only factor affecting occupational distributions within ethnic populations. For each equation the appropriate proportion of the total male workforce in the particular occupation has been added as an independent variable in addition to indexes created with a factor analysis of other relevant independents.[36] In the case of German laborers (Y_{GL}) and carpenters (Y_{GC}), a comparison of beta weights indicates that the proportions of Germans in these occupations were significantly related both to the relative size of the laboring and carpentry share of urban occupational structures (X_{11},X_{13}) and to the level of homeownership

(X_{12}), conditions which we could expect to be especially high in maturing frontier cities. In the case of Irish laborers (Y_{IL}) much the same influence existed, except that among Irish carpenter proportions (Y_{IC}) the city age factor was a relatively more important independent variable than homeownership levels. As we have seen, homeownership levels fluctuated cyclically as young cities "aged". The lesser influence of homeownership levels on the proportions of Irish who were carpenters (compared to Germans) thus may be an indicator that that the Irish were less concentrated in those cities with peak homeownership levels in 1890 than were the Germans.

Local and Regional Implications

With the information we have gained of the major structural influences upon household formation, homeownership and occupational distribution at the national urban level we may now address the other major issue of this chapter: how representative were demographic patterns in St. Paul of the region's or the nation's cities? Table 72 presents household headship rates for St. Paul in 1860 and 1895 for the same age and sex groups for which we measured nuptiality levels. The decline in headship during this 35 year period in St. Paul is not surprising if we refer to Easterlin's demonstration that the curve of

Table 72

Household Headship Rates, Men and Women Born Outside of Minnesota, By Place of Birth and Age, St. Paul, 1860, 1895

	Ireland	German States	Other Foreign	U. S.	Total	N
Men, 25-34 Years						
1860	81.1	69.2	62.7	69.2	71.4	336
1895	41.7	61.4	37.4	35.8	40.7	114
% Change	-39.4	- 7.8	-25.3	-33.4	-30.7	
% Departure from Average Change	- 8.7	+22.9	+ 5.4	- 2.7		
Women, 20-29 Years						
1860	71.1	74.2	64.9	70.9	71.0	286
1895	33.3	48.9	41.4	32.6	38.9	239
% Change	-37.8	-25.3	-23.5	-38.3	-32.1	
% Departure from Average Change	- 5.7	+ 6.8	+ 8.6	- 6.2		

Significance levels: Men, 1860 - .10; Men, 1895 - .05; Women, 1860 - NS; Women, 1895 - NS.

Cramer's V: Men, 1860 - .14; Men, 1895 - .18.

Source: Sample data.

rising-then-falling economic expectations in frontier areas was compressed into a shorter time period for areas settled late in the century.[37] Though St. Paul was founded about 1850 it had largely completed its frontier developmental cycle by 1895, principally because its population was drawn from a larger Midwestern population nearby. The headship ratios for Midwestern cities displayed in Table 73 confirm that city headship levels were similar in the Midwest by 1890. Recalling the regression equations for headship(Y_H) in Table 70, and examining the observed values of the independents from this equation for the cities listed in Table 73, we may also conclude that St. Paul's headship ratio in 1890, slightly lower than average when compared to other large Midwestern cities was related to St. Paul's high level of employment among young women (40%) and its low level of manufacturing employment (28%).

Another economic factor, to which we referred in an earlier chapter, the depression of the early 1890's, seems to have had relatively little net effect on the headship ratio in St. Paul from 1890 to 1895 (from sample data, the ratio in 1895 was 41%).[38] The apparent reason for the steady levels of headship despite the worsening depression from 1890 to 1895 in St. Paul can be found by

Table 73

Observed Values of Variables for Six Selected Cities of 100,000 Population or More in 1890

	St. Paul	Minneapolis	Chicago	Milwaukee	St. Louis	Philadelphia
Male Nuptiality	50	52	59	67	57	60
Sex Ratio	111	118	105	82	86	85
Female Employ.	40	36	33	33	31	39
Mfg. Employment	28	32	42	52	44	50
% M. Workers, German	13	6	20	32	22	10
% M. Workers, Irish	6	3	9	1	7	13
City Age	40	30	50	50	70	100
% Pop. Growth, 1880-90	224	251	119	76	29	24
Female Nuptiality	53	52	58	52	54	47
% Homeowners	40	31	29	42	20	23
% German M. Work. Laborers	19	17	18	20	15	7
% German M. Work. Carpenters	7	6	6	8	6	3
H. Headship Ratio	41	40	42	47	44	38

referring to Table 74. The likely drop in homeownership levels from 1890 to 1895 (associated with a drop in headship in the regression equation) was offset by a temporary decline in the prime age male/female ratio, caused by both a net out-migration of prime age males and a net in-migration of prime age females. Though we cannot estimate the marital composition of these migration streams because of lack of data on marital status for 1895, we might speculate that most of the female migrants were single young women attracted by clerical or factory operative positions, and perhaps most of the males were unemployed single men escaping the depressed construction or other sectors. If so, then the net effect of the depression years was to temporarily alter the sex ratio toward a more balanced marriage market among young adults in St. Paul, offsetting the negative influence on headship ratios of depressed economic conditions.

The ethnic differences in headship rates among migrant men in St. Paul in 1860 (Table 72) are difficult to explain on the basis of structural considerations. Assuming that immigrant marriage markets were largely endogomous (as we discovered in Chapter One), our regression equation for male nuptiality suggests that above average levels of German and Irish male headship probably would be the result of: a) more balanced Irish

Table 74

Net Migration Rates, Prime Marriage Age Cohort of 1895 in St. Paul, 1890 - 1895, 1895 - 1900

Cohort Ages in 1890	Reported or Estimated Number[a]			Survival Ratios[b]			Net Migration Rates[c]		
	1890	1895	1900	1890	1895	1900	1890-95	1895-00	1890-00
Males									
20 - 29	17673	14799	22563	.837	1.525	1.277	-11.1	+57.7	+38.1
Females									
15 - 24	15450	15480	14958	1 002	.966	.968	+ 7.2	+ 3.6	+10.7
Sex Ratios	114	96	151						

[a]Estimate for 1895 from sample data.

[b]Ten year national survival ratios, or the ratio of survivors of a cohort in a latter census per original members of the cohort in a census ten years earlier, were taken from: Everett S. Lee, *et al.*, *Population Redistribution and Economic Growth, 1870 - 1950* (3 vols.; Philadelphia, 1957-1964), Vol. I, *Methodological Considerations and Reference Tables*, Table 1.1, p. 17; five year survival ratios were estimated by dividing the 1890-1900 ratios by two.

[c]Percentage difference between five year survival ratio for the city and the five year national survival ratio estimated as in "b".

and German sex ratios; b) lower levels of female employment for Germans and Irish; or c) higher levels of manufacturing employment. We have found in Chapter 1, Table 13, that "a" was not true. High German headship rates might be explained by "b" and "c", but the extraordinary high male Irish headship rates in 1860 certainly could not, since young Irish women were employed as domestics at a high rate and Irish men were over-represented in unskilled labor. Two other possible explanations are ethnic differences in the marital composition of migration streams to St. Paul or in cultural values about household formation.

Since we lack marital status and age-sex breakdowns for individual ethnic groups in St. Paul in 1890 we are unable to compare the composition of ethnic migration streams during the depression years 1890-95, but the possibility exists that ethnic differences in headship in 1895 were the result of differences in migration streams in response to the depression. The relatively high German male headship rates in 1895, for example, may have been the result of a temporary exodus of single Germans from the city during the depression. Another explanation, as we suggested in earlier chapters, may have been differences in cultural norms about household formation.

Turning next to homeownership levels in St. Paul in the 1890's, we note by referring to Table 75 that St. Paul's level in 1890 was among the highest in the country (40%) among large cities, though the decline of 10% in St. Paul by 1900 placed the city's homeownership level near the average for the Midwest. The decline of homeonwership in St. Paul, 1890-1900, fits the predicted cyclic pattern of frontier city development outlined above. In addition, our regression equation for homeownership (Table 70) indicates that the steepness of the decline in the 1890's was probably affected by high female employment activity and low manufacturing employment in St. Paul during the decade (Table 73).

As for ethnic differences in homeownership levels in St. Paul in the 1890's, the only indicator available in the data is "residence in single household dwellings" by ethnic group in 1895, as we suggested in Chapter Two. If this indicator in fact reflects patterns of homeownership in 1895, the ethnic differences among immigrants and native-born migrants discovered in Chapter Two cannot be explained further by our regression equation for ownership. Because controls for household relationship and occupational sector were applied, the major independents of our regression already have been employed in the analysis presented in Chapter Two. The positive associa-

Table 75

Homeownership Levels Among Cities of 100,000 Population Or More in 1890, Comparing Public and Private Households in 1890 With Private Households Only in 1900

	1890	1900	% Change
Chicago	29	23	-6
Philadelphia	23	20	-3
New York City[a]	11	12	+1
St. Louis	20	21	+1
Boston	18	18	0
Baltimore	26	25	-1
San Francisco	22	23	+1
Cincinnati	19	20	+1
Cleveland	39	36	-3
Buffalo	40	31	-9
New Orleans	22	22	0
Pittsburgh	28	27	-1
Washington	25	24	-1
Detroit	42	39	-3
Milwaukee	42	36	-6
Newark	22	21	-1
Minneapolis	31	29	-3
Jersey City	19	20	+1
Louisville	24	26	+2
Omaha	26	28	+2
Rochester	44	38	-6
St. Paul	40	30	-10
Kansas City	23	24	+1
Providence	21	21	0
Denver	29	28	-1
Indianapolis	33	34	+1
Allegheny	27	26	+1

[a]Brooklyn included with New York City in 1890 for comparison with consolidated city in 1900.

tion of German population proportions with city homeownership levels (and the negative association of Irish proportions) in the regression equation also conforms to conclusions about ethnic differences drawn on the basis of individual level data in Chapter Two. The convergence of both of these sets of data strongly indicates the existence of ethnic norms about residence in single household dwellings and(perhaps as a result) of homeownership at early family life cycle stages, though as we have indicated above, the overall effect of such differences upon city homeownership levels was relatively small.

Lastly, we turn to our regression equations for German and Irish laborers and carpenters (Y_{GL}, Y_{GC}, Y_{IL}, Y_{IC}) in Table 70 to see whether they shed light upon the ethnic differences in occupational concentration for St. Paul which we noted in Chapter Four (see Table 60). Among the Germans of St. Paul, Table 60 indicates that their relative concentrations in labor increased, while their proportions in construction decreased, 1860-1895. Looking at the beta weights for independents in our equations for proportions of Germans in labor (Y_{GL}) and in carpentry (Y_{GC}), we see that the equations predict lower concentrations in labor and in carpentry for Germans as homeownership levels decline.[39] The <u>increase</u> in the proportions of Germans in labor in St. Paul,

1860-1895, therefore, was the result either of temporary or purely local factors (which we discussed at length in Chapter Four) while the decrease in construction was expected for structural reasons.

Among the Irish, we discovered in St. Paul that their proportions in labor declined slightly and their proportions in construction increased from 1860-1895. (Table 60). We note from our equations (Y_{IL}, Y_{IC}) that, contrary to the case of the Germans, high Irish proportions in labor and construction were associated with low homeownership levels. In part, this result was a reflection of the fact that the Irish were more heavily settled in older cities with low homeownership levels in the East than was the case in the newer Western cities. The case of St. Paul, however, suggests another possibility: because the proportions of Irish in construction increased from 1860 to 1895 as the city aged, the regression equation may also indicate a secular trend in Irish occupational concentrations based on specific ethnic factors, such as the putative role of ethnic resource networks which we discussed in Chapter Four. In other words, the proportion of Irish employed as construction workers increased as cities aged despite the decreasing importance of construction jobs in the employment sectors of such cities for reasons peculiar to the Irish but not to the Germans.

Conclusions

In comparison to other large cities in 1890, then, St. Paul's household headship level was about average nationally, though slightly below average for large cities in the Midwest, primarily because of its relatively small manufacturing sector and high level of employment for young women. St. Paul's homeownership level was among the highest in the country in 1890, but the level had fallen to an average among Midwestern cities by 1900 as St. Paul completed the developmental cycle for frontier cities. The city's demographic patterns thus were for the most part typical for its stage of development and regional location, so far as we can distinguish from comparisons with other large cities near the end of the frontier era. The ethnic differences in headship and single-household-dwelling-residence which we discovered for St. Paul in Chapters One and Two thus were not strongly conditioned by eccentric local conditions. Though it is possible that ethnic differences in headship in 1895 in St. Paul were partially or wholly the result of differing ethnic migration patterns, the downward trend of both headship and homeownership clearly followed a typical regional pattern for new cities during the late nineteenth century.

The rather small, but nevertheless statistically significant and analytically interesting contribution of Irish and German proportions of large city populations which we found with individual level data for St. Paul also appeared among all cities of 100,000 population or more in 1890. German populations tended to increase male and female nuptiality and homeownership, while Irish population tended to decrease city levels of headship and homeownership. Though the contributions of these immigrant groups to marriage, headship and homeownership levels were in part the result of their distinctive settlement patterns among large cities (Irish in the oldest cities, Germans in cities with high manufacturing employment levels) we discovered that a small independent effect of "Irishness" and "Germanness" could be measured. While these independent effects were small they were without exception in the same direction as the differences noted at the individual level in earlier chapters for St. Paul's ethnic populations.

Perhaps the most important result of our ecological analysis of large cities in this chapter has been to set the influence of immigration within a larger national framework of urban development in the nineteenth century. Though the nation's large cities on the average were just beginning to follow a long trend of gradual increases in nuptiality and household headship inaugurated in the 1890's (and a trend to increased homeownership originating at least as early as the 1870's) a cyclic "frontier-filling" pattern can be discerned for younger Western cities in 1890. In response to declining sex ratios and economic expectations which accompanied the filling up of available land resources with suitable levels of population in frontier cities about 60 years or less after their founding, the nuptiality, headship, and homeownership levels of the younger cities were temporarily moving contrary to the national pattern in 1890. The primary engines of change in this developmental pattern were demographic and economic. The relative scarcity of appropriate marriage partners, of immediate economic resources, and of promising long term economic prospects imposed overwhelming structural constraints upon the markets within which immigrants made personal and household decisions. The relatively high male nuptiality, household headship and homeownership levels of Milwaukee in 1890, for example, had much less to do with its large proportion of German immigrants than with its relatively low sex ratio and female employment level and its high rate of manufacturing employment (see Table 73). Without our comparative analysis of these structural conditions, we would have had no measure by which to gauge the representativeness or the importance of the patterns discovered for Milwaukee, St. Paul or other Midwestern cities during the late nineteenth century.

Footnotes

[1]Brooklyn and New York City combined in 1890 for accurate comparison with the combined city reported in the census of 1900.

[2]The proportion of a young adult population ever married, often expressed as a percentage of women aged 20-24 or of men aged 25-29, reflecting the sex difference in average age at first marriage.

[3]John Modell, Frank F. Furstenberg, Jr., and Douglas Strong, "The Timing of Marriage in the Transition to Adulthood: Continuity and Change, 1860 - 1975", forthcoming in the *American Journal of Sociology*, 1977.

[4]Ernest R. Groves and William F. Ogburn, *American Marriages and Family Relationships* (New York, 1928), 286-287. The lack of significant relationship between nuptiality and income levels at the state or city levels in 1921 is described on pp. 287-294; also see Modell, Furstenberg and Strong, *ibid*., above for similar conclusions.

[5]Modell, Furstenberg and Strong, *ibid*., footnote 2.

[6]Richard A. Easterlin, "Factors in the Decline of Farm Fertility in the United States: Some preliminary Research Results," *Journal of American History*, LXIII (December, 1976), 607.

[7]A thorough discussion of sex differences is in Groves and Ogburn, *American Marriages*, 193-218. On the declining influence of the sex ratio as a determinant of nuptiality at the state level in the twentieth century see Modell, Furstenberg and Strong, "The Timing of Marriage in the Transition to Adulthood," Table 6. See also: Alan Freiden, "The United States Marriage Market," *Journal of Political Economy* 82 (March/April, 1974), Supplement, S34-S35; and Samuel H. Preston and Alan T. Richards, "The Influence of Women's Work Opportunities on Marriage Rates," *Demography*, 12(May,1975), 209-221, for current comparisons of the relationship at the level of SMSA's.

[8]Preston and Richards, *ibid*., 217; Freiden, *ibid*., S43-S52; and Glen H. Elder, Jr. and Richard Rockwell, "Marital Timing in Women's Life Patterns," *Journal of Family History*,1,(Autumn, 1976), 37-48.

[9]*Ibid.*

[10]David M. Heer, "The Marital Status of Second-Generation Americans," *American Sociological Review*, 26(April, 1961), 233-241.

[11]I.e., the relative shares of owner-occupied or "sales" demand and rental unit demand.

[12]Burnham O. Campbell, "Population Change and Building Cycles." *University of Illinois Bulletin*, 64(October 7, 1966), 75; percentage change in the total required sales and rental additions, calculated from data in Table 4, were: +31.7% for the 1870's to the 1880's and +15.6% for the 1880's to the 1890's.

[13]*Ibid*.

[14]*Ibid.*,115-117, 192.

[15]Easterlin, *Population, Labor Force, and Long Swings in Economic Growth: The American Experience* (New York, 1968), 32.

[16]Taken from Manuel Gottlieb, *Estimates of Residential Building: United States: 1840-1939* (New York, 1964), 61-62,65.

[17]"Population Change and Farm Settlement in the Northern United States," *Journal of Economic History*, XXVI (March, 1976), 63-70; and Easterlin, "Factors in the Decline of Farm Fertility in the United States: Some Preliminary Research Results," 607,611.

[18]Richard F. Muth, "Urban Residential Land and Housing Markets," in Harvey S. Perloff and Lowdon Wingo, Jr., eds., *Issues in Urban Economics* (Baltimore, 1968), 287; the heady atmosphere of real estate value inflation in St. Paul's early years is described in Henry S. Fairchild, "Sketches of the Early History of Real Estate in St. Paul, *Minnesota Historical Society Collections*, X, Part 1, 418-423.

[19] Muth, "Urban Residential Land and Housing Markets," 286.

[20] Campbell, "Population Change and Building Cycles," 18-19, 188; the trend in peak ages for renters has declined since the nineteenth century.

[21] *Ibid*.

[22] On life expectancy, see *ibid*., 36-38; on the effect of improvements in transportation, see the general discussion in Werner Z. Hirsch, *Urban Ecomomic Analysis* (New York, 1973), 49-60.

[23] Lee Soltow, *Patterns of Wealthholding in Wisconsin Since 1850* (Madison, 1971), 31-43.

[24] Modell, Furstenberg and Strong, "The Timing of Marriage in the Transition to Adulthood," Table 7. Campbell also observed the trend in age-specific headship, 1890-1950, "Population Change and Building Cycles," 16-17.

[25] Modell, Furstenberg and Strong, *ibid*., Table 9.

[26] John Modell, Frank Furstenberg and Theodore Hershberg, "Social Change and Transitions to Adulthood in Historical Perspective," *Journal of Family History*, 1 (Autumn, 1976), 14,26.

[27] Campbell, "Population Change and Building Cycles," 46-48.

[28] *Ibid*., 48-49.

[29] See, for example, the assumption (*ibid*.,192) that "as the immigrant population is assimilated, a lagged impact on required additions would be expected as the applicable headship rates adjust toward the norm of the nonimmigrant population."

[30] Scattergrams with accompanying correlation coefficients and measures of statistical significance were run to determine both the existence of significant linear associations and the form of curvilinear associations, if any; see Table 68.

[31] Norman H. Nie, *et al*, *Statistical Package for the Social Sciences* (2nd ed.; New York, 1975), Chapter 24.

[32]Though a linear regression technique understates the strength of curvilinear associations, the purpose here is to provide a rough estimate of causality only. The scattergrams indicated that only city age and rate of population growth were associated with our dependents in an obvious curvilinear fashion; hence the influence of these closely inter-related factors is understated in our linear regression equations. Only factors which "loaded" strongly on the underlying structural dimensions were incorporated into the index for the dimension. See discussion in Nie, *et al*, *SPSS*, 487-489.

[33]Cf. correlation coefficients among independents in Table 70 with the coefficients in Table 69. Since the sex ratio was known to be a crucial determinant of nuptiality and very probably of headship, this variable was introduced separately into the equations for interpretive clarity; the same procedure was used to clarify the role of the occupational structural variable in the equations on German and Irish proportions in carpentry and labor.

[34]The "regression coefficient (B)" is a numerical value describing the relative influence of an independent variable upon the dependent variable, and its sign indicates the direction of influence; thus, a coefficient of -1.0 indicates that an increase of 1 unit of the independent variable is associated with a decrease of one unit in the dependent variable. Since the units used to scale the independents were usually not the same for each, standardized regression coefficients ("beta weights") are also provided, expressing the relative influence of each independent in terms of standard deviations from a mean of zero. Standard errors also are provided to indicate the relative reliability of statistically nonsignificant regression coefficients. For further discussion of method, see: Hubert M. Blalock, Jr., *Social Statistics* (2nd ed.; New York, 1972) 367,453, *passim*.

[35]Groves and Ogburn, *American Marriage and Family Relationships*, 193-201.

[36]Including: age of city, proportion of workforce in manufacturing, homeownership level, population growth rate, growth rate of capital per manufacturing employee, male unemployment rate, and male nuptiality level.

[37]Easterlin, "Population Change and Farm Settlement in the Northern United States," 52-55.

[38]See also Table 7, Chapter 1, where a somewhat different headship ratio (heads per 100 adults aged 20+) also indicates essentially similar ratios for 1890 and 1895 in St. Paul.

[39]Strictly speaking, regression equations using cross-sectional data cannot predict change over time, though the apparent developmental pattern can be demonstrated for rural frontier populations with time series data as well: see Easterlin, "Population Change and Farm Settlement in the Northern United States," 55-59.

CONCLUSION

Briefly stated, the purpose of this study was to provide answers for four basic questions:

-how much difference actually existed in the rate at which Irish and German immigrants formed households, lived in single family dwellings, and took up occupations in specific sectors, as compared to migrants of native parentage in St. Paul from 1860 to 1895?

- how much of this ethnic difference can be attributed to either economic or demographic circumstances and how much to a common ethnic characteristic (represented by specific place of birth)?

-what evidence is there that the Irish and German immigrants in Midwestern cities actually shared ethnic group values about household formation, homeownership and occupational position?

-what effect did such ethnic differences have upon the development patterns of American cities, particularly in the Midwest?

The general conclusion of this study is that real ethnic differences existed among German and Irish immigrants and urban migrants of native parentage in St. Paul with regard to household formation, residence choice and occupational sector but that these differences only marginally affected the rate of development of Midwestern cities such as St. Paul. More important explanatory factors included the level of female employment, sex ratios, level of manufacturing employment, and the age of the city involved. In St. Paul, the study found that German immigrants tended to form husband-wife households at greater rates, to reside in single family dwellings more often, and to take up occupations in the manufacturing sector more often as compared to the Irish and migrants of native origin. The Irish also formed husband-wife households at high rates during 1860 but postponed household formation more than others in 1895 in response to slowed economic expansion in the latter year. By 1895 the Irish also lived in multiple family dwellings at above average rates. Despite shrinking opportunities in the construction sector, a higher than average proportion of Irish were concentrated in that sector in 1895. In general, both Irish and German immigrants contributed a greater than average share of demand for housing and consumption expenditures generally during the early years of St. Paul's development.

The study of St. Paul also uncovered an apparent 60 year developmental cycle for new frontier cities in the Midwest in the latter half of the nineteenth century.

Household headship rates temporarily moved downward in the latter half of this cycle in St. Paul and other cities in response to a temporary "filling up" of available local opportunity. The low point of a long swing in housing construction also contributed to a shift in tenure composition toward multiple family dwelling rentals during the down side of this cycle. This cycle clearly influenced the opportunities of both Germans and Irish in St. Paul, though the Irish were more seriously affected. The cycle also suggests that Richard Easterlin's recent discovery of such a cycle among rural residents of the Midwest during this period also applies to frontier cities in the area.

At the national level, both the apparent differences in Irish, German and "native" behavior and the temporary cyclic decline of opportunity in frontier towns of a certain age are found to be of relatively minor importance for urban development generally. German and Irish household forming and housing consumption behavior -- while real -- had little impact compared to other demographic and economic factors. The long trend of urban development was characterized by increasing household formation rates, increasing homeownership, and broad shifts in occupational structure toward semi-skilled manufacturing positions by the end of the nineteenth century. While

German and Irish immigrants may have speeded these developments by their higher than average rates of household formation and single-family housing consumption, the effect was clearly marginal overall.

The study of occupational distributions in St. Paul from 1860 to 1900 also revealed that ethnic resource networks may have been more influential than ethnic occupational values in explaining the concentrations of Irish and German workers in "typical" sectors. The fact that many of their countrymen were employed in such sectors as construction or manufacturing had a more visible impact on Irish and German workers than their apparent preferences. This was particularly the case for the Irish, who remained concentrated in the construction sector in 1895 long after opportunities had shrunk drastically in this sector of St. Paul's economy. The study of values about marriage and homeownership also indicated that German tendencies toward a higher consumption profile may have been to cultural values linking marriage and property-holding to personal respectability in the community, but a more comprehensive analysis of further data is needed in this area.

Though ethnic differences in consumption or occupational behavior clearly were not as important as the sheer size of the immigration itself in American urban development, this study has revealed that real ethnic differences existed apart from explanations provided by demographic circumstances or economic constraints. Within the context of the social history of America's immigrants, this study also has posed several lines of inquiry about the adaptation of the Germans and Irish to American society. The intimate family context of the daily interplay of value and constraint in economic decision-making needs further study if we are to understand the adaptation of immigrants in all of its complexity.

APPENDIX

This appendix summarizes the crucial decisions which were necessary for designing the samples of households and workers, for classifying the characteristics of the population and manufacturing firms, and for producing comparable economic data for St. Paul's economy. The author will gladly provide more complete technical information upon request.

1. Sample Design

The objectives of this study required that information be gathered on characteristics of the population of St. Paul, both individuals and households. Information on housing type and workforce also was required. To meet these needs, the initial intention was to select randomly a sample of 500 households in the federal census manuscript schedules for 1860 and 1880 and the state census schedules for 1895. Within each of the sample households, a separate punch card was prepared for each individual aged 15 years or older. The cards for each adult included information both on personal characteristics of the individual and a summary of the total number of persons in the household (by 5-year age and sex groupings). Where possible, both the type of residential dwelling unit and the apparent type of household structure also was coded on the card for each individual adult selected.

Limitations of the data for each census year required several adjustments of the initial sample design, as follows:

<u>Census of 1860</u>:

Each household in the census manuscript schedule for 1860 in St. Paul was numbered sequentially from first to last household visited as required by U. S. Census Bureau. However, street addresses were not included for each household, which prevented identification of multiple household dwellings. The only distinction which could be made among types of residential dwelling units was to separate hotels (labelled by name) from boarding houses (defined as any household which contained more than three adults whose last names were not the same as the male and/or female household heads) from all other dwelling unit types. Because the census takers were instructed to list separately all households occupying separate "tenements," it was possible also to identify those households which contained more than one family unit.

The actual selection of households in 1860 was

done by selecting 500 random numbers between the first and last sequential numbers in the manuscript schedule, using a random numbers table. The list of numbers was placed in sequence and the corresponding households chosen from the schedule.

Census of 1880

Street addresses were provided for most households in the manuscript schedules of St. Paul for 1880. Households were numbered sequentially within each of 24 enumeration districts. For all but 3 of the 24 districts, several groups of individuals were appended to the end of the regular numbering sequence without street address identification. A total of 123 such groups of persons (for the most part unrelated adults) were listed. Though a published population total was available for the city and its wards, the total number of households was not published.

Because of these limitations, the sample was drawn first by manually counting the total number of households listed, including both the households in the regular sequential numbering system and the groupings of individuals listed at the ends of enumeration districts. An overall sampling fraction was then calculated (6803 households divided by 500). Using a random numbers computer program, a set of random numbers were selected for each of the 24 enumeration districts, based on the total households in each district and the city-wide sampling fraction. The coding scheme used was essentially the same as for 1860, except that the street address listings for most households allowed separate identification of single and multiple-household dwelling unit types.

<u>Census of 1895</u>:

Because the manuscript schedules of the federal census of 1890 were destroyed accidentally while in the custody of the Census Bureau, the manuscript schedules of the Minnesota State Censuses of 1895 and 1905 are the only available manuscript census sources for the end of the nineteenth century for St. Paul. Neither census was conducted with the same care as the federal censuses, judging from the arrangement of the data. The 1895 state census was selected over the 1905 census for this study because the latter did not as clearly identify households. The 1895 census schedules presented several obstacles for sample design purposes:

- -households were not numbered;
- -in a few cases, long lists of unrelated adults were given for a street address, without indication that the dwelling was a hotel or institution;

-some households were crossed out with a line through each name;

-pages of the manuscript for Wards #5, 6, 7, 8 and 9 were out of sequence;

-portions of the listing of hotel tenants for the same hotel were in some cases scattered throughout several pages of the manuscript, though the portions were labelled;

-no published total for households was available, though total population figures for each ward were published.

Given these limitations, the first step in drawing the sample of households was to estimate the average household size for St. Paul in 1895 by interpolation from 1880 to 1900. This estimate of household size was then applied to the published population total to produce an estimate of 27,241 total households. Using a random numbers computer program, 500 random numbers were selected between the numbers 1 and 27,241 and listed in numerical order. Beginning with the first household, all households in the manuscript were counted manually, and the sample of households was selected in sequence (during the count) from the corresponding list of random numbers. To deal with the problem of pages out of sequence, a page index was developed for Wards #5 - #9 so that the count of households could proceed sequentially for each ward. Using the federal census scheme, all groups occupying flats or apartments were considered to be separate households, but not groups identified by "room" number. Groups listed as occupying "floors" were considered separate households. Any long list of persons with a single street address was considered to be an hotel and counted as only one household if no internal blank lines, labels or other designations were provided within the list. Separate groups of people listed sequentially with the same street address repeated in the margin for each group were considered to be separate households occupying apartments in a multiple household dwelling. Any household in which all persons were "crossed out" were skipped in the count.

As it happened, the estimate of 27,241 households was short by 2,826 of the actual total of 30,057 households counted using these rules. After exhausting the list of 500 random numbers, the remaining households following the 500th sample household were counted, and a sampling fraction determined by dividing the 500 sample households already selected by the total number of households counted so far (27,231). An additional sample of 52 households was selected for the remaining households using the random numbers computer program.

Possible Sources of Sample Bias:

The samples produced by this procedure were as follows:

Census Year	Sample Households	Total Persons Aged 15 years+	All persons in Sample Households	Average House-Hold Size
1860	501	1436	2418	4.83
1880	508	1972	2827	5.56
1895	552	1045	2882	5.22

Very little published data on the characteristics of the total population in each year is available, making an evaluation of these samples difficult. Using the manual counts of total households in each year and the published population totals yields the following:

Census Year	Total Households Counted	Published Total Population	Implied Household Size
1860	2,168	10,401	4.80
1880	6,803	41,473	6.10
1895	30,057	140,292	4.67

The household sizes produced by the samples follow a more reasonable trend than these figures when compared to published data for 1875, 1885 and 1900 as indicated in Table 7 of Chapter 1. The reported household size in 1900, for example, was 5.3. Because of the disorganized condition especially of parts of the 1895 census manuscript, it is possible that the published population totals were overcounted in 1880 and undercounted in 1895. Another possibility is that the manual count of total households was too low in 1880 and too high in 1895.

A further check on the quality of the manual count of total households for 1895 is provided by calculating the implied average household size for each ward, using the published population of each ward as follows:

Wards	Total Households (Count from MSS.)	Population (Published)	Household Size (Implied)
1	3972	17,995	4.53
2	2988	14,296	4.78
3	1380	6,596	4.78
4	1911	11,106	5.81
5	3462	15,683	4.53
6	3435	15,755	4.59
7	2822	13,119	4.64
8	5837	25,823	4.42
9	2795	12,748	4.56
10	793	3,762	4.74
11	646	3,409	5.28
Total	30,041	140,292	4.67

None of the implied household sizes above are unreasonable, especially in view of the fact that all "households" such as large hotels, hospitals and other institutions are included in the count. The published data also provides a check on the sex ratio of the sample; according to published totals, St. Paul's population had 101 males per 100 females, compared to 104 males per 100 in the sample (including children under 15 years old). In general, it seems reasonable to conclude that though some roomfuls of lodgers in hotels may have been counted mistakenly as separate households, thus inflating the real count of households in 1895, the magnitude of this possible error is not large in the sample drawn for this study. Mistakes in the published figures for total population seem equally as likely a possibility.

A further source of sample bias is a result of the sample structure. The sample is a simple random selection of households, but a random clustered sample of individuals of age 15 years or more. Since the random <u>clusters</u> of individuals are persons in households, the sample probably overrepresents related individuals. The effects of this source of bias are presumed to be similar in both 1860 and 1895, however, and should not change the direction of trends measured between these two census years.

2. Classification Systems

To be meaningful, the characteristics of individuals listed in the census schedules were aggregated into a few classes. Besides the characteristics reported directly, several characteristics had to be inferred from the arrangement of the data or by making reasonable assumptions about the relationships among firms or individuals in a household. This section summarizes some of the critical distinctions which were made to classify the following:

-relationship to head of household;

-occupational category, by type of industry and level of skill;

-type of residential dwelling unit;

-type of family or household;

-ethnic generation;

-type of manufacturing firm;

Rules for distinguishing classes or types are given and illustrated with a few examples in some cases. A detailed listing is available from the author.

a. Relationship to Head of Household:

The term "head of household" in this study applies to both the first adult listed in the household and to his/her spouse if present. If a household consisted of adults with different last names and if the first person listed was less than 20 years old with no real or personal property, the "head" was considered to be the oldest adult, regardless of sex. In general, the relationship of members of the household to the head or heads of the household was inferred from last name identity, sex, age, placement in the list of household members, and place of birth for the censuses of 1860 and 1895. The inclusion of family relationship designation in the 1880 census allowed a more refined delineation of family types in that year. In some cases, adults with different last names from the male head of household were coded as "mother-in-law" or "father-in-law" when a comparison of ages and place of birth with the wife of the male head reasonably suggested such a relationship. All other adults whose names differed from the heads of household were considered "lodgers or boarders" except when a secondary family (with identical last names but different than the head of household) was listed. All members of secondary families were coded in terms of their relationship to the head or heads of the secondary family. The term "family" here includes only persons related by blood, marriage or adoption with identical last names.

b. Occupational Category:

The occupational classification system used in this study followed closely the system used in Theodore Hershberg, *et al*, "Occupation and Ethnicity in Five Nineteenth-Century Cities: A Collaborative Inquiry," *Historical Methods Newsletter*, Vol. 7 (June, 1974), 187-190. The "vertical" or level of skill classes and a few important examples of occupations within each class for St. Paul in 1860 were:

I. Professional and High White Collar.
Banker (2), Civil Engineer (4), Grocery Merchant (7), Lawyer (12), Merchant(5), Physician (5).

II. Proprietors and Low White Collar.
Clerk (38), Farmer (16), Bookkeeper (7), Grocery Store (9), Hotel Keeper (2), Lagerbeer Saloon (5), Music Store (3), Saloon (4), School Teacher (3).

III. Skilled Manual.
Blacksmith (15), Carpenter (50), Master Carpenter (9), Painter (9), Plasterer (5), Shoe maker (13), Tailor (6).

IV. Semi-skilled Manual.

Barkeeper (9), Drayman (5), Deckhand (12), Gardener (3), Hostler (4), Lumber Men (3), Servant (81), Warehouseman (3), Teamster (22).

V. Unskilled Manual.

Daylabor (112), Laborer (15), Washerwoman (13).

Similarly, the classes for 1895 were:

I. Professional and High White Collar.

Attorney (2), Capitalist (3), Clergyman (2), Doctor (2), Lawyer (6), Merchant (4).

II. Proprietors and Low White Collar.

Bookkeeper (13), Clerk (54), Contractor (9), Clothing Merchant (3), Conductor (24), Farmer (4), Milkman (3), Public Teacher (3), Salesman (8), Stenographer (6), School Teacher (7), Traveling Salesman (13).

III. Skilled Manual.

Blacksmith (12), Barber (10), Baker (4), Carpenter (33), Cigarmaker (5), Dressmaker (15), Engineer (13), Machinist (3), Moulder (3), Painter (21), Printer (10), Shoemaker (10), Tailor (6).

IV. Semi-skilled Manual.

Brakeman (7), Coachman (6), Driver (6), Fireman (11), Gripman (6), Janitor (6), Servant (19), Teamster (19), Waiter (6).

V. Unskilled Manual.

Common labor (17), Domestic (54), Laborer (133).

The industrial or "horizontal" classification of occupations also followed the five cities scheme cited above. Some important examples of classifications for 1895 are:

Class	Occupation	Number
Agriculture	Farmer	4
Manufacturing	Engineer	13
	Moulder	5
	Shoe Maker	10
Construction	Bricklayer	8
	Carpenter	33
Labor	Laborer	133
Commerce	Bookkeeper	13
	Clerk (Unspecified)	54
	Merchant	4
	Salesmen	8

Class	Occupation	Number
Transportation	Brakeman	7
	Car Inspector	3
	Clerk (Railroad)	3
	Conductor	24
	Expressman	4
	Gripman	6
Public Service	Barber	10
	Cook	10
	Elevatorman	2
	Lamplighter	3
Domestic Service	Coachman	6
	Porter	6
	Domestic	54
Profession	Doctor	2
	Lawyer	6
Education and Government	School teacher	7
	Student	5

c. Type of Residential Dwelling Unit;

The major classes adopted were hotel, boarding house, single household dwelling, and multiple household dwelling. The term "boarding house" was defined to mean any household which contained more than three persons whose last names were not the same as the head of household, unless the household was labelled an "hotel" or an institution such as a hospital or jail. A household was considered a "hotel" only if so labelled. The Census of 1895 provided the street address of each household, which allowed identification of "multiple household dwellings," defined as dwellings which contained more than one household with identical street addresses. Because street addresses were not provided for the Census of 1860, only "residential dwellings" were identified.

d. Household Composition and Family Type

Only a relatively simple classification scheme for family types and household composition was possible for the Censuses of 1860 and 1895 because neither census provided direct information on the relationship of each individual to heads of family or household. Using the rules for classifying household relationships listed above, families were identified as:

-nuclear family only (husband-wife pairs with children or single parents with children)

-nuclear with lodgers (same as above but with other adults present with different last names and no apparent kinship ties)

-extended (one or more members judged to be kin from place of birth and age data)

Households thus were classified into those which contained the three types of "families", plus those containing only adults with different last names, and all other households such as hotels, jails and hospitals.

e. Ethnic Generation:

The Census of 1895 provided information on the place of birth of each individual, but indicated only whether the father and mother of each individual were foreign-born or native born. Second generation Irish or German children living with their parents could be identified directly, but second generation adults could be identified only generally by an indication that one or both of their parents were foreign-born. To identify second generation Irish or German adults specifically, lists of distinctive Irish and German surnames were developed, and all native-born or Canadian-born male adults or single adult women whose fathers were listed as foreign-born and whose last names were present on the respective lists of distinctive ethnic names were coded as second generation Irish or Germans. The lists of distinctive Irish and German last names were developed from four basic sources:

- -the last names of persons born in either Germany or Ireland in the 1860 census sample for this study;
- -the last names of persons born in either Germany or Ireland in the 1895 census sample for this study;
- -Robert E. Matheson, _Special Report on Surnames in Ireland, With Notes as to Numerical Strength, Duration, Ethnology and Distribution_ (Dublin, 1894);
- -American Council of Learned Societies, _Report of Committee on Linguistic and National Stocks in the Population of the United States_, published in the American Historical Association's _Annual Report_ for 1931.

f. _Manufacturing Firm Type_:

The manuscript schedules of the federal manufacturing censuses of 1860 and 1880 listed numerous types of manufacturing firms in St. Paul. For analytic purposes, these types of firms were aggregated into 21 major categories:

1. Machinery, Tools
2. Hardware
3. Printing, Engraving
4. Metal
5. Construction
6. Furniture
7. Clothing
8. Baking
9. Shoes
10. Harness
11. Meat
12. Blacksmithing
13. Wagons
14. Beverages
15. Flour
16. Cigars
17. Leather, Fur
18. Lumber
19. Drugs
20. Household, Personal products
21. Cooperage

Examples of sub-types within these broad categories include:

1. Machinery, Tools:

   Machine shops

   Boiler works

   Agricultural Implements

   Cutters and Grinders

2. Hardware:

   Gunsmith

   Fireworks

   Wire Works

   Tinsmith

   Locksmith

3. Printing, Engraving:

   Photography

   Bookbinding

   Engraving

   Lithographing

   Type Foundry

   Stereotyping

   Publishing

   Job Printing

BIBLIOGRAPHY

I. MANUSCRIPT COLLECTIONS

(Dates listed for materials used in this thesis only.)

Chicago Foreign Language Press Survey. Microfilm copy deposited at the Immigration History Research Center, University of Minnesota.

Ignatius Donnelly Papers. Minnesota Historical Society.

State of Minnesota. Manuscript schedules of the State Census of 1895. Minnesota Historical Society.

U. S. Census Bureau. Eighth Census, 1860. Manuscript schedules of the population census for St. Paul. Minnesota Historical Society.

U. S. Works Projects Administration. Minnesota Papers, 1939-1942. Minnesota Historical Society.

Wenzel Petram Papers. 1849 to 1890. Minnesota Historical Society.

II. PUBLIC DOCUMENTS

1. City of St. Paul

City of St. Paul. Annual Reports of the City Officers and City Boards. St. Paul, 1886-1900

R. L. Polk and Company. St. Paul City Directory. 1890-91.

St. Paul Building Inspector. Reports. St. Paul, 1885-1899.

St. Paul Chamber of Commerce. Annual Report of the St. Paul Chamber of Commerce. St. Paul, 1869-1884.

Public Documents (continued)

2. State of Minnesota

Minnesota Bureau of Labor. Biennial Reports. 1893-1900.

Minnesota Secretary of State. Minnesota Executive Documents. St. Paul, 1865-1886.

3. Federal Government

U. S. Census Bureau. Eleventh Census, 1890. Vol. 1, Population, Part 2.

U. S. Census Bureau. Eleventh Census, 1890. Vol. 4, Report on Vital and Social Statistics in the United States, Part 2

U. S. Census Bureau. Eleventh Census, 1890. Vol. 13, Report on Farms and Homes. Washington, D.C., 1896.

U. S. Census Bureau. Twelfth Census, 1900. Vol. 2, Population, Part 2.

U. S. Census Bureau, Twelfth Census, 1900. Special Report - Occupations. Washington, D.C.

United States Immigration Commission. Reports. 42 vols., Washington, D.C., 1907-1910.

III. BOOKS AND PAMPHLETS

Address of the Minnesota Irish Emigration Convention, Held in the City of Saint Paul, Minnesota, January 20th, 1869, to the People of Ireland. St. Paul, 1869.

Anderson, Harry H., ed. German-American Pioneers in Wisconsin and Michigan: The Frank-Kerler Letters, 1849-1864. Milwaukee, 1971

Anderson, Michael. Family Structure in Nineteenth Century Lancashire. Cambridge, England, 1971.

Andrews, C. C. History of St. Paul, Minn. Syracuse, New York, 1890.

Books and pamphlets (continued)

Arensberg, Conrad M. The Irish Countryman: An Anthropological Study. Gloucester, Massachusetts, 1959.

Aronovici, Carol. Housing Conditions in the City of St. Paul. St. Paul, 1917.

Berkhofer, Robert F., Jr. A Behavioral Approach to Historical Analysis. New York, 1969.

Carpenter, Niles. Immigrants and Their Children: 1920. Washington, D.C., 1927.

Chudacoff, Howard P. Mobile Americans: Residential and Social Mobility in Omaha, 1880-1920. New York, 1972.

Clark, Dennis. The Irish in Philadelphia: Ten Generations of Urban Experience. Philadelphia, 1973.

Cole, Donald B. Immigrant City: Laurence, Massachusetts, 1845-1921. Chapel Hill, 1963

Covello, Leonard. The Social Background of the Italo-American School Child. Leiden, 1967.

Dollar, Charles M. and Jensen, Richard J.,Historian's Guide to Statistics. New York, 1971.

Easterlin, Richard A. Population, Labor Force, and Long Swings in Economic Growth: The American Growth: The American Experience. New York,1968.

Ernst, Robert. Immigrant Life in New York City, 1825-1863. New York, 1949.

Esslinger, Dean R. Immigrants and the City: Ethnicity and Mobility in a Nineteenth-Century Midwestern Community. Port Washington, New York, 1975.

Faust, Albert B. The German Element in the United States. 2 vols., Boston, 1909.

Fishman, Joshua A., ed. Language Loyalty in the United States. The Hague, 1966.

Books and Pamphlets (Continued)

Fuess, Claude M. Carl Shurz: Reformer, 1829-1957. New York, 1932.

Glick, Paul C. American Families. New York, 1957

Gordon, Milton. Assimilation in American Life. New York, 1964.

Gottlieb, Manuel. Estimates of Residential Building: United States: 1840-1939. New York, 1964.

Greeley, Andrew and Rossi, Peter H. The Education of Catholic Americans. Chicago, 1966.

Greeley, Andrew M. That Most Distressful Nation: The Taming of the American Irish. Chicago, 1972.

Greeley, Andrew M. Why Can't They Be Like Us? America's White Ethnic Groups. New York, 1971.

Groves, Ernst R. and Ogburn, William F. American Marriages and Family Relationships. New York, 1928.

Hagedorn, Hermann. The Hyphenated Family: An American Saga. New York, 1960.

Hartsough, Mildred L. The Twin Cities as a Metropolitan Market. Minneapolis, 1925.

Hill, Reuben. Family Development in Three Generations. Cambridge, 1970.

Hirshler, Eric E., ed. Jews from Germany in the United States. New York, 1955.

Hoffmann, Charles. The Depression of the Nineties: An Economic History. Westport, Connecticut, 1970.

Jordan, Terry G. German Seed in Texas Soil: Immigrant Farmers in Nineteenth-Century Texas. Austin,1966

Katz, Michael B. The People of Hamilton, Canada West: Family and Class in a Mid-Nineteenth-Century City. Cambridge, 1975.

Kennedy, Robert E., Jr. The Irish: Emigration, Marriage and Fertility. Berkeley, 1973

Books and Pamphlets (continued)

Kohn, Melvin L. *Class and Conformity: A Study in Values*. Homewood, Illinois, 1969.

Korman, Gerd. *Industrialization, Immigrants and Americanizers: The View From Milwaukee, 1866-1921*. Madison, 1967.

Lebergott, Stanley. *Manpower in Economic Growth: The American Record Since 1800*. New York, 1964.

Lee, Everett S. *Population Redistribution and Economic Growth, 1870-1950*. 3 vols., Philadelphia, 1957-1964.

Levine, Edward M. *The Irish and Irish Politicians: A Study of Cultural and Social Alienation.* Notre Dame, Indiana, 1966.

Lieberson, Stanley. *Ethnic Patterns in American Cities*. New York, 1963.

Luebke, Frederick C. *Bonds of Loyalty: German-Americans and World War I*. Dekalb, Illinois, 1974.

Luebke, Frederick C. *Immigrants and Politics: The Germans of Nebraska, 1880-1900*. Lincoln, 1969.

Mindel, Charles H. and Habenstein, Robert W. *Ethnic Families in America*. New York, 1976.

National Bureau of Economic Research. *Output, Employment, and Productivity in the United States after 1800*. New York, 1966.

National Bureau of Economic Research. *Trends in the American Economy in the Nineteenth Century*. Princeton, 1960.

Nau, John Frederick. *The German People of New Orleans, 1850-1900*. Leiden, 1958.

Niehaus, Earl F. *The Irish in New Orleans, 1800-1860*. Baton Rouge, 1965.

Perloff, Harvey S. and Wingo, Lowdon, Jr., eds. *Issues in Urban Economics*. New York, 1968.

Books and Pamphlets (continued)

Potter, George. To the Golden Door: The Story of the Irish in Ireland and America. Boston, 1960.

Sennett, Richard. Families Against the City: Middle Class Homes of Industrial Chicago, 1872-1890. Cambridge, 1970.

Shannon, James P. Catholic Colonization on the Western Frontier. New Haven, 1957.

Shannon, William V. The American Irish. New York, 1963.

Soltow, Lee. Patterns of Wealthholding in Wisconsin Since 1850. Madison, 1971.

Still, Bayrd. Milwaukee: The History of a City. Madison, 1948.

Thernstrom, Stephan. The Other Bostonians: Poverty and Progress in the American Metropolis, 1880-1970. Cambridge, 1973.

Thernstrom, Stephan. Poverty and Progress: Social Mobility in a Nineteenth Century City. New York, 1964.

Thernstrom, Stephan, and Sennett, Richard, eds. Essays in the New Urban History. New Haven, 1969.

Vecoli, Rudolph J. The People of New Jersey. New York, 1965.

Walker, Mack. German Home Towns: Community, State and General Estate, 1648-1871. Ithaca, New York, 1971.

Ward, David. Cities and Immigrants. New York, 1971.

Wittke, Carl. The German-Language Press in America. Lexington, Kentucky, 1957.

IV. ARTICLES AND PERIODICALS

1. Newspapers, Directories

Catholic Citizen. Milwaukee,

Irish Standard. Minneapolis,

Northwestern Chronicle. St. Paul,

St. Paul Pioneer Press. 1860-1895. St. Paul, Minnesota

2. Miscellaneous Articles

Bodnar, John. "Immigration and Modernization: The Case of the Slavic Peasants in Industrial America." *Journal of Social History*, 10 (Fall, 1976), 44-71.

Campbell, Burnham O. *Population Change and Building Cycles*. University of Illinois, Bureau of Economic and Business Research, Bulletin No. 91, 1966, 118-143.

Clark, Terry Nichols. "The Irish Ethnic and the Spirit of Patronage," *Ethnicity*, 2 (1975), 305-359.

Deininger, Marion and Marshall, Douglas. "A Study of Land Ownership by Ethnic Groups from Frontier Times to the Present in a Marginal Farming Area in Minnesota," *Land Economics*, 31 (November, 1955), 351-361.

Easterlin, Richard A. "Factors in the Decline of Farm Fertility in the United States: Some Preliminary Research Results," *Journal of American History*, LXIII (December, 1976).

Easterlin, Richard A. "Population Change and Farm Settlement in the Northern United States, Journal of Economic History, XXXVI (March, 1976), 63-70.

Elder, Glen H., Jr. and Rockwell, Richard. "Marital Timing in Women's Life Patterns," *Journal of Family History*, 1 (Autumn, 1976), 37-48.

Articles and Periodicals (continued)

Elkins, Stanley and McKitrick, Eric. "A Meaning for Turner's Frontier: Part I: Democracy in the Old Northwest," Political Science Quarterly, LXIX (September, 1954), 321-353.

Fairchild, Henry S. "Sketches of the Early History of Real Estate in St. Paul," Collections of the Minnesota Historical Society, 17 vols. (St. Paul, 1872-1920), Vol. X, Part 1, 418-423.

Ferber, Robert. "Consumer Economics: A Survey," Journal of Economic Literature, 11 (December, 1973), 1303-1342.

Furstenberg, Frank F., Jr., Hershberg, Theodore, and Modell, John. "The Origins of the Female Headed Black Family: The Impact of the Urban Experience," Journal of Interdisciplinary History, 6 (Spring, 1975), 211-233.

Hansen, Marcus L. "The Third Generation in America," Commentary, 14 (November, 1952), 493-500.

Hareven, Tamara K. "The Family as a Process: The Historical Study of the Family Cycle," Journal of Social History, 7 (Spring, 1974), 32.

Heer, David M. "The Marital Status of Second-Generation Americans," American Sociological Review, 26 (April, 1961),

Hershberg, Theodore. "Free Blacks in Antebellum Philadelphia: A Study of Ex-Slaves, Free-born and Socio-Economic Decline," Journal of Social History, 5 (Winter, 1971-1972),183-209.

Hershberg, Theodore. "Occupation and Ethnicity in Five Nineteenth-Century Cities: A Collaborative Inquiry," Historical Methods Newsletter, 7 (June, 1974), 174-216.

Knodel, John. "Law, Marriage, and Illegitimacy in Nineteenth-Century Germany," Population Studies, 20 (1966-1967), 279-294.

Articles and Periodicals (continued)

Kohn, Melvin L. and Schooler, Carmi. "Class, Occupation, and Orientation," American Sociological Review, 34 (October, 1969), 659-678.

Laslett, Barbara. "Household Structure on an American Frontier: Los Angeles, California, in 1850" American Journal of Sociology, 81 (July, 1975), 109-128.

Laurie, Bruce, Hershberg, Theodore, and Alter George. "Immigrants and Industry: The Philadelphia Experience, 1850-1880" Journal of Social History, 9 (Winter, 1975), 219-248.

McLaughlin, Virginia Y. "Patterns of Work and Family Organization: Buffalo's Italians," Journal of Interdisciplinary History, 2 (Autumn, 1971), 299-314.

Modell, John. "Family and Fertility on the Indiana Frontier, 1820" American Quarterly, 23 (December, 1971).

Modell, John and Hareven, Tamara K. "Urbanization and the Malleable Household: An Examination of Boarding and Lodging in American Families," Journal of Marriage and the Family, 35 (August, 1973), 467-479.

Modell, John, Furstenberg, Frank and Hershberg. "Social Change and Transitions to Adulthood in Historical Perspective," Journal of Family History 1 (Autumn, 1976),

Modell, John, Furstenberg, Frank F., Jr., and Strong, Douglas. "The Timing of Marriage in the Transition to Adulthood: Continuity and Change, 1860-1975," American Journal of Sociology,

Mortimer, Jeylan T. "Patterns of Intergenerational Occupational Movements: A Smallest-Space Analysis," American Journal of Sociology 9 (March, 1974), 1278-1299.

Articles and Periodicals (continued)

Mott, Frank L. "Portrait of an American Mill Town: Demographic Response in Mid-nineteenth Century Warren, Rhode Island," Population Studies, 26 (March, 1972), 147-157.

Olson, Sister Audrey. "The Nature of an Immigrant Community: St. Louis Germans, 1850-1920," Missouri Historical Review, 66 (April, 1972), 342-359.

Pleck, Elizabeth H. "The Two-Parent Household: Black Family Structure in Late Nineteenth-Century Boston," Journal of Social History 6 (Fall, 1972), 1-31.

Ryder, Norman B. "The Cohort as a Concept in the Study of Social Change," American Sociological Review, 30 (1965), 843-861.

Schnaiberg, Allan. "The Concept and Measurement of Child Dependency: An Approach to Family Formation Analysis," Population Studies, 27 (March, 1973), 69-84.

Vecoli, Rudolph J. "Ethnicity: A Neglected Dimension of American History," in Herbert J. Bass, ed., The State of American History (Chicago, 1970), 70-88.

Vecoli, Rudolph J. "European Americans: From Immigrants to Ethnics," International Migration Review, 6 (Winter, 1972), 403-434.

Vecoli, Rudolph J. "Prelates and Peasants: Italian Immigrants and the Catholic Church," Journal of Social History, 2 (Spring, 1969), 217-268.

Walkowitz, Daniel J. "Working Class Women in the Gilded Age: Factory, Community and Family Life Among Cohoes, New York, Cotton Workers," Journal of Social History, 5 (Summer, 1972), 464-490.

Wilner, Daniel M., The Housing Environment and Family Life: A Longitudinal Study of the Effects of Housing on Morbidity and Mental Health. Baltimore, 1962.

Articles and Periodicals (continued)

Williamson, Jeffrey G. "Consumer Behavior in the Nineteenth Century: Carroll D. Wright's Massachusetts Workers in 1975," *Explorations in Entrepreneurial History* 2nd. Ser. 4 (Winter, 1967), 98-135.

V. DISSERTAIONS

Conzen, Kathleen Neils. "The German Athens: Milwaukee and the Accomodation of its Immigrants, 1830-1860," Doctoral Dissertaion, University of Wisconsin-Madison, 1972.

Dobbert, Guido. "The Disintegration of an Immigrant Community: The Cincinnati Germans, 1870-1920." Doctoral Dissertation, University of Chicago, 1965.

Glasco, Laurence A. "Ethnicity and Social Structure: Irish, German and Native-born of Buffalo, New York, 1850-1860." Doctoral Dissertation, State University of New York at Buffalo, 1973.

McLaughlin, Virginia Yans. "Like the Fingers of the Hand: The Family and Community Life of First-Generation Italian-Americans in Buffalo, New York, 1880-1931." Doctoral thesis, State University of New York, 1970.

Massman, John C. "German Immigration to Minnesota, 1850-1890." Doctoral dissertation, University of Minnesota, 1966.